"A Little Revolution"
How Most Federal Powers Are Returned To The Towns

A Political Novel
by
C.F. Speer

I.   NSA Spy; Law School Dean
II.   Mister Chief Justice
III. Mister President

Introduction

"I hold it that a little rebellion now and then is a good thing, and as necessary in the political world as storms in the physical." (Thos. Jefferson, 1787).

The first premise of my book is that our towns are in a much better position to take care of their townspeople than either the State, or the Federal Government. My second premise is that our Constitution is the only *written contract* between *We The People* and our *Federal Government*- and that *every* government official and *most* citizens have taken a solemn oath to 'preserve and protect' it.

I recognize that convincing the 'best and brightest'- those who have demonstrated the leadership talent to *'make things run'*, and *'get things fixed'*- to volunteer a few years of their lives as *'citizen politicians'*, will not be easy, because of the stigma attached to *'career politicians'*.

I should add that exceptional leaders have always emerged *when we need them most*, and that we Americans are always at

1

our very best when things are at *their very worst!*- as in the first dark days of WWII, and sadly, at the present time.

After 14 Presidents, I have created my own fictional 15th – a central Illinois farm boy named Jack Fitzgerald- 4-time *All-American*; 2-time *Heisman Trophy* winner; a great leader, and *'The Architect'* who first re-designs 21st century American domestic politics, and then our relations with foreign nations. Here are a few examples:

* Town-paid tuition (age 3-Ph.D.) at *any* school, especially adult education;
* Town-paid jobs ($100/day; $12.50/hr min. wage), age 16- retirement age 70;
* Town-paid healthcare, performed mostly by 'House-Call Docs', at much lower cost.
* A *Single* 10% *Tax* on *all purchases; asset transfers*; and *corporate mergers*- paid to town tax accounts *daily- no exceptions*, and no *double taxation*, such as debt repayments and pension distributions. Tax revenues in year one are $5 trillion (vs. $2.6 trillion today) - divided 50% town; 10% County; 10% State, and 30% Federal. Those with the most money pay 85-90% of tax revenues;
* *No tax* on earnings; profits; or property- No *IRS;* tolls; duties; fees, or even parking meters;
* No EPA; no VA bureaucracy- Agency/sub-agencies reduced from more than 600 to less than 50, mostly related to national security;
* Substantial increases in military personnel; military hardware, and national security personnel;
* Conversion of Social Security, and *all other pension plans*, to *Personal Pension Accounts* (PPAs) in T-Bonds, managed by the Treasury Dept., averaging $700,000 at retirement age 70, and funded by past *net* contributions, plus employer-paid

10% contributions on wages, and 10% pay-in on net earnings by independent professionals;
* 'Private Sector'-level salaries for all political offices (e.g. $50 million/year for President, on down the line to Councilperson); office holders pay for personal staff, personal travel, and their political campaigns;
* 2-term limit for *all* offices; no cash campaign contributions, but unlimited candidate support by individual initiative;
* Elections by *popular vote only*- no 'Electoral College'.

With regard to the details of these new *Domestic* policies and new *Foreign* policies, President Jack Fitzgerald creates the "*American Commonwealth*" – (common Constitution; common currency; common prosperity, and common defense).

I invite you to read my book to learn how he handles the *'D.C. Mafia'*, and *Local Political Mafias*; wipes out nuclear 'rogue nations' North Korea and Iran; eliminates ISIS and all other Islamic terrorist organizations (*'Muslim Crazies'*); drug cartels, and provides a path to citizenship for 7 million *'Foreign Invaders'* (illegal immigrants).

About The Author

Speer was born in Manhattan in 1936; graduated from M.I.T in 1957; and completed his military service as a U.S. Naval Officer at 6th Fleet Headquarters in Naples, Italy in 1961. He was then recruited as a management consultant, and moved to Milan, Italy.

He worked for the next 10 years during the *'Italian Miracle'* of the 1960's, and left his position as Manager in the Management Consulting Department of KPMG to return to Southern California with his wife and 3 children in 1971. He bought a small electronics firm, and turned it around within one year.

He earned his CPA certificate in 1978, and worked as a sole practitioner, specializing in 'high-tech start-up' company consulting; 'interim CFO'; corporate accounting and taxation. He moved his family to San Francisco in 1989, where he continued his private practice until his retirement in 2010.

He now resides on Singer Island in West Palm Beach.

I

NSA Spy; Law School Dean

Chapter One

The tower clock in Harvard Square struck 5 o'clock as the heavy-set man in the dark blue suit entered *Ryan's* pub, the Law School's unofficial watering hole; spied his target seated at a back booth; approached him, and introduced himself:

> "Jack, I'm Mike McMahon, an old friend of your boss, Dean Bernstein. He's been impressed for quite a while with your Constitutional Law skills, and also as his 'go-to guy'. My job is to recruit talent for the *National Security Agency,* and he was kind enough to suggest that I talk to you."

Jack Fitzgerald sat back, lit a cigarette, and took a long swallow of his *Guinness Stout*, while Mike (the image of actor Brian Dennehy in his 40's) lit a Cuban cigar, and took a sip of his Irish whiskey. 'I'll be dammed', Jack thought, 'never dreamed the *NSA* was into Constitutional Law'. The lean, 200 pound, six foot four, blonde, 25- year- old ex- Illinois farm boy (a much taller and younger version of actor Robert Redford) took a full minute before he replied:

> "Mike, you've got my attention, but what can I do? I'm just an ordinary Harvard Law Professor, with no particular knowledge of national security."

> "Right now you can't do much," Mike answered evenly, eyes fixed upon the young man:

"Just position yourself for a future time, and, don't be so damned modest, because there is absolutely nothing 'ordinary' about you since your first day in high school- Captain of the football team; captain of the baseball team; Valedictorian; full scholarship to the University of Illinois where, as Captain of their football team, you led them to a National Championship; a four-time *All American* wide receiver; a two-time winner of the *Heisman Trophy*; Captain and All-Star center fielder for their baseball team, which won the *College World Series*; graduated *Summa Cum Laude*; and, repeated this academic feat in just two years at the Harvard Law School, while keeping in shape as a member of their top-ranked Rugby Club squad, a sport which you continue to play; Olympic gold medalist in track; Full Professor in Constitutional Law; Professor in International Economics, and publisher of the Harvard Law Review. Oh yes, I almost forgot that you turned down a $2 million contract to play professional football for the *Chicago Bears*, and a $5 million signing bonus to play for the *New York Yankees*."

Jack sensed that Mike had reviewed his file from the day he was born, in the central Illinois farmland town of Cissna Park, pop. 632, an hour east of the U. of I. campus. Jack's father was the local vet and his mother was a schoolteacher, both working overtime to give their six kids the promise of the *American Dream*- doctor; lawyer; engineer; scientist; or any other profession they should choose.

Their current six hundred and forty acres of farmland, a full section, planted with corn and soy beans in rotation, had been added to the original sixty-four acres by each Fitzgerald generation. This farmland is now cultivated by, and profits shared with, a nearby neighbor before heading to the town's co-op silos. The Fitzgerald clan consider themselves to be just an average mid-Western farm family, and figure that the rest of America must be working just as hard as they to get ahead in this great land of opportunity.

It all began with Jack's great-great-grandfather, Sean Fitzgerald, who had not disembarked, as did most of his Irish countrymen, in Boston or New York, but rather in Baltimore-gateway to the pioneer farmlands, plowed flat with dark, rich soil by the latest ice- age glaciers, 10,000 years earlier. He and his bride Maureen had saved enough for one- way passage, and to bring a meager array of family heirlooms, including a bit of sod from their blight- infested Irish potato patch in County Cork. The year was 1842.

They had headed West with an eye on California, but despite the odd farm job, they ran out of money 2,000 miles short, at a quiet farmland village named Cissna Park, population 312. This proved to be the end of the line, because Maureen was now carrying Jack's great-grandfather, Aidan Fitzgerald, and there were only 200 dollars left for fees to acquire a homestead grant of sixty-four acres- four acres for a house and barns; and the rest to clear, plow, plant, and reap.

They were the first Catholic family to settle in this Protestant community, but quickly found that their religion was their own affair amongst the majority of their conservative neighbors, and in fact, the whole town turned out to help put up the framing for their house and barns.

Mike McMahon suddenly skipped the small talk, and went directly to his point.

> "Jack, we need you to infiltrate Harvard's left- wing activists on campus; confirm their leader; determine whether he's preaching Socialism or Communism; and stick to him like a tick on a dog. We've already fingered the *Harvard Law Review* editor, a light-skinned black guy named Barry O' Hara, but we're not yet sure if he's a potential future political star to be reckoned with. He's got an I.Q. that's off the charts; and an inspiring rhetoric in favor of the 'fundamental transformation' of America- whatever the hell that means- and a radical far-leftist upbringing on both sides of his family." Jack then queried:

> "Mike, as you know, I'm Barry's publisher and faculty advisor on *The Law Review*, and he plans to practice law in Chicago next Fall. How do you expect me to infiltrate his inner circle in the time remaining?"

> "You'll figure it out Jack, and I'll stay in close touch. In the meantime, think long- term commitment, with me and the NSA 'greasing the skids' for you from a safe distance. I'll need to have your answer soon and remember, you don't have to be a WWII combat super- hero like your father in order to serve America."

With this parting remark, the elder man stood, shook Jack's hand, and left silently by the tavern's back door.

Jack returned to his campus quarters knowing he would not sleep until he had reached a decision about becoming an undercover spy. Reading between Mike's lines was not that difficult- it would be a very long, tough assignment if Barry O'Hara should become a top Democrat Party leader. At the same time, his assignment seemed to be without any apparent danger to himself or his family.

NSA's 'shadow spooks' were far removed from *James Bond,* not that Jack was afraid of physical combat. At age 21, after graduation from U. of I., he had often thought of joining his dad's WWII 1st Marine Division, and earning just half the medals and ribbons his father had brought home after beating the Japs, including two Navy Crosses; three Purple Hearts; and the Congressional Medal of Honor for leading his troops, while bleeding badly from a bullet in his left leg, on that final killing charge to the summit of Mt. Suribachi, in order to plant the American flag for the whole offshore fleet to see that Iwo Jima's key objective had been conquered. After nearly four years of jungle combat, Jack Sr. was carried back down the mountain and put aboard a hospital ship for the long voyage home, where he would sell War Bonds to finance the $80 billion cost of combating Germany; Japan; and Italy.

At 6:30am next morning, after a fitful sleep, Jack rang his boss, Law School Dean Aaron Bernstein, a budding Supreme Court Justice candidate and his mentor, for a pre-class meeting.

> "Jack, you must have spoken with Mc Mahon", the middle- aged, balding man observed in their sleepy-eyed phone conversation.

> "Yes Aaron, and as always, I need counsel. Your study chambers in an hour?"

"I'll be there. Coffee or tea?"

"I'll bring triple espressos, and almond *croissants*."

The two colleagues were alone in an empty building, as Jack opened the conversation, while both sipped, and lit their cigarettes.

"Mike said you referred me to the *NSA*. Why me?"

"Because you're my best and brightest, and my hope is that someday you may join me on the *Supreme Court* bench, which is where my Senate supporters say I'll wind up my career. In the meantime, life is all about serving others, in the roles our common God has designed for us. Your Jesus Christ, whom we Jews consider a great Rabbi, preached much the same theme during his short life in my ancient homeland."

"Aaron, I'm greatly encouraged by your visionary 'end game' of the Supreme Court bench, but my road to *Calgary* appears to be quite bumpy. I see mostly a *Garden of Gethsemane,* with *Judas Iscariot* lurking in the background, clutching 30 pieces of silver- namely, my ass. Have I got the picture?"

"Jack, you're a very 'quick study', as most of my previous *NSA* referrals have been, but to date we have not hit the 'mother lode'- that is, a future left- wing Presidential candidate with superb rhetoric, but we have both spotted him, and his name is Barry O' Hara. Mike will spell out the detailed game plan."

Mike was seated in the reception room, next to Bernstein's attractive young secretary, and arose to greet Jack as he emerged from the Dean's chambers.

"Thought I'd catch you before your afternoon classes. Let's go get an early beer at a nearby pub, and I'll try to fill in the blanks."

Jack nodded somewhat mystified, as they headed for Harvard Square, and a quiet back table at *Ryan's,* otherwise empty at this early hour, and ordered two *Guinness Stouts* and corned beef sandwiches. The elder man led off:

"Jack my boy, Aaron and I have thrown a lot of stuff at you, but if we didn't think you could handle the chin-high fastballs and outside curves, you would not be on our 'A- list'. As you'll learn from this file, Barry O' Hara is an exceptionally shrewd target- radical commie/ racist upbringing, and backed to the hilt by Chicago's *political Mafia.* He's never paid a dime for his education- scholarships all along the way, plus living allowances and he's now engaged to a very attractive, very intelligent, medium light-skinned African-American gal from Yale. He hasn't missed a beat so far." Mike continued:

"He's almost white enough to 'pass', and just close enough to 'black' to claim 'African- American'. My point is that Barry can appeal to people of all color shades; from pure *Blacks*; to *Latinos*; to white left- wing liberals- all in all, a powerful combination of voters, destined to lift him as high as he can go with his God-given talents.

"Your mission Jack, will be to follow this guy along the way, by 'morphing' into his trusted liberal *confidant*."

"Mike, I 'm in this ballgame, and you damn well knew it from the get- go that this is my chance to show my father's kind of patriotism- ass on the line for however many years this mission demands."

Jack shelved his NSA thoughts, and after classes spent the rest of the day contemplating just how he could win the hand of the only woman he yearned for. He had fallen in love at first sight, over a brief coffee break with tall (5 foot 10), flaming red-haired, sparkling green- eyed Kathleen O' Malley. 'I need look no further for my life mate' Jack thought- she could double for a young Maureen O'Hara. He also knew that his *Illini All-American* football hero courting tactics would never work with this beautiful, quiet *coleen*. Until now, he had remained a backdrop in Kathleen's steady advancement to Constitutional Law Assistant Professor at age 23, having also completed Law School in just 2 years, quite an accomplishment for this ivy-laden, antique Cambridge establishment called Harvard University.

Kathleen was assiduously courted by every rich, handsome, East Coast son of both *very old,* and *very new,* money. When she sloughed them off, one by one, Jack took courage. 'No', he told himself, 'she is definitely not impressed by family fortune heirs, but exactly what magic do I need to win her'? The opportunity was provided in the form of a faculty cocktail party- a quarterly obligatory affair complete with live dance band.

Jack's footwork on the gridiron might have been *All-American,* but he was no Fred Astaire on the dance floor. However, the band obliged him as he took Kathleen in his arms for the first time, with Cole Porter standards- *Night and Day, Begin The Beguine,* and other slow, romantic dances.

"Kathy", he blurted spontaneously, "I've waited a long time for this moment".

"No need to equivocate, Jack. If I didn't feel the same way, I wouldn't be trying to keep up with your clumsy feet. However, did you get dubbed by football writers as *The Dancing Ghost-* catching impossible passes, and making death- defying end- run blocks for your running backs- the *Illini's* best player since Red Grange more than half a century ago?"

"Kathy, that was four years ago. I was a team player then, and nothing has changed. I now have a new team in mind- Jack Fitzgerald and Kathy O' Malley- how does it sound?"

"I thought you'd never ask", she replied with a knowing, gorgeous smile.

Jack proposed to Kathy later that evening- on the outdoor veranda, under starry skies, after a long session of kissing and petting, during which she confided that she had saved her virginity for her wedding night.

Jack spent the entire next day studying NSA's extensive file on O'Hara, most of which dealt with Barry's family, friends, associates, and mentors. The list was a *Who's Who* of 'radical lefties'. It all began with 'Big Burt' O' Hara's third marriage to a white, left- wing activist, one Sarah Kapinsky, also a South Side Chicagoan, whom he had met at a *Black Panther* gathering. Both advocated violent overthrow of the American government.

True to form, after two previous divorces, Barry's dad split when he was two years old, and his mother left Barry a year later, in the hands of his maternal grandparents- both active revolutionaries, recently converted to radical *Islam* by 'The Reverend' Jedidiah White, who spewed forth his racist venom from the pulpit each Sunday morning, at the largest Baptist Church in the country. 'God damn America', and 'kill *Whitey* and his *Cracker* babies', he roared into the ears of young Barry O' Hara and a few thousand others. In all fairness, Jack deduced, the kid never had a chance to learn American core values.

This early indoctrination, and later Socialist tutelage, would form Barry's political vision. His exceptional I.Q. and oratorical skills would always place him at the head of his class, and his complexion would allow him the luxury of playing both ends against the middle- depending on his audience.

Whatever Chicago *political Mafia* juice might be required along the way was readily available when he would begin his political career after Harvard Law School. This was the way Jack figured it from Mike's *dossier*. The personal hitch was that Jack had always disdained politics and most politicians in general. He was a fiercely independent thinker who never joined any club except Harvard's Rugby team, dominated by ex-professional players from Wales; Britain; Australia; New

Zealand, and South Africa. Jack was content to play outside wing, and scamper like the wind until he lateralled the ball to his buddies for their 'touch downs' beyond the goal line- a now very familiar role for the lone *Yank* on the team.

It was with some trepidation that he would join Harvard's '*Young Democrat Club*', headed by Barry O' Hara, who was quick to corner him a few days later in *Ryan's*.

Barry led off with an innocuous comment:

> "Never figured you for a liberal Jack, what's your story?"

> "Just looking forward, Barry, just looking forward." Jack replied evenly, and then continued. "I don't like the way our country is going, and want to be part of the changes that I feel must come to put us back on the right track. I decided to start with your club since Democrats have historically been the promoters of change- simple as that."

Barry gauged Jack a somewhat reserved country boy with no personal political agenda. 'Jack just teaches class', Barry mused to himself, '*old school style* perhaps, but Jack never preaches'- a rare quality among young Professors in this tumultuous Harvard atmosphere. 'After Bob Clanton leaves office', Barry reasoned, 'a downstate Illinois guy like Fitzgerald might come in handy at some point along the line'. Even as he pondered, Barry was thinking of a U.S. Senate seat, and the importance of the crucial Mid-and-Southern Illinois conservative vote to get there. Barry figured Jack as a potential major asset in his future political plans, and told Jack:

"O.K. Jack, you're in our club. Perhaps in time you'll learn something about the dynamic jungle world of politics."

When first Jack, then Barry, became re- settled some months later in *Chicagoland,* Jack recounted to Kathy his 'back story' with O' Hara one evening over a delivery Chinese dinner. His new bride was still struggling with her mother's recipe books, but happily for Jack, Mary O' Malley, husband Bill in tow, came by for dinner every Sunday after Mass. She and Kathy disappeared into the kitchen, while Jack and Bill disappeared into the family den for football and *Jameson's* Irish whisky.

Several hours later, the feast was put before the two men of the house- leg of lamb; prime rib roast; and all the trimmings. The senior Irishman and his new son- in- law honed their carving knives, and proceeded to serve the ladies- Bill's wife nibbling, and daughter Kathy gorging to feed her blossoming fetus.

The same ritual prevailed on Thanksgiving day, when the entire Fitzgerald and O' Malley clans once again drove or flew into the Chicago suburban town of Naperville, where Bill and Mary held sway in their 6- bedroom, 6- bath mansion, complete with billiard/card room; cigar room for the gents; big spa for all; and indoor swimming pool for the kids, who were housed in the back yard guest cottage with their nannies. The O' Malley clan was slightly older but just as prolific as the Fitzgerald's.

Bill O' Malley, at age 86, was the eldest of the two patriarchs, and 'Big Jack' Fitzgerald, now 75, was not far behind. Each had made their money during many years of hard work- Jack the retired veterinarian and gentleman farmer; Bill the retired squire, a home and church builder in upscale *Chicago* suburbs.

Neither had inherited a dime- just rambling old family homes, and a little land.

During what would be Bill's last Thanksgiving, he and Jack the elder shared the meat carving honors, while elder daughters Kathleen and Maureen dished out plates to the combined clans of fifteen adults at the 'big table', while nannies tended to another thirty grand and great - grandkids in the huge kitchen, which resembled a small restaurant.

After dinner, Bill called the combined family members into his grand salon, and lit the timber in his marble-faced fireplace. He spoke for the last time to his and Jack's families. He was dying from heart disease, but had vetoed a transplant. It was time to meet his Maker, with no regrets for his extraordinary life.

> "I will not be with you this coming Christmas, so I pass the baton to Jack, who in turn will pass it along to one of you who truly believes in *The American Dream.* And a glorious dream come true it has been for myself and Mary. I judge myself the luckiest man on the face of the planet, so please don't weep for me when my time comes- I will go to a far better place."

True to his word, Bill passed away quietly in his sleep on Christmas Eve, to the sounds of downstairs family carolers belting out *Adeste Fideles, Silent Night*, and *White Christmas*.

Christmas day arrived, and the clans entered Naperville's Sts. Peter and Paul Church in mourning wardrobe, and were seated in the O'Malley family pews. Bill had built this glorious church twenty years earlier, as well as the adjoining school, for pure cost, a fact not lost on the Archdiocese of Chicago, which had received a phone call at midnight, announcing Bill's demise. The Church may often seem to act at a snail's pace, but on this Holy Day proved to be the contrary, as Cardinal William Flynn mounted the sermon pulpit.

> "Today we celebrate the birth of Jesus, and sadly acknowledge the death of our benefactor, William O'Malley, who built this church and this school, as well as many others in our Archdiocese. Bill was a man of few words and many deeds- a true friend of mine during his lifetime, and a true friend of our Church. I pray that all of you may follow his generous spirit."

Cardinal Flynn became clearly emotional as he concluded his surprisingly brief sermon, as most of the large gathering, outwardly or inwardly, teared with him.

> "Let us now inter our brother William O'Malley in his family crypt in our backyard cemetery- the only favor he had ever asked from his Church."

The Cardinal then led the solemn procession 'Inter- Mass'- a ritual unheard of in the Catholic Church- especially upon the birthday of Jesus Christ.

But then, Cardinal Flynn was as bold a mortal as his close friend, and would one day be elected *Pope Luke I*- the first American successor to Saint Peter, and oddly enough, the first Pope to adopt that *Disciple's* name, after two millennia of Luke's Biblical chronicle of Christ's life; times; and death on a Roman cross.

Cardinal Flynn's words of eulogy at the O'Malley crypt were as simple as his sermon had been some minutes earlier.

"Dear Lord in Heaven, please accept my brother into Your Eternal Kingdom. Let us now return to our Christmas Mass for Holy Communion."

Chapter Two

At their next meeting, McMahon quizzed his young 'asset' about his Harvard pub meeting with Barry O' Hara, and the events in Naperville.

"If I understand you correctly, your father has inherited the families' patriarchal mantle, and you are next in line. But tell me more about Barry."

"He plays his cards very close to the vest- definitely not the spontaneous type. His every move appears to be well- calculated, including his approach to me, even after two years of working together on the *Law Review.*

"He's clearly a European-style *Socialist*, with the central government taking care of the people from cradle to grave. My only question is whether his revolutionary Commie 'fellow- travelers' can swing him further to the left, but I think he's too clever to move to the fringe elements publicly, before he masters the great middle class of voters during his quest for political power- in other words, a decidedly left of center position on domestic and foreign political issues."

"Jack, I have an update for you. My South Chicago informants tell me that he will quickly hang his 'shingle' in their neighborhood, and be launched by several community activist clients. He will make big bucks in his private law practice, and modest bucks at the University of Chicago Law School, starting next September as an Assistant Professor of Constitutional

Law. His political fast track is well greased, from Mayor Daley on down. My best guess is that he'll run for State office as soon as he consolidates his base in Chicago and Cook County as a 'Community Organizer'.

"Bill, that means that I'll just have to stay one step ahead of him. I'd like you to arrange for a position as Assistant Dean at the University of Chicago Law School, and a Full Professorship in Constitutional Law and International Economics- which on the surface appears a normal career move from Harvard. To belay any suspicion on Barry's part, you can throw in an International Economics Professorship. That way, he won't know whether I'm shooting for a big 6- figure job on Wall Street, or Law School Dean at a major university."

"Judas Priest, Jack! How the hell do you come up with all this stuff?"

"Just a God-given talent Bill, plus, Kathy is pregnant, which means I'll need a much larger home and a much larger paycheck."

Kathy was ecstatic when Jack gave her the news over pre-dinner cocktails. She was going back to *Chicagoland* after nearly 15 years of 'Back East' schooling and teaching- Miss Randall's prep in Manhattan; Wellesley; then Harvard Law, where she was courted by many an eligible bachelor son of the landed 'East Coast Establishment'. She could have married banks; railroads; oil fields; or shipping lines, but she chose Jack, halfway through their second dance- by the same lightning bolt that hit Jack. She gave him her heart and soul, because he asked for nothing, except her hand in marriage before the evening was over.

The rest of her lifemate selection had been easy- they both knew it instinctively, and never argued with their *Guardian Angels*. It was a grand marriage made in Heaven, ceremony performed by Chicago's Cardinal William Flynn, full choir and 2,000 guests. Later that night, or perhaps during their Hawaiian honeymoon, they would create a baby.

"Where shall we live?" Kathy asked. "My elder brother Michael has an empty nest in Naperville, but it would mean commuting to Chicago."

"I think not, honey. First, a house with two women is a house divided, and when I exchange ideas with Michael, we can do it at his downtown club over lunch or 'happy-hour' cocktails. No, I think it best to buy a place in Lake Forest- the schools are the best in the country; my commute will be 20 minutes, and I like the idea of some day driving my own *BMW* roadster."

"Darling, you're talking about a very expensive lifestyle!"

"Not to fret dear, my salary will double to 80 grand for current living expenses, and Mike McMahon has agreed to double our *Credit Suisse* payment to 4 grand per month to cover our children's' future prep schools and college educations."

"So be it Jack," she said with a curious smile on her face, remembering that she and Jack came from *Great Depression* families that somehow managed to put food on the table; make the mortgage payment; and save for their kids' college educations.

A few of Kathy's younger brothers and sisters had moved west to California, landed in Southern Orange County, and worked their way up to San Francisco, where they practiced law; public accounting; medicine; and architecture- all bread-winning professions. Her elder brother Michael was bent on building new homes; schools; malls; churches, and office buildings just like his father, and had left his corporate law career in favor of *O'Malley Construction*. He would carry on in Bill O'Malley's giant footsteps, complete with political and Catholic connections at the highest level.

Jack and Mike McMahon next met in Boston's downtown *Sheraton* bar, to discuss the details of Jack's pending Chicago move. Bill spoke first:

> "Jack, 'the game is afoot', as *Sherlock* would say. You've got your Assistant Law School Deanship; your professorships in Constitutional Law and International Economics, and a friendly banker to finance your Lake Forest home. The rest is up to you."

> "I shall not fail" Jack responded quietly. "You've given me the tools, and I will now plow the land, as my father, grandfather, great-grandfather, and great-great-grandfather before me. It's strictly a question of family honor, without the medals my dad earned in the South Pacific, or my granddad at *Belieu Wood* in WWI France."

Jack's family was almost a mirror image of Katie's. Sean had cleared his fertile farmland with lots of neighborly help. Jack's *Illini-* educated father continued to farm the 'corn patch' with neighbor share- croppers, while practicing vet medicine and restoring ancient automobiles as a hobby- many dating back to the early 1900's, including a 1903 International Harvester flat-bed milk truck, and a 1904 Buick touring sedan. Yes, his dad definitely knew how to work with his hands, while 'Little Jack' knew how to work with his brain.

'Big Jack' Fitzgerald had graduated from nearby U. of Illinois on his G.I. Bill, and all six kids followed him- one doctor; one nuclear engineer; one high school principal; one pharmacist; one high school English teacher; and the eldest, a Harvard Law Professor, about to become a U. of Chicago Assistant Dean and 'Double Professor', just two hours North of his hometown roots in Cissna Park, central Illinois.

After that bittersweet Christmas two years earlier, Jack the elder had just one problem- how to take Bill O'Malley's place as patriarch. Jack the younger had just one problem- how to convince Barry O'Hara that he was gradually converting to *Socialist* dogma, and not just shadowing him. In the dead of night, he made one of his infrequent phone calls to Mike McMahon.

> "Mike, I just thought of something. I need my Chicago appointments ahead of O'Hara's, not behind- otherwise he might smell a rat."

At two in the morning, Bill grudgingly awoke and fired back.

"Jack, I'm way ahead of you. Barry will make his move after June graduation, and you will start in two weeks to begin Spring semester. I've found you a lovely home on the lake, complete with boat dock and friendly financing. I'll move to my Chicago office at the same time, because we may have found the 'mother lode'. Now let me go back to sleep."

Jack returned to bed, and Kathy's sleepy embrace.

"Honey, our timetable has moved up, but don't worry. Bill has arranged everything in Chicago for us- Lake Forest house and my University job, beginning in two weeks with Spring semester. Do you mind terribly giving up your Harvard job and becoming an ordinary pregnant housewife in an upscale Chicago suburb?"

"Dearest, I seem to recall that we recently vowed to share our lives, in sickness and in health, for better or for worse, 'till death do us part'. Is there anything about this vow that you are still vague about?"

"Nothing, my treasure, absolutely nothing."

The Lake Forest home Jack and Kathy moved into was perfect for a growing family- 4 bedrooms, 3 baths, and big living areas on the ground floor overlooking Lake Michigan and their boat dock. Jack's first drive in his pre- owned, metallic blue *BMW Z8* roadster was down to the University campus for his formal interview with Law School Dean, Sheldon Goldberg.

"Jack, we welcome you to one of America's top Law Schools- and perhaps *the* top Economics School- you won't be disappointed with the challenges we offer for your long- range career plans. I'll be your law boss, and *Nobel Laureate* Milton Friedman will take you under his wing on the International Economics side. You shouldn't be bored. By the way, you can call me "Shelly", but Milton prefers *not* to be called '*Uncle Miltie*'- to him an unwelcome reference to the 1950's T.V. king of comedy, Milton Berle, which his rowdy students have bestowed upon him."

Jack reflected for a long moment before responding to the man frequently referred to as a future Supreme Court Justice.

"Shelly, I'll try my very best not to disappoint you, nor Milton. But tell me, how did all of this come about?"

"By way of the *Oval Office*," Goldberg said simply, "and I never argue with our President."

Dean Goldberg then turned in his swivel chair; opened his back desk *credenza*; pulled out a bottle of very old *Armagnac*, a box of Cuban *Monte Cristo* cigars, and two finely etched crystal snifters.

"Jack, I have an idea that we will both bring honor to our University, so let's light up, sip, and enjoy the moment."

When Jack returned home, Kathy was waiting with baited breath. He quickly recounted the day's events calmly and surely, as was his nature. Kathy suppressed her delight while serving their evening cocktails. Later, pillow to pillow, she whispered.

"Jack my love, do you realize what this reception, backed by the White House means?"

"Not yet darling, not yet."

Jack met Mike in the Drake Hotel cocktail lounge ten days later, and as usual, Mike led off:

"Satisfied with my arrangements?", as he sipped his aged single malt Scotch, and lit up his contraband Havana cigar.

"Bill, I don't know how the hell you pulled all these strings, but Kathy and I are overjoyed with our new lives."

The elder man answered *sotto voce*:

"Jack, you have no idea of the power that has been concentrated in Washington and Wall Street since the Civil War. Our supposedly 'Sovereign States' have been castrated, slowly but surely. It's become a steady march towards *new age autocracy* at best, if O'Hara and his buddies ever gain the power they seek- the dark road to fulfillment of the prophecies of Author/ philosopher Ayn Rand, half a century ago in her novel *Atlas Shrugged*. They are collectively a dangerously incompetent lot that *must* be slowed down should they ever gain entry into the Oval Office. This is the only reason I don't retire tomorrow morning- and you are my 'mole' should that happen."

"I agree Mike. Our Constitution has been systematically trashed- only Ronnie Reagan stepped up to the plate and took action to defend our Constitution, while defeating the Russians in the 50-year '*Cold War*'."

"It looks like it will be up to guys like you and me to help defend that unique document invented by our Founding Fathers."

If Mike had any remaining reservations about Jack's unwavering dedication to family, God, and country, they were all dispelled. 'This kid has got the '*right stuff*' for his mission- I just hope I'm still around when he pulls it off', were Mike's final thoughts before they departed home to their waiting women.

The University of Chicago venue was as far afield from Harvard as the East Coast mentality was from middle America- or for that matter, the California 'Left Coast'.

Jack began his new professorial tenure by joining the University *Young Democrats Club*, much to the chagrin of mentors Milton Friedman and future Supreme Court Justice Sheldon Goldberg- both staunch conservatives. Jack just bit his lip and swore never to discuss politics in their presence. 'Good Lord'! he thought to himself, what a 'fearsome threesome' we would have made under different circumstances, with me as the fiercely independent balance. Little did Jack know what his destiny had in store for him!

Kathy was, as always, pure practicality when they discussed dilemmas over pre- dinner cocktails.

"Jack darling," she began, "we both have to bite the bullet and tether our tongues, especially in front of our families and friends. They must never get a hint of your undercover life, which precludes my writing about our adventures in my spare time, even in fictional form."

"Kathy, you never cease to amaze me with your brains and beauty, but I never imagined you yearned to write. Guess you'll have to settle for family diaries to pass along to our kids and grandkids- no memoirs until after I'm retired for at least 10 years, and even then I'll need NSA approval. Of course, your daily notes will be very helpful when the time comes, but make sure you keep them under lock and key."

As the Spring semester unfolded, it didn't take Jack long to begin making his well- balanced mark amongst movers and shakers. His Constitutional Law classes emphasized the original writings of our *Founders,* and the limiting flexibility of the Constitutional Amendment process. Jack proved to be an indulgent teacher- wide open to every meritorious challenge from both left and right viewpoints. His law students quickly dubbed him 'Solly', in reference to Hebrew King Solomon of Biblical fame, because Jack just taught, and never preached.

His International Economics classes took this same approach- always two sides to every issue worth debating, from Keynesian Central Government supremacy, to the 'free open market' doctrine promoted by Milton Friedman, who frequently used *Hong Kong* and *Singapore* as prime examples of great economic success when government stays the hell out of commerce.

When Barry O'Hara entered the scene in September, he would find his former mentor the most popular young professor on campus. Fitzgerald's classes were fully booked, unlike Barry's classes, designed for far- left wing Democrat boosters. Barry would end up sermonizing to his choir, in preparation for his political career just around the corner, and soon put out a law shingle in South Chicago's ghetto, specializing in 'Community Organizing', and selected Jack to be his *'go-to guy'* behind his political comet.

Jack and Kathy, who was now very pregnant with their first baby (to be named Mary), slid into their young family lifestyle without any major hiccups, and kept mainly to themselves, except for mandatory social occasions with their neighbors, many of whom slugged it out every day on the Chicago Mercantile Exchange, only to flame out before they hit forty- well off financially, but with premature grey hair and stomach ulcers, resulting from their hectic lives in the commodity 'trading pits'.

Not surprisingly, the Fitzgerald's were the only 'academics' on the block, and their friends were not shy in pumping them for clues about their 'secret wealth'. Jack's typical answer was that he worked two professorships, and invested his spare change in gold- backed, Swiss Franc- denominated common stocks- pharmaceutical firm *Roche,* and giant bank *Credit Suisse*. Sometimes he added that the Swiss Franc had been revalued upwards from 28 cents to 40 cents in the late 60's; was now at 60 cents, and over time would reach parity with the American dollar. Those who chose to follow Milton Friedman's *acolyte* would make out like bandits, because the Swiss Franc revaluation upwards would continue for many years to come.

Kathy's answer to neighborhood sleuthing housewives was equally vague.

"My husband is a great provider and a great lover- no sane woman could ask for more. It's the luck of the Irish- The O'Malley/Fitzgerald clans are a force to be reckoned with, and like all our men, Jack is self- made."

Afternoon housewife bridge games broke up at tea time- their men were coming home exhausted, and the last thing they wanted to discuss was female gossip about marriages in trouble, or *boy- toys* like fast cars and restored *Criss Craft* teakwood motorboats with twin inboard *Chrysler* diesel engines from the *Roaring Twenties*- it was *nuveau riche* bragging that Kathy disdained most.

It was an unwritten rule that religion and politics, which ran the gammit, were never debated. Everyone knew of Jack's involvement in the grass roots *Young Democrats Club*, and Kathy's charitable work for *St. Vincent De Paul* parish. But no one suspected that this was just an interim strategy in preparation for Barry O'Hara's arrival on the Chicago scene- the perfect cover for the 'perfect mole'.

Barry was so involved in his first professional job, and in renewing political contacts, that he failed to question Jack's previous move back to their common Illinois home turf. 'Pure coincidence', Barry told himself. 'Moreover', he thought, 'Jack could prove to be quite useful when dealing with down- state farmer conservatives'.

Thus, the idea of Jack Fitzgerald as his 'go- to' guy was born in Barry's mind, and would remain there throughout his many political campaigns, leading to the Oval Office some years later- against all odds and against any American born outside the lower Continental forty- eight; the odds against a Chicago political machine product; and the odds against a Socialist far left- winger. America was disgusted with the *status quo,* Barry reasoned, and was ready for fundamental changes. His oratorical skill, together with his unusual intelligence, proved to be a winning combination for the mass of middle class voters, who were otherwise not likely to vote for a black man.

As in most 'rags- to- riches' sagas, it would all begin innocuously enough with a *de facto* 'appointment' as a South Side Chicago councilman under Mayor Daley's umbrella. Although little skill was required for this *walk in the park* campaign, Jack accepted Barry's invitation to run things out of a vacant shoe store. Jack and Barry had a ball together, and none of O'Hara's fellow black Baptist inner circle took exception to his choice of a white Catholic as his right hand man. Jack was considered beyond suspicion, and would remain so.

Just one year later, a State Senate seat was put in play, and the O'Hara machine was tested by a rich young Italian businessman backed by the Irish and Polish - controlled unions, and the Catholic Archdiocese of Chicago. All in all, it presented a formidable obstacle for the young politician.

> "Well coach," Barry would start out at their daily late afternoon faculty bar brain storming sessions "what do we do now?"

Barry knew perfectly well what he would do to swing Cook County his way, and so did Jack- they would play the 'race card' for all it was worth, complete with raving Sunday sermons in the jam- packed Baptist Church, courtesy of 'The Reverend' Jedidiah White. Any black in South Chicago not voting for Barry would be ostracized. The power of O'Hara's racial duality won the day- by a meager eight hundred votes, cast by 'Tombstone' voters from the dearly departed, lodged in the large Baptist cemetery behind the church. The mandatory recount changed nothing- it was rigged from the get- go.

Barry's victory party was held in the local High School auditorium, amidst frequent choruses of "Bar- ry! Bar- ry! Bar- ry!" for their newly- anointed State Senator. As he climbed the lectern steps to his favorite microphone venue, O'Hara was the picture of a humble servant of the people.

> "Soon I will leave for Springfield" he said, "to begin changing the face of Illinois politics, in favor of you folks here tonight, who refuse to accept second- class citizenship as the answer to the American Dream of equal opportunity, and not just for the privileged few in up-scale manors in rich suburban towns."

Chapter Three

For the next 5 years, Jack and Kathy concentrated on creating their family. After Mary, a healthy 9lb, blonde haired, blue eyed image of her father, but with her mother's unique facial beauty and nascent stature. A year later, Kathy had a first trimester miscarriage of a baby boy, who would have been named Michael. Not to be deterred, 2 years later Kathy gave birth to twin boys, Mark and Matthew, both of whom inherited the flaming red hair and green eyes of their mother, and the handsome facial features and stature of their father.

The millennium New Year's day came and went, and on a whim Jack and Kathy decided to take an *impromptu* Swiss skiing trip to St. Moritz, leaving Mary, Matt, and Mark in the care of grandma Mary O'Malley, who, if she was bored with her widow's life, would soon be more than challenged by the antics of 2- year- old twin boys, and a 5- year- old girl.

She would later recover by taking a 6- month 'seniors only' cruise around the world, where she would meet any number of very interesting folks, most of whom were more than willing to recount their lives, and brag about their kids and grandkids- especially the elderly gentlemen, who were attracted to her ageless Irish beauty.

Meanwhile, Jack and Kathy gloried in their new honeymoon at the St. Moritz *Palace*, and made their fourth and final baby- a 7- month, four pound 'preemie' boy to be named Stephen, who barely survived his feet- first womb exit- and a traumatic incubator time which convinced them to end their baby-making.

When he returned to the real world, Jack found that Springfield was much the same small city it had been in Abe Lincoln's time, as were many other seemingly sleepy State Capitals. Jack drove down each Monday morning, met with Barry and staff, and returned Tuesday evening for his mid-and late-week classes.

In stark contrast, the action inside Government chambers was far from sleepy, as downstate and suburban conservatives fought mightily against Chicago's Cook County 'machine', on rare occasion with the help of a Republican Governor.

Jack's job as Barry's Chief of Staff was to convince one and all that his man was basically a mainstream kind of guy, as reflected in his prepared oratory- a strategy that apparently worked to everyone's amazement, since O'Hara's voting record proved just the opposite. When cornered from time to time, Jack would slough off tricky questions with a standard reply that went something like this:

> "State Senator O' Hara is just trying to appeal to a broad spectrum of Illinois voters, in preparation for a future run for the United States Senate."

It was a lame answer, but most media people were sympathetic towards a populist candidate with undeniable appeal to many voters- it worked even with his one-sided, left-wing voting record. But in 2004, when Barry and his fellow Democrats won control of the House and the Senate, Jack's focus was as ever, upon the future ascent of Barry O' Hara to the Presidential nomination of his Party in 2008.

Kathy was always quick to put in her two cents worth over cocktails, the dining table, and their nighttime pillow talk.

"Jack darling, we've been carrying on this *charade* for almost 10 years. When does it end?" Jack thought for a moment and replied:

"My best guess is in about 2 years, after the 2010 mid-term elections. Barry will win the nomination over Eleanor Clanton because of his oratorical skill, and again win against the likely Republican nominee, John McCall. The fact that he proposes an agenda of 'radical change' will win the day momentarily, but will not survive the grand test of economic reality when he attempts to 're- distribute' our national wealth.

"I believe that his Socialist agenda will be perceived as leading to Federal bankruptcy, and that the Wall Street guys who have so far backed him, will run for cover when Fannie Mae and Freddie Mac present a trillion-dollar bailout request to cover 'non-performing' home loans. It will not be a pretty picture, no matter how he may claim that the fault lies with previous President Bushnell.

"There will be a counter- revolution not seen since Newt's 'Contract with America' in 1994, which stymied former President Bob Clanton in a dramatic heartbeat, and balanced the Federal budget for 4 straight years, while reducing unemployment to below 5%.

"At that point, my mission will be complete with Barry O' Hara. He will be faced with a relatively conservative House and Senate, and will accept my resignation to take a Law School Dean's position someplace calm and quiet. His failure to 'fundamentally transform' America will be our final victory."

Sure enough, Jack followed Barry to the U.S. Senate- a 'slam dunk' election compared to the Illinois State Senate race some years earlier- no Italians; no Irish; no Catholic Church intervention- a pure victory for Chicago's Democrat dominance of Illinois politics.

Washington D.C. proved to be a brand new ballgame, played by big- spending lobbyists and special interest Congressional caucuses. Barry O'Hara learned his new Senatorial role quickly, as befitting his talent, and Jack Fitzgerald backed him up as his Chief of Staff, thoroughly vetting Barry's inner circle of advisors to assure their far left Socialist sympathies, including billionaire George Soros.

Two years into his first Senate term, Barry popped the question over dinner at Jack's home.

"Jack, I've been advised by close friends to make a run for the Presidency in 2008- what's your thinking?"

"Barry, I think your timing is perfect for great national change. Bushnell's compromising policies with our Democrat majority in Congress are dead in the water.

"Except for die- hard Southerners, your mixed racial heritage will ignite a lot of fervor amongst voters eager to once and forever rid their consciences of our days of Southern slavery and segregation.

"The Republicans will have lost their juice with the demise of the Bushnell policies- Iraq and Afghanistan included.

"Keep in mind Thomas Jefferson's prediction that occasional revolution is a healthy sign that our Constitution is working well."

At the start, Barry was challenged by Eleanor Clanton, who automatically inherited the legacy of her husband Bob's very successful, compromising economic policy with House Speaker Newt Gingrich. Halfway through the nomination campaign, Barry was trailing in every voter pole. Eleanor had his number on the main issues, and hammered at his voting record. The left- wing base they both appealed to was listening more to oratorical skill than the same old basic issues, and when Barry predictably pulled out the 'race card' late in the battle, the game was over.

The ensuing campaign against quiet- spoken combat hero John McCall, and his vociferous surprise running mate, obscure Alaskan Governor Susan Paulson, proved to be just another 'walk- in- the- park'. The economic collapse, coupled with Barry's impossible promise of revolutionary 'redistribution of wealth', won the day.

The new, and old, Democrat Congress quickly passed a trillion dollar Federal 'bailout bill' for banks and companies 'too big to fail'; together with a quarter- trillion dollar 'stimulus package', containing every *boondoggle* imaginable, little of which got spent on infrastructure.

Two years later, it was clear that the 'bailout' had not worked as planned, but American workers and investors rose to the occasion, as we always have in times of National crisis. 'Bailout' loans were being repaid to the Treasury faster than they could count, and Wall Street was in a *Mini Bull* market, amidst a general recession not seen since the 1930's *Great Depression*.

Unemployment 'froze' at nine percent- more in key States. The ill- conceived boondoggle 'stimulus' had failed to stimulate a damn thing, because new EPA regulations and a Presidential vow to increase tax rates confused the entrepreneurs responsible for seventy percent of new job creation.

When Jack and Barry next discussed this in the Oval Office, all of the President's inner circle were present.

Barry led off:

> "Jack, how do we get out of this mess before the mid-term elections, which are likely to give me a conservative Congress, just like Harry Truman in 1948, and Bob Clanton in 1994?"

Jack knew that the advice Barry was continually fed by his 'leftist buddies' had steeled him against any and all contrary views. Jack easily fell into line, as he had for the past dozen years, with minor comments only- just to show everyone that he was using his formidable brain power.

"Mister President, the only dramatic move you can make between now and Election Day is to support continuation of the tax cuts for everyone- rich and poor alike- until the recession is over, and perhaps propose even greater incentives for job-creating entrepreneurs.

"The men and women who drive our economy would gain confidence in the near future, and you would give up very little of your long- term plan to re- shape America."

O' Hara allowed his minions to take over this insider debate. Predictably, no one else took Jack's side. The President then spoke after all the debating was over.

"Jack, ol' buddy, you have suggested a course of action that is contrary to my vision, and promotes compromise with the East Coast landed aristocracy, whom I view as a privileged class which has little place in my transformation of America."

The O' Hara inner *clique* was overjoyed by their victory, and Jack was pleased with his answer. He had gone as far as he could go, commensurate with his patriotic mission to lead Barry down the garden path to domestic policy failure.

When Jack met Mike McMahon in Chicago's Drake Hotel bar that evening, he was surprised to learn that his 'handler' was still way ahead of him.

"Jack, you've gone much further than I would have ever dreamed of when we first met", observed the now partially grey- haired man with the permanent Bahaman tan, taking a long sip of his usual well-aged single malt

Scotch, while lighting his Havana and offering another to Jack, which he quickly accepted. Jack's occasional cigars were otherwise limited to much cheaper *Dominican* transplants." Mike continued:

"We think it is time for your graceful exit, which should come on the heels of the probable Republican Congressional gains next month. Ironically enough, you'd probably be the best guy to make peace with a new conservative Congress, and give O' Hara a big boost for a second term, but my people think it best to leave him to his own devices, and play out his hand."

"Mike, Kathy and I have been waiting a long time for this moment to arrive. We sincerely thank you and your people for making the journey as painless as possible."

The elder man responded:

"Your Country thanks the two of you for your dedication and stamina. Tonight, you can tell Kathy that she will be a Law School Full Professor, while you will be the new Law School Dean of the University of San Diego- a top rated Jesuit Law School. You will have no continuing mission for my *NSA-* and I might add, a good stepping stone for the Supreme Court in a few years.

"On the financial side, you have enough socked away in *Credit Suisse* gold Francs to last you a lifetime and provide for your kids' college and post- graduate education.

"Alas, there will be no medals to honor your service to our Country, but something tells me you and Kathy knew this from the start."

Jack responded quietly.

"Yes Mike, we did, but as always, the ends justify the means in everything but screwing around with our Constitution. Too many brave men and women have given their lives or limbs to preserve our God- given freedoms, and we're just one secret footnote to our glorious history- two Americans doing what others have done before us."

Jack related the day's events to Kathy over pre- dinner cocktails.

"I can't believe it!" she shouted when Jack told her of their new life in San Diego.

"Me a Law School Professor and you the Dean of the Law School?"

"Yes, darlin' Kathy", Jack replied with elation, "we are going to our new home in San Diego."

After dinner, they made love 'til dawn, with Kathy screaming out as never before with each orgasmic climax. They were as if reborn in marital bliss.

When Jack and Barry next met in the Oval Office, some of the President's key advisors and Cabinet members had resigned.

"Jack", Barry began, "you're the only trustworthy guy I have left".

"Before you go any further, Barry, I'll stick with you until the start of next semester at the University of San Diego, where I will be the new Dean of the Law School, and Kathy a Full Professor. We'll be leaving at the end of January. It's been a great ride for these many years, and I wouldn't have missed it for the world."

O' Hara was surprisingly graceful at the news.

"Thanks Jack for all your advice along the way- you've played a big part in getting me into the Oval Office, and no politician could ask for more. I shall miss you greatly, and can only wish you and Kathy the best of everything."

The President then went to his liquor cabinet, pulled out two crystal brandy snifters and two Cuban cigars.

"Let's drink to the coming changes that we must both face, and to our success in dealing with them."

Jack's 'mission' had not followed the *NSA* script. Barry O'Hara did not self-destruct, but rather would be re-elected by a very narrow margin in 2012. However, his 'fundamental transformation of America' and 'redistribution of wealth' European-style Socialist agenda had been stopped cold by the representatives of *We The People*.

As predicted during Dean Bernstein's Harvard Law days, Jack's mentor had become Associate Justice of the Supreme Court, then nominated Chief Justice by President Bob Clanton, one of his last acts before giving way to incoming President Greg Bushnell. Clanton proved to be the consummate politician, notwithstanding his personal scandals. When they

44

got together during the late 2000 transition period, the main topic of conversation was the selection of a new Chief Justice nominee to submit before the 'lame duck' Senate.

"Bob", Greg began, "we've had a few Jewish Justices on The Court, but never a Chief Justice." Clanton responded after deep contemplation:

"Well Greg, we never had a Catholic President before Jack Kennedy. These shibboleths are antiquated. It's as true today as it has been since day one- the man makes the job, as you will soon find out, and there is no lawman in America as qualified as Aaron. I guarantee you that he will defend our Constitution with his dying breath."

"Bob, your word is good enough for me- consider it done."

The two Presidents laid down their Cuban Cigars; inhaled the rest of their *Bristol Cream* sherry, and shook hands. Aaron Bernstein would prove to be the best Chief Justice in more than a century.

Jack's credentials as President O' Hara's former *Chief of Staff* quickly made him the most popular teacher on campus, although as always, he never pushed anything but conservative Constitutionalism, much to the chagrin of a few of his brainwashed left-wing students. Jack's classes nonetheless had a long waiting list, which meant that he taught the best and the brightest, mainly those who had survived their first year.

The thankless mission of selecting the 'best and the brightest' for Jack fell to his wife Kathy, who was quickly dubbed 'the

Redhead'. Her classes overflowed with those unable to qualify for 'The Man', but she taught much the same Socratic approach to the Law as Jack.

Jack and Kathy's transition from Washington to San Diego was greased as always by Mike McMahon, who located a 5-bedroom home with a backyard pool, sitting atop the 15th fairway of the Solana Beach Golf and Country Club- twenty minutes from their law school domain down Pacific Coast Highway.

Jack had learned many years before to never look the NSA's gift horses in the mouth- whether a handsome Lake Forest chalet on Lake Michigan, with private boat dock, or a handsome golf course home. His NSA 'mole' mission was now over, but his service to his country would soon continue in a very different vein, as Associate Justice on the Supreme Court, under the leadership of Chief Justice Aaron Bernstein.

Jack's nomination came as a bolt from the blue. He had divorced all ties to the political arena, and as far as he knew, had no continuing sponsor of any importance. Mike McMahon was enjoying retirement at his beachside abode in the Bahamas, and Jack had cultivated no prominent figures in San Diego. The very thought of political intrigue had become anathema to Jack, and Kathy shared his feelings.

> "Jack, you've taken care of our family- the kids will be going through prep school and college; we have an easy life; no money worries; and our grand- kids are just a few years away. Why should you even consider a lifetime appointment to the Supreme Court?"

"Honey, our Constitution is in constant jeopardy from those who wish to change America from the basic individualism of common folks that our *Founders* envisioned, and make them into robots- looking to the *'D.C. Mafia'* to care for their every want in life, from cradle to grave.

"I refuse to sit back in relative luxury, and not come to the aid of my country- assuming of course, that my brain still has something to offer. Otherwise, we can all retire to our Cissna Park farm and watch the corn grow. I believe the time has come for yet another big change- and it's either our High Court, or our low farm land. Let's get our families together and take a vote."

The O'Malley's and the Fitzgerald's met in Cissna Park for the Thanksgiving weekend of 2013. President Barry O'Hara had followed Chief Justice Bernstein in recommending Jack for Associate Justice, never suspecting that he was a former *NSA* 'mole' in Boston, Chicago, Springfield, Washington, and the White House-always supporting O'Hara's bull-dog, wealth-sharing, anti- capitalist, ideological agenda.

The Thanksgiving 'family vote' was unanimous, which was rarely the case between the suburban O'Malley's and the farmland Fitzgerald's.

'Justice Jack' was humble in his family welcomes at what he termed *'the corn patch'*. Kids and nannies slept in the refurbished barn and watched the corn grow, and the dinner conversation centered upon the education of each family's children. The O'Malley kids were a few years older and were attending top Catholic Universities across the country- from

Santa Clara near San Francisco; *Notre Dame* in Nothern Indiana, to *Boston College* on the East Coast.

Jack and Kathleen would chose different schooling for their teenagers- *St. Johns Prep School* for Matt and Mark; *Eton* for Stephen; and *The Julliard School of Music* for daughter Mary. Their NSA-funded *Credit Suisse* bank account would take a mighty hit along the way, but this is what Jack and Kathy had saved for.

The adults in the combined families were careful to avoid any question put to Jack that might smell of political bent. After leading Easter dinner grace, Jack said simply:

> "I don't know when Kathy and I will be free for another family reunion like this, so let's enjoy our short time together. I leave you for the toughest job I have ever contemplated, because our Constitution has been under constant attack for the past 150 years, and I promise that I will do my utmost to re- establish it for this 21st century and beyond. I ask that you all pray for my success along the way."

Two days later, when the combined clans had scattered to the four corners of America, Jack and Kathy took solace in their old familiar Georgetown manor, purchased during his two years as Chief of Staff to Barry O'Hara. One by one, they renewed old acquaintances, including a private dinner at the White House.

Contrary to popular belief, there is no 'Book of Secrets'- the NSA had never revealed Jack's previous undercover mission, so conversation quickly drifted to the 2014 mid-term elections.

"How do you figure it, Jack?" Barry queried.

"Much tougher than 2012, Barry. You can't rely on your controversial healthcare bill to carry the day, so you have to come up with something new that can pass the new conservative Congress, and I can't think of anything that would be acceptable to you or your other close advisors. We went through this routine four years ago, when I suggested a 'middle road', but House Speaker Rowan is no Newt Gingrich, and he now controls the spending. So I guess you've got to invent something entirely new, and very popular across the board- especially for the average taxpayer."

Jack and Kathy's first Georgetown dinner party was with Chief Justice Bernstein and wife Sarah. Aaron opened the conversation over cocktails:

"Jack, in the past few months you've seen only the tip of the iceberg, as it were- several lower court decisions quickly overturned or sent back for further review. In the larger scheme of things, small pickings. But right after New Year's Day, we have some Constitutional 'blockbusters' to deal with- *"U.S vs. Arizona"*, *"U.S vs. Texas"*, and *"Florida et al vs. U.S."*, to name just three cases.

"I'd like you to work at my side during the coming months, and to represent me when necessary, because I'm not well, and may not have the energy required to convince our colleagues of the answers we two may come up with. I'm sorry you haven't had a few years more under your belt Jack, but then, you've always been a 'quick study', as I recall."

"Aaron, you're taking a big gamble relying on me to push through these conservative decisions- I have little or no standing with these older guys and gals- I'm the 'new boy on the block'."

"New boy or not, you're the *only* boy who knows where I want this 5-4 split Court to go in future years in order to preserve and protect our Constitution. Jack, I'm dying of colon cancer, and have maybe 6 months left, so my choice is rather limited. It's now strictly up to us to get the job done in the next 90 days. We have these three cases before us, and thank God they don't require anything but interpretation of the law- no witnesses, just Constitutional arguments. Of course, you realize that if we are successful, this will probably kill any chance of you taking my place when I'm gone. O'Hara will be as mad as a hornet."

"Whoa, Aaron, let's take this one step at a time- you're way ahead of me. Why would I ever be considered to take your place?

"Because you have the keenest Constitutional mind in the country, and everyone of importance knows it."

Chapter Four

Jack shared his day with Kathy, over a double vodka *Martini*.

"I'll just vote with the usual conservative 5 to 4 majority in *U.S vs. Arizona,* and *U.S. vs. Texas,* and refrain from any substantial additional comments in my written brief, such as Federal gross negligence in protecting our borders. Then we have *Florida et al* vs. U.S. in the matter of *O' Haracare.*"

"Jack, Aaron's terminal illness comes as a great shock. He has been the backbone of The Court for more than a decade, and for him to even think of you as his successor is a great compliment.

"I think a lot will depend upon your effectiveness in pinch-hitting for him during the coming months, and your persuasiveness in leading your fellow Associates- especially on the Federal healthcare overreach, which we both know to be clearly unconstitutional.

"No government legislation can oblige us to purchase any product. And for the government to include regulations requiring coverage for either abortion or birth control- against any healthcare providers' religious beliefs- is outright blasphemy." Jack sipped his cocktail, took a long drag on his cigar, and responded:

"Kathy my love, I wish it were that simple, but the political ramifications of O' Hara's entire healthcare bill, and his 'legacy' with it, brings enormous pressure on the Supreme Court. Aaron and I don't want another 5 to 4 vote- it's got to be much closer to unanimity, say 7 to 2."

"Jack, the political side of this case can take forever, but the Constitutional side is straightforward. Suggest to your colleagues that they go back and research the original intent of our *Founders*, when they debated the now infamous 'commerce clause'. You'll find most of your internal discussion clues in that history. You've got to convince them that the fundamental precepts of our Constitution are at stake. There must be a limit imposed upon the power of the Federal Government-or the State Governments for that matter- or else *We The People* will be in danger of losing the freedoms our *Forefathers* fought and died for."

As they passed their children's empty bedrooms on the way to their love chamber, Jack suddenly thought to himself 'what have I done to deserve this brilliant and beautiful woman?'

As they began listening to the opening arguments from both counsels, Jack and his colleagues realized that they were about to redefine the Constitutional limitation placed on Federal powers; but also knew that they were not alone when it came to this task. They were just following the lead of many High Courts before them, which had grappled with similar Constitutional questions regarding the delegation of authority to the Federal Government, and the separation of powers between the 3 branches.

Jack believed that past actions constituted a giant bureaucratic step- *not* along the *Yellow Brick Road* towards the *Emerald City*- but rather, the dangerous road leading to the *autocracy* described by author/philosopher Ayn Rand in her prophetic novels, *The Fountainhead a*nd *Atlas Shrugged.*

Chief Justice Aaron Bernstein, before he died, once again summoned Jack Fitzgerald to his chambers for a private chat regarding *Florida et al vs. The U.S.*, which centered upon *The*

Affordable Healthcare Act, known as *O'Haracare-* which had turned out to be neither affordable, nor did it provide freedom of choice for healthcare recipients.

> "Jack, this is the most important case you or I will ever preside over, because it goes to the very heart of our Constitution's separation of powers between the States and the three branches of Federal Government, and between Church and State.

> "I'm not saying that Abe Lincoln was wrong in combatting Southern State secession with every means he could muster to save our Union, including freedom for several millions slaves. Abe did what he had to do, and never looked back, and neither should we at this time. Future generations will judge us on our collective wisdom during the coming weeks, and we dare not fail them, so I'm handing you my *de facto* powers to lead my Court. I'm dying Jack, simple as that."

Sure enough, Chief Justice Bernstein passed away just a few days after his fellow *Supremes* had agreed to an historical verdict, by a 7 to 2 majority, which read in part:

> "Neither the Federal Government, nor any other Governmental entity can require the purchase of *any product*, including health insurance. Nor can they abrogate the religious rights of citizens, such as requiring Catholic health institutions and doctors to provide for abortions and contraceptives. Therefore, this Court has decided that the entire *Affordable Healthcare Act* is unconstitutional and therefore null and void."

Both Jack and Barry attended Aaron Bernstein's burial services in Arlington Cemetery, after which Jack pulled the President aside.

"Barry, if you're interested, I've developed a few new solutions for universal healthcare and other domestic issues which could leave you with a legacy greater than you have ever dreamed. Whenever you have the time, I'd like to discuss them with you."

"No time like the present, Jack. Hop in my car and we'll go back to the Oval Office, and along the way you can also tell me how you and Bernstein managed to torpedo my Healthcare Act."

"There was absolutely nothing personal, Barry- it was strictly business-which is what I get paid to do when it comes to our Constitution. Our only mistake, if you can call it that, was in taking far too much time to bring this case to our Bench- we should have found an excuse to jump in at the very beginning, and quashed it out of hand.

"In hindsight, it was clearly unconstitutional overreaching, and as it turns out, the administration of that 2,500- page law has been a nightmare, as everyone has witnessed. How the devil did you think you and your Democrat Party could get away with this? The good news is that I have come up with a better solution, and one that should please you." A few minutes later, in the Oval Office, Jack would explain:

"Barry, how would you feel about giving full responsibility for free healthcare; free schooling; and guaranteed daily employment at $100 per day to the villages, towns, and cities- in other words a return of social services powers to the local level- with the Federal Government sticking to its Constitutional mandate for national defense; foreign representation; foreign trade; and national money management?"

"It almost appears as if you have become a Socialist, Jack. Apart from the revenues required, it sounds great to me, although the shift in power strikes me as being somewhat revolutionary."

"That's exactly what our *Founding Fathers* decided more than two centuries ago, when they voted to cut the umbilical cord with England. Thomas Jefferson later observed, after the Constitution and Bill of Rights were finally ratified, 'I hold it that a little rebellion now and then is a good thing, and as necessary in the political world as storms in the physical'. This brings up the basic question of whether or not you believe, as I do, that the American people are quite capable of managing their own day-to-day lives, with little or no intervention from either Washington, nor from their State Capitals. For purposes of this discussion, let's pretend that you do.

"Now, about the money that would be needed. I have a solution which will yield about $5 trillion of tax revenues in year one, as opposed to current revenues of about $2.6 trillion at all levels of government, and at the same time reduces our current 88,000- page *Machiavellian* tax code to just a few paragraphs."

"Exactly what do you have in mind?"

"Simply stated, the essence of paragraph one would go something like this:

"There shall be enacted by the Congress a Single 10% Tax on *every financial transaction in our economy*- with no exceptions or exclusions- and no 'double taxations', such as debt repayments. Debts are taxed when incurred. Paragraph two would read as follows:

"This Single 10% Tax shall be paid daily, and collected

daily by local governments, which shall retain 50% of the gross tax proceeds, and transfer the remainder to the Counties (10%); States (10%); and the Federal Government (30%). All governmental entities shall operate with a positive cash flow budget- all future domestic and foreign borrowings are specifically prohibited.

"Local governments shall be responsible for free healthcare to every resident, supervised and managed by newly- established *Municipal Medical Councils*; free public and private school tuition, from age 3 through PhD, including adult education, supervised and managed by *Municipal School Councils*, and guaranteed day work to the otherwise unemployed residents, at the minimum wage rate of $100/day, $12.50/hr; supervised and managed by *Municipal Jobs Council*.

"In short, local governments- not Federal, nor State nor County governments- would be responsible *for taking care* of their local residents. Counties would be responsible for county institutions; county infrastructures; and county environment.

"States would be responsible for State Parks; prisons; freeways; the protection of their borders with foreign countries, and the repayment to local governments of the net present value of future State insurance liabilities, such as State unemployment and disability.

"The Federal government would retain responsibility for national defense; foreign representation; foreign trade agreements; management of the nation's finances; and the repayment to local governments of the net present value of all future Federal insurance liabilities, including Social Security, which would be distributed into new

Personal Pension Accounts, in the form of 30- year Federal T-Bonds, earning compound quarterly interest at the then- prevailing rate for such bonds; or upon death, in which case the proceeds shall be distributed to that person's designated beneficiaries.

"There would be *no other sources* of governmental revenues, including but not limited to, personal or corporate taxes on earnings and profits; property taxes; tolls; fees; customs duties; excise taxes; licenses; assessments; alcohol, gasoline, tobacco, and luxury taxes. There would be no tax placed upon the repayment of debt.

"The sole exceptions shall be governmental lotteries, including a new *National Daily Debt Reduction Lottery,* based upon the last several digits of total collections from the Single 10% Tax receipts for that day. Each winning ticket would receive $1 million for their $1 ticket (plus 10 cents tax). The remaining net proceeds be used exclusively for the reduction of our National foreign debt, and thereafter for the reduction of our domestic debt.

Barry broke in for comments:

"Hold on a minute Jack, surely you don't mean *all* financial transactions and asset transfers. What about charitable donations? Purchases of homes? Purchases of stocks and bonds? Acquisitions and mergers between corporations? Federal purchases of military hardware? - just to name a few." Jack replied quickly:

"Barry, how do you think it otherwise possible to almost double governmental tax revenues in year one without taxing a lot of people and entities that have never been taxed before, because of existing tax code exemptions.

Our current tax code is a monster, and has got to be *dumped*!

"You have always advocated a *'fair tax'*, which is clearly aimed at the people and entities with most of the money. Well, I've given you what you said you wanted, because they will pay 80% or more of all governmental tax revenues- and on a daily basis, which will put governmental tax *cash flow* at a level that will never again require borrowing a dime from either the American people, or much less, foreign countries like China, Japan, or the European Union. The only new T-Bonds that will be issued in the future are those that go directly into Personal Pension Accounts every payday.

"Furthermore, I don't believe that there is a person or entity in this country that will risk 2-5 years in jail for a lousy 10%, considering that all of their *'back-end profits' are* tax-free.

"I further estimate that more than 1,000 foreign corporations will transfer their headquarters to various American cities because of the 'no tax on profits' embodied in our new tax code- bringing several million new jobs to America- and because our cost of labor would be 10% on wages, and 10% on PPA contributions, as compared to 50% or more in the European Union." Barry then queried:

"So what happens to the IRS?" Jack countered:

"Barry, they fade into oblivion like a bad dream after the current fiscal year. Many adept field investigators will no doubt find employment with their towns, and the others will eventually find *'productive'* employment in various administrative jobs. I say *'productive'*, because the collection of taxes; tolls; license fees; and parking meter quarters is, by definition, 'none-productive' for our national economy. The same goes for some half million tax accountants and tax lawyers- they add absolutely nothing to our country's productivity- *'Gone With The Wind'*, Barry, just like the Old South."

"What happens to the health insurance companies?" Jack responded:

"There will still be plenty of health- related insurance business. First of all the towns will be looking for 'catastrophe coverage' for cancer patients, plagues, such as Ebola, and other epidemics. On the individual level, many families will choose to be covered by 'disability and Sick Pay policy' which is not provided for by the towns, although the Municipal Medical Councils negotiates for the lowest rates."

"What about home buyers and their mortgages?"

"Once again my answer is both simple and easily understood by 99% of Americans. The 10% tax is 'folded' into the mortgages; the payback of which debt, as I told you before, is a *nontaxable* transaction, as are all debt repayments, including payments from PPAs, which is repayment of national debt owed to retirees.

Barry then asked about the replacement of Social Security Insurance (SSI) by Personal Pension Accounts (PPAs), to which Jack replied:

"Barry, we both know that *'Social Security'* is no security at all- in fact, it is *unfunded* by about $100 trillion- the greatest domestic debt ever created by our Federal Government. I have created a new way out of this inevitable fiscal disaster by designing a 50-year plan, whereby the employer pays a contribution of 10%

of each paycheck into a personally-owned account, administered by the Treasury Secretary, which goes something like this:

"All existing Pension Accounts- private; union; and all other government employee plans, must be converted within the next 12 months into T-bonds for deposit into *Personal Pension Accounts*, which shall be subject to 'default' claims by all creditors, including bank home loans. Each Personal Pension Account shall receive a quarterly statement which includes the previous account balance; additions; T-Bonds interest earned; and any withdrawals.

"Existing Pension Accounts related to future benefits such as health, unemployment are to be actuarially calculated at their net present value, and distributed in the form of T-Bonds to the local governments of the members' current addresses, since the towns now bear responsibility for the welfare of their residents. T-Bonds issued shall be used only for existing Local and State debt repayment, and 'rainy day' reserves.

"Jack, tell me how *'10% on everything, paid everyday'* results in about 22% of Gross Domestic Product."

"Great question, Barry. Let's take the simple example of the 'tax life' of a loaf of bread. 'Sam the seed store owner' buys a bushel of seed from 'George the grower', pays him cost, plus a 20% profit mark-up, and then a 10% tax. 'Farmer John' buys wheat seed from Sam, and pays cost, plus a 20% profit mark-up, plus 10% tax. After harvesting his crop, 'Farmer John' sells it to his local 'Co-op' in Nebraska, which pays him an additional 10% tax, after his 20% profit mark-up. The local 'Co-op' ships a rail car of wheat grain to 'Mike the miller' in

Springfield, Illinois at cost plus 20% profit mark-up, and another 10% tax.

"'Mike the miller' processes wheat grain into flour and ships it to 'Bob the baker' in Chicago at cost plus 20% profit mark-up, plus 10% tax. 'Bob the baker' converts the flour into loaves of bread and ships them to a nearby supermarket chain, at cost plus 20% profit mark-up, plus 10% tax.

"The supermarket chain then trucks the loaves of bread to their outlet in Naperville, which pays them cost plus 20% profit mark-up, plus 10% tax. Finally, 'Carol the customer' goes to the check-out counter and pays them their cost plus 20% profit markup, plus 10% tax. The total tax collected along the way is about 30% of the final retail price.

"At the other end of the spectrum, we have 'Bob the billionaire', who decides to acquire several companies during the year at a total price of $50 billion in cash and stock, and pays a $5 billion tax on the purchase.

"Next, we have 'Joe the plumber'- an independent businessman who, with every other independent 'mom and pop' enterprise, independent professionals, and their employees represent about 60% of our work force. Assuming that they spend about $100,000 per year to support their families, this group will yield about $10,000 each in tax revenues plus another $50,000 each for the sale of their goods and services.

"Now Barry, let's take your Federal Government, which, in the future will receive about a $1.5 trillion share of total tax revenues- more than enough to defend America; support our foreign embassies; manage our remaining Federal Government; maintain our national monuments and parks, and begin to pay the quarterly interest on Personal Pension Accounts. In addition, the *Daily National Debt Reduction Lottery* should bring in close to $1 trillion per year from patriotic Americans anxious to become one of several dozen 'instant millionaires' every day.

"Finally, let's look at Wall Street. I estimate that at least $10 trillion in year one will be newly invested in American companies. This would mean about $1 trillion in additional taxes from stock exchange transactions. Summing it all up Barry, 'all-out capitalism' is the necessary means to provide the money required to make every family in America secure in their healthcare; schooling; employment; and fully funded retirement at age 70.

"Politically speaking, left-wing Socialist Liberals and Progressives will love you for the free domestic programs; Conservatives will love you because there is no tax on corporate profits; personal incomes; or property. People like myself will love you because you will be sponsoring bi-partisan legislation."

"Jack, it looks like you are forcing me into a kind of 'Bob Clanton box' of having to join hands with the conservative side of Congress."

"You're right Barry, that's exactly what I had in mind in order to get the Federal Government off its backside. You'll have to convince the Congress that these proposals are strictly non-partisan, and in the best interest of the American people."

"Jack, are there any Constitutional conflicts of interest you can think of that would prevent you from being at my side during these political negotiations with

Congressional leaders?"

"Barry, the fact that it's never been done before does not mean that *'Tri-partite'* efforts in the interest of the American people is on the face of it unconstitutional- I can assure you that it is *not*. Furthermore, I suggest that after you have laid the groundwork, we all meet in *my* conference room, as a symbolic gesture of political neutrality, and Constitutional equality.

Three weeks later, this historic gathering was opened by the President:

"My purpose in requesting this extraordinary meeting of the three independent branches of government is to answer the many questions you must have regarding the basic framework of the most important legislation put to the Congress since FDR's *New Deal* eighty years ago. I'll now refer your comments to Associate Justice Fitzgerald, who is my *Chief Architect* on these domestic solutions." As was his custom, Jack rose as he spoke:

"As I look around the table, I see that we have all known each other for several years, and in the spirit of friendly cooperation I think we can dispense with formal titles-you can call me 'Jack'. I believe we are in the same position today that our *Founding Fathers* found themselves in 1776, when they cut the 'umbilical cord' with England.

"In our case, it boils down to cutting the 'umbilical cord' with Washington, as far as our day-to-day lives are concerned. We must believe, as our *Founders* believed, that the American people are fully capable of taking care of their neighbors and their fellow townspeople. I don't think I'm overstating the situation when I tell you that this 'package' of Legislation is the equivalent to a second *Declaration of Independence* for the average American. In order to make it Constitutionally 'bullet proof', you will need to secure a 67% approval by both Houses of Congress.

"The solutions being offered for your approval have taken several years to develop fully, including every side-effect I could think of. So, why don't we start with the most important social issue-family healthcare- which at a cost of $1.6 trillion is the single most important item in our economy." House Minority Leader, Anna Palmeri, predictably raised her hands first:

"Jack, please tell us about the newly-established Municipal Medical Councils," To which Jack responded:

"Good question, Anna. That's where families go to sign up for the type of medical service they prefer- they can choose between a 'house-call doctor', armed with a medic van and nurse/driver; bi-monthly family visits to nip illnesses in the bud, by examining and taking blood samples from each family member on the same visit.

"My best guess is that this timely type of action could eventually save the health system about $500 billion per year. Alternatively, families can sign up to retain their existing 'office doctors'; drive back and forth for each family member; receive exactly the same examinations, and the same referrals to specialists when required. Thus, the health provider service is essentially the same- the basic difference being that the 'house-call doc' will probably be a young, up-to-date, ex-hospital resident intern.

"The second responsibility of the Municipal Medical Council is to settle all malpractice complaints. Finally, all families would be free to change doctors at any time-no questions asked. Personally, I would opt for the young 'house-call doc', because I would be able to observe the tests performed on my family, and the doctor's comments.

"In conclusion, a 'house-call doc' will cost the community about $300,000 per year for giving basic health services to about 300 families- at the rate of $100 per family medical visit, paid by local government, plus $10 tax on the visit paid directly to the doctor for local tax deposit. There would also be a 10% tax on any prescribed medication, also paid for by the local government. On the other hand, a successful 'office doc' would cost about $500,000 per year, at the same rate of $100 per single family member visit.

"In the same manner, towns would provide free tuition to any school-public; private; or parochial- from age 3 through PhD, and any required adult education, with the oversight of newly established Municipal School Councils, which would function in much the same way as Municipal Medical Councils.

"In the case of advanced schooling, the town paying the tuition would be the location of the school, since they would be receiving the bulk of the expenditures and taxes from the students' new residence for about 9 months out of the year.

"I think we are all aware that both healthcare and school tuition have become unaffordable for the average American family, because of abnormal inflation in these two areas- in many cases the cost of public schools is greater than that of private and parochial schools.

"One last point, free tuition applies to adults of any age

as well as to young people. The overriding theme of this proposal is that of 'continuing education' for everyone- night school; online school; professional seminars; or any other means. In other words, I firmly believe that basic and continuing education is the future of our country." Anna quickly followed up:

"Jack, are you telling us that Medical Services and schooling are to be taxed?"

"Anna, *everything* is taxed- no exceptions, because the minute we start adding exceptions or exclusions, the politically inspired list will never end. It's '10% on everything', paid every day, or the newly proposed tax system will inevitably fail- first healthcare tax; then tuition tax; then charitable donations; then gifts; then inheritances; and then just about everything else on the long list of *taxable transactions.* The general idea is that *everyone* has to pay their fair share.

Senior Senator John McCall was the next to raise his hand, and received Jack's nod:

"Jack, I think this *Global Free Trade Act* is a big gamble, and I would like to know your reasoning."

"It's quite simple, John. We represent about 25% of the global marketplace, and would have no tariffs on foreign imports. To create a level playing field, we require reciprocity from all our trading partners. We can live *without them*, but they cannot live *without us*. Therefore, we must *insist* that there be no tariffs or other restrictions on the export of American goods and services.

"For example, if China should decide against reciprocity of unrestricted free trade on any single American product or service, they would be barred from exporting even one 'fortune cookie' to our country.

"We should have enacted this same law at the end of World War II, but did not, because the rest of the world was in shambles. Well, today the rest of the world is no longer war-torn, and in the interim we have spent tens of thousands of hours negotiating trade agreements with individual countries, most of whom still have politically-inspired restrictions on American goods and services. You're right John, it's a bit of a gamble, but we must remember that we are the 'only gorilla in a jungle full of chimpanzees'."

Speaker of the House was next:

"Jack, I thought we were limited to discussing domestic policy." To which Jack replied:

"John, this *is* domestic policy, because the price of imported goods must be kept down, otherwise we will face inflationary pressures due to our $100 per day minimum wage; full employment; and the effects of $10 trillion in new foreign and domestic investments, plus another $3 trillion in tax-free repatriation of foreign profits of American companies. In addition, it is likely that the dollar will appreciate in value against foreign currencies at the rate of about 10% per year.

The Senate Minority Leader was next to inquire:

"What will happen to Federal employees now working for the IRS; the EPA; and other Federal Departments, and the more than 600 agencies and sub-agencies?"

"Glad you asked, Hal. Many competent IRS field investigators will likely be hired by local government to assist in collecting taxes from houses of gambling and prostitution, as well as illicit trafficking in drugs. Broadly speaking, most displaced Federal employees will no doubt return to their home towns to likewise assist local governments- some will take early retirement, but remember that there would be no such thing as unemployed, because everyone in the country over age 16 and under age 70 would be guaranteed employment in one capacity or another, even if its only temporary town jobs until they are gobbled up by the Private Sector.

"You have to remember that $10 trillion in new foreign and domestic investments, plus foreign corporation transfers of their headquarters and manufacturing operations, will create about 20 million new jobs. Do you realize that many foreign corporations are now paying 50% or more for employee benefits? This would compare to 20% in the U.S.A."

The Secretary of Homeland Security next voiced his concern:

"Jack, how can we expect our foreign country border States and local governments to be responsible for border protection?"

"Good question, and my answer is in two parts. Firstly, the Federal government has failed miserably to keep out what I call *"Foreign Invaders"* which is to say, they are *foreign* and they are *invading* our country. Politically incorrect as this may sound- it's the simple truth.

"My solution has nothing to do with immigration law, because my Court does not make law, it only interprets existing Constitutional law, which we recently upheld by agreeing with the States of Texas and Arizona, which deputizes all border landowners and their personnel to work in conjunction with State border protection stations- in other words, no fences, just the *militiamen* authorized by our Constitution." he then added:

"How does this solution fit in with Islamic terrorists attempting another 9/11?"

"Quite directly, although I prefer to call them *'Muslim Crazies'*, because they are *Muslims*, and as far I'm concerned, fanatically *crazy*. They constitute the modern equivalent of the *'Manchurian Candidate'*- completely brain-washed through indoctrination, and prepared to do anything upon command, including suicide bombing of innocent women and children.

"Make no mistake about it, these *'Muslim Crazies'* have declared war on all Western countries, and especially America. It is high time that our Congress declare war on these extremists, because we *are* indeed at war. They have little to do with their religion's basic teachings of peaceful coexistence- as do all other religions, including Christianity; Judaism; Hinduism; Buddhism; and the others.

"In conclusion, it is difficult to say which part of this 'Federal legislative package' is more important- jobs for everyone; healthcare for every family; which concerns the present- or extensive schooling, which is our country's future. Of course, none of these benefits can occur without first passing the Single 10% Tax Act. Barry, I think that's about enough for one session, don't you?"

"It looks to me that you legislators have a big job to do during the six months remaining before the mid-term elections, so I suggest you stay in session until these measures are passed, and that we plan to meet here again in about two weeks."

The President pulled Jack aside before they left the conference room:

> "Jack, something tells me that what you've come up with so far is just the tip of your '*solutions*' iceberg." To which Jack replied:

> "Barry, you've always been a 'quick study', and you're right, there is much more to this 21st century 'revolution'. But let's agree to take first things first, because if this legislative package doesn't pass The Congress there will be no point in going any further."

> "Jack, after today's meeting it would not take that kind of majority to approve your nomination as Chief Justice of the Supreme Court."

II

Mister Chief Justice

Chapter Five

It took Jack about two hours and two vodka *Martinis* to recount all of the details of the day's meeting to Kathy, including his nomination for Chief Justice. She jumped up, fell into his arms and smothered him with kisses.

"Oh Jack darling, you've finally realized your dream! Barry is certainly the sharpest politician in a generation- he has once again put himself in a position to accept none of the blame for a Congressional failure, but to rather claim all of the credit if it passes."

"Kathy, it doesn't make any difference to me who takes the credit, and I certainly cannot directly influence legislative decisions to pass this 'package'- it is entirely in the hands of Congress to thoroughly debate every detail of these issues- and when their votes are counted, I'm not quite sure there will be the overwhelming majority I would hope for. Giving up most of the power they have accumulated over the past century or so will probably turn out to be like pulling teeth."

Jack's words would prove to be prophetic. Three days before the next scheduled meeting of the 'Round Table', Jack once again found himself sitting in the Oval Office for a private conversation with the President.

"Jack, I'm running into problems with my own Democrat Party, not to mention the Republicans- and it's all about money and power. I hope you have some good answers for me."

"I think I might have something to resolve the 'money

problem', but I'm not so sure about the 'power problem'. What if elected offices such as yours were to receive salaries equivalent to those of our top corporate executives- say $50 million per year for President; $10 million for Senators, and $5 million per year for Representatives? In return, all elected offices, would, like yourself, be limited to two terms, including the present term.

"In addition, office- holders would be required to pay out-of-pocket for their personal staffs, and their political campaigns- no direct cash contributions to any candidates, nor to any PACs or Party National Committees. The objective of course is to 'buy' votes with pure capitalistic incentives- compensation based upon level of responsibility. By the way, you would be paid *less* than most top corporate CEO's, and *much less* than those on Wall Street, since there would be no stock or cash yearly bonuses- office holders will be well paid to perform at a very high level.

"There would also be the standard 10% contribution to their Personal Pension Accounts- which should be more than adequate to make their retirement quite comfortable, even if they spend most of their salaries for their personal staff and re-election campaigns. In short, if money is indeed the answer, then this is the solution. In the future, winning elected office would be a very attractive proposition for our country's best and brightest leaders, and would give the American people 'new young blood' every election day.

"Although direct cash campaign donations, which in my mind are tantamount to bribery, would be prohibited, individuals would be free to spend as much money as they wish supporting their favorite candidates- a billboard on every highway, and a full page ad in every newspaper if they so desire- which satisfies the Constitutional 'Freedom of Speech' question.

"With regard to State and local government offices, I would propose that each state Legislature determine the salary of their governor- say $10 million per year in big states like New York; California; Texas; and Florida. Likewise, local governments should determine the annual salaries of their mayors and other elected offices- say $5 million per year for the mayors of big cities like New York; Los Angeles; Miami; Chicago; and Houston, and so forth on down the line." Barry thought for a long moment before giving his answer:

"Jack, in the true sense of the word, money will lead to some kind of power. Therefore, I think this just might fly in our next meeting. As always, you have independently balanced out 'the pros and the cons'- I would have expected no less from my new Chief Justice nominee. So let's see what happens." The 'Round Table' assembled that Friday afternoon, and the President took charge:

"It is my understanding that you have hit a number of 'road blocks' concerning the return of responsibility, and tax revenue collection to our local governments. Once again Jack, you have come up with a compromise solution."

Barry proceeded to lay out the money solution proposed by his *'Chief Architect'*, whereupon all jaws dropped. Anna Palmeri was again the first to raise her hand:

"If I understand you correctly Barry, you are proposing that *all* elected offices be put on a compensation par with the private sector, and that direct cash contributions to candidates, and their PAC's, and their National Committees be prohibited." Then turning directly to Jack, she asked:

"Isn't this a limitation on our freedom of speech?" Jack was quick in his reply:

"You're wrong Anna, it's simply a ban on political bribery for past and future favors, and I'm quite sure that my Associates Justices will stand behind me in this matter." Anna again rebutted:

"Then tell me how Abraham Lincoln, a relatively poor country lawyer, could ever be elected President."

"Anna, Lincoln would have been elected in *any* generation, because he had the right vision for America at the time, and a God-given talent for eloquent debate, which is now what is required of you Congressional leaders at this very moment. Believe me that future candidates for elected office will be this country's best and brightest leaders, and will bring the new blood required for the constant renewal of our country. Furthermore, capitalist compensation for winning candidates is necessary to attract the best talents America has to offer."

Congress spent the next several weeks in committee, determining the exact wording of this multi-part legislative 'package' before bringing it to the floor for open debate. To his surprise and delight, Jack found that there had been no attempt in committee to 'gut' any of his proposals, beginning with the Single 10% Tax Act, which would be debated first in early June, although his several paragraphs had now become several pages.

As they sat quietly in their Georgetown manor, sipping pre-dinner cocktails, Jack and Kathy reviewed the first draft, and silently smiled when they discovered that Jack's ideas had not been distorted to any great extent. Jack was the first to speak:

"I'm very encouraged, darling." Kathy replied:

"Just wait 'til it hits the floors of the House and Senate-dozens of amendments will be offered, and each will have to be debated and voted upon- which will probably take until Labor Day." To which Jack answered:

"Kathy, as far as I'm concerned, the more debate the better- rewording the 1913 Tax Act Amendment deserves the utmost scrutiny, because that's where the money is to fund the three new main social benefits. In the meantime, why don't we get out of here for a long Summer vacation. Unlike the Congress, I don't have to be back to work until the first Monday of October"

"Honey, I'm way ahead of you. I've found a beautiful hilltop villa just outside a Tuscan small town, half-way between Florence and Siena."

"*Brava, amore*. Let's get all the family together and fly over in a few days."

Kathy did a double take.

"Where did you learn Italian?"

"You left your language disk in our laptop more than a month ago," Jack replied with a broad smile. "What a beautiful language!"

"Oh Jack, *tesoro,* you knew!"

"*Si',* *cara Caterina,* I knew that something was afoot, and your choice of *Chiantiland* is perfect."

Three days later, the whole family, less Mary, who was training at *La Scala,* landed in Florence via Frankfurt; rented a large SUV, and drove the thirty miles to *Greve's* main piazza to meet their landlord's agent, Giorgiana. As the three of them sat sipping a *Negroni apperitivo* under the large cafe outdoor awning, munching on *antipasti*; and listening to the church chimes calling parishioners to evening worship, a middle-aged American couple approached their table.

"Excuse the interruption, but aren't you Chief Justice Fitzgerald? My name is Tom Mauldin from Cissna Park, and this is my wife, Berta. We own the local Ford dealership, but we've never met, probably because we have no Catholic Church in town."

Jack was momentarily taken aback, but quickly recovered and rose to shake hands with his fellow townsman and his wife.

"Yes Tom, I'm Jack Fitzgerald, and if my memory still works, we went to grade school together more than a few years ago. What a pleasant surprise! My, my, *little Tommy* Mauldin, our feisty second baseman and star bunter in Little League baseball. I insist that you and Berta join us. We decided to skip the farm this summer, and have rented a large villa, two miles up the hill. What brings you to this remote village?"

"Berta and I decided to tour Europe and just happened to land here for a few days to see the Siena *Palio,* but that town is booked to the hilt."

"Then please follow us up the hill while we open up the villa with my agent, Giorgiana, and be our guest for your stay," Jack replied earnestly.

"Right behind you, Jack; to heck with the tour; we'll pick it up in Rome; or Venice; or Vienna; or Prague; or Budapest. We're so glad to be rid of that tour bus and find a prominent American neighbor after four weeks in London, Paris, Brussels, Berlin, Geneva, Milan, and Florence. We're dead tired, and gratefully accept your hospitality. But how the devil do you recall our young baseball days, 'Joltin' Jack' Fitzgerald?"

"Baseball has always been my passion, Tom, so it's easy."

Seventyish, distinguished- looking landlord 'Bepe' Annichini, a Florentine merchant, along with the Villa's housekeeper/cook, Ursola, met them at the front door with hearty handshakes. Bepe spoke English, and had visited America on several occasions. Ursula spoke only Tuscan and Neapolitan dialects, and a few English phrases, so she was overjoyed when Kathy responded to her in decent Italian, while the three women toured the hilltop mini- mansion. Bepe escorted the men through the giant living room onto the spectacular terrace, which overlooked the entire valley and the hills beyond; now bright orange as the sun set into the Mediterranean Sea thirty miles away. Bepe spoke:

"Gentlemen, allow me to welcome you to my ancestral home, originally built in 1412, before our Cristoforo Colombo sailed the ocean blue to discover your *New World*."

Bepe then went to the decanter, and poured four goblets of his twenty-year-old Special Reserve Chianti, saying softly as he served:

> "This is a humble wine I have made from my vineyards below. It is made with great heart, but I have never been able to win first prize away from *Brunello Di Montalcino.* Perhaps next year," the elderly man sighed, as they raised their glasses and Bepe toasted "*Benvenuti in Toscana,*" and then in English, "welcome to my little piece of paradise."

'Men's talk' then went on for another half hour before Ursola returned with the ladies, each carrying a tray of goodies loaded with thinly- sliced, cured wild boar and *prosciutto*; and a vast array of cheeses- all from the farmhouses and forests below, accompanied by Ursola's own kitchen- baked Tuscan bread.

Two hours later, after the sun had long set and a bright full moon began to rise in the vast starry sky, Jack pulled Kathy aside to smoke his evening cigar, while she lit up a cigarette.

> "*Amore,*" he began, "you've outdone yourself. You couldn't have picked a more beautiful spot for another honeymoon. *Grazie, tesoro.* I'm already so relaxed I can't believe it." Kathy replied:

> "I think your wine is beginning to speak, *marito mio,* and so is mine, as I tell you I haven't been happier in years. We are finally out of the 'spy business' and into the 'justice business' until your retirement."

Then they kissed deeply under the silvery moon, well aside from the others, who continued to chat about this and that.

Ursola entered at precisely 9pm to announce a 'light' supper menu of home- made *tagliatelli* with fresh *porcini* mushroom sauce; a garden salad; home- grown fruits from the villa orchards; more cheeses; and a double espresso with *Cognac* 'correction'. Jack and Kathy looked at each other knowingly, as if to say, 'we've got to slow down, or we'll both come away 20 pounds heavier'.

Early the next morning the entire party left for Siena, 25 miles to the South to attend the world-renowned *Palio*- a 'Wild West'- type bareback horserace with each jockey clothed in Medieval garb, and bearing the colors of his neighborhood- and very few 'rules of engagement'. One after another of the jockeys either could not make the sharp turns of the central square race course, or were otherwise jostled off their mounts by one or more of their competitors, onto the thick strata of dirt laid down for the event. As a consequence, just six horses with jockeys managed to finish, as the late afternoon sun dipped behind the adjoining buildings of this early Renaissance *piazza*.

After the closing ceremony, Jack's group, which had been seated on the mayor's balcony, departed for the nearby Medieval town of Cortona, which was offering an evening concert of operatic arias, classic Italian songs, and orchestrations, by a popular Dutch *maestro* and his company, which was held in the central *piazza* to a audience of more than ten thousand villagers and tourists.

Once again, Jack and his group viewed the performance from the Mayor's balcony. On the way back to the villa everyone commented on what they had seen and heard that long day- Jack and Kathy didn't have a clue as to how or why they had been treated in such a royal manner- but would very soon find out that very important people in high places were well aware of their arrival in Italy.

Chapter Six

A few days later, Jack received an unexpected phone call from Prime Minister Dino Cecchi, whose English was nearly perfect.

"Chief Justice Fitzgerald, I would never disturb you on your vacation if I didn't urgently need your advice. I would be very grateful if you would receive our Chief Justice Lino Zanussi, for a brief half-day chat about your Constitution and your Court's recent decisions. As you Americans so aptly put it, I am 'up to my ass in alligators' because of my so- called 'austerity program' to avoid default on our national debt. Actually, I call it my 'fiscal sanity program' but too few are buying this line. Italy cannot afford to lose the first centrist Parliamentary coalition we have had in years. In fact, we currently have a *super majority,* which prompts me to tackle the question of a new Italian Constitution.

"Lino is a 60-year old conservative from the Venice region and has come to the conclusion that our existing Constitution, put in place right after WWII, has become both outdated, and basically unworkable in this 21st century. He needs help, and so do I."

Jack absorbed the essence of Cecchi's plea before responding.

"Dino-may I call you Dino?"

"Yes, Jack, You may." Answered Italy's Chief of State.

"We Americans, myself included, have favored Italy since the time of Garibaldi, and I see no reason to break that tradition."

"Well spoken, Jack. I'll tell Lino to be at your villa first thing in the morning, with security escort, of course. His life has been threatened 6 times in the last 3 months."

"Of course, Dino; *Ciao* for now, and perhaps we shall meet sometime after his visit."

"Indeed we shall, *amico mio*, indeed we shall," concluded the Italian Prime Minister.

Jack was still deep in thought as the group sat for their evening cocktails at their usual outdoor table at the central *Piazza Café,* and chatted about their coming tourist trip to Florence.

After dinner on the villa patio, where they viewed the end of yet another glorious Summer Tuscan day- cooling breeze from the North, and orange sun diving into the Med. Jack drew Kathleen aside for their now ritual terrace 'smoke break', and laid out his 'phone conversation with Dino Cecchi.

"Can't do any harm, and might just do some good for our host country,
Kathy replied promptly, "and if we return here next year, it won't hurt to be on a first name basis with the 'main man'."

Jack and Kathleen returned to the outside bar, and quietly informed the others that the Italian Chief Jusice would be arriving in the morning, and that their day trip to the local Medieval museums would not include Jack.

'Quiet meeting indeed'! Jack thought later the next evening. At 7am, a Secret Service *Alfa Romeo* showed up with four 'Men in Black', who awoke everyone for a living room briefing. At 8am, six *Carabinieri* motorcyclists woke up everyone else in the area, as they blasted their way up the one mile dirt road from the main highway. The black armored Fiat limo arrived seconds later, trailed by two other security *Alfa's*. This quiet little hamlet hadn't witnessed so much commotion since car horns blared when Mussolini was kicked out by King Victor Emanuel II in the Summer of '43, only to be rescued later by German paratroopers, and brought to Hitler's side in Munich.

The Italian Chief Justice descended, and was escorted to the front door by yet another duo of 'Men in Black', while Jack opened the front door and greeted them. "Mister Chief Justice, you may call me Jack," They shook hands, and the elder man replied quietly. "My friends call me Lino. You may marvel at my security measures, but I have learned to be very patient, and very cautious. Mine is not an easy life in these times of strife, and I would never have left my summer villa in the Alpine foothills if it were not for a mission of great importance."

Jack observed that Lino also spoke perfect English, no doubt a result of his Cambridge University education.

> "Why don't we go to the *terrazzo,* have a *doppio espresso,* and my cook's homemade *bignet* pastries."
>
> "Gladly, my boy, and I noticed that you have bothered to learn a little *Italiano.*"
>
> "Comes with the territory, Lino. Did you expect less?"
>
> "Frankly, yes. Most of the Americans I've met don't give a rat's ass about learning foreign languages, much less foreign culture. They seem to parachute in, and then quickly fly away."

Ursola arrived with the coffee and *bignets*, which prompted Lino to ask if she was from French- influenced Torino, with its

Napoleonic castles and Savoy Italian Kings.

> "No, *Signor Giudice,* I was born in *Napoli* and came
> North for a better life in *Toscana, con mio marito
> Toscano.*"

> "*Brava, bravissima!* Ursola", replied the white- haired
> head of the nation's justice system.

Jack was quite pleased that Lino had taken a moment to
compliment a servant woman- it showed him that the man
sitting before him had heart, as well as the courage to take on a
job that day- by-day threatened him, and his family.

Both men now sipped, and munched on their Continental
breakfast. Jack broke the silence:

> "Dino tells me that you have a number of Constitutional
> problems, and are open to my advice. So tell me."

Lino Zanussi thought before he answered- these Americans are
always so direct- not an ounce of diplomacy or deviousness in
their bones- just 'give me the facts', they always say.

The Chief Justice arrived at the bottom line an hour later, after
minutely explaining the major differences between the Italian
Constitution of 1948, and the American Constitution of 1789.
He then concluded:

> "Dino and I are at wit's end- it just doesn't work
> anymore! Our *Socialist* society of 'entitlements' can't be
> financed anymore with foreign debt- it is falling apart,
> and could possibly lead to anarchy. Then Dino and I
> studied your Court's recent decisions, and were
> flabbergasted by America's ability to stop on a dime and
> change direction. It's unheard of in Italy! More

importantly, our informants tell us that you are the main man behind the 'legislative package' being submitted to your Congress for approval."

Jack did not delay his answer:

"Lino, you and Dino are asking me to advise you about a country I know little about, just as though I were born here- but here goes:

"You have the regional structure that parallels our States, but the government in Rome must divest most power back to the villages; towns; and cities, with ample tax revenue to take care of their own citizens without asking Rome for anything but national defense; treasury functions, and foreign representation. That's the Constitution we had after adding the Bill of Rights, and before our Federal 'power grab' began more than a century ago."

For the next 2 hours the two Chief Justices discussed the changes currently being debated in the American Congress, plus those applicable to Italy. Jack spoke first:

"Lino, you don't need the Amendments regarding slavery nor prohibition. However, I propose that you change the wording in the Federal Tax Amendment to read as we have discussed, and also that of the two-term limitation on the Office of the President to include *all* elected offices.

"Furthermore, I suggest you keep your election days of Saturday and Sunday, say the first weekend in November- with Inauguration Day shortly thereafter- perhaps November 15th, to avoid the confusion of 'Lame Duck sessions'. Lastly, I propose that you eliminate our

Electoral College method, in favor of election by total popular vote only, which is how you do it today.

"So you see Lino, your coalition government with its 78% majority has a unique opportunity to adopt our American Constitution, with the changes I have mentioned, and become one of the leading nations of Europe. Should you also decide to adopt the American dollar to replace the Euro, your finances will improve dramatically, because our dollar is destined to appreciate by about 10% per year against all other foreign currencies, once our Congress has approved the new tax law, and the new Global Free Trade Law.

"You'll also find that foreign investments will increase ten-fold, thus providing enough new jobs to wipe out your unemployment in 2 years, and your foreign debt in 5 years, because there is no tax on profits, and only 20% tax/ pension contributions on labor, instead of the current 60%.

"Jack, if I understand your solutions correctly, we dump our Constitution and adopt yours, with your proposed changes, including those you have not as yet formally proposed to your own President and Congressional leaders. Further, you propose we adopt the American Dollar as our national currency, in anticipation of greatly improving our future national finances."

Jack realized that if Italy should adopt his proposals, they would become the perfect 'trial run' for what he would soon propose to the President and the Congress.

"Bottom line Lino, you can't bring Italy into the 21st century as a newly- solvent nation without what our Thomas Jefferson termed 'a little revolution now and then', which confirms the basic tenants of our original Constitution as an everlasting expression of faith in the common people, with reliance on God's guidance along the way."

The elder man thought and responded.

"Jack, your clarity of thought is an eye- opener. I will convey your ideas to Prime Minister Cecchi." To which Jack replied:

"My family plans to spend some time in Rome before sailing home from Naples. By that time, I will have developed many more details to this plan, so why don't we get together- you; me; Dino; our Ambassador Rollie Giordano; and your Finance Minister Gino Venturi?" To which Lino replied:

"I'll arrange everything, including your stay as guests of our Prime Minister. The hotels are packed during the Summer, because everyone wants to see Rome before they go home."

That evening, over pre-dinner cocktails with Kathy, Jack summarized his long meeting with Chief Justice Zanussi, and commented:

"Perhaps I went too far with Lino, but Italy has been technically bankrupt for several years, not to mention their unfunded future pension liabilities. They need all the extra financial help and new foreign investments they can get." Kathy observed with a frown:

"Jack, do you realize that you've broken State Department protocol? I think you should call Ambassador Rollie Giordano first thing in the morning, and then call the President and explain yourself. It shouldn't be that hard, since the Prime Minister called you for ideas- you did not call them- and after all, we are summer guests in this very friendly nation." Kathy continued:

"On the other hand, you'll have to apologize to Barry for not letting him know about the additional proposals you have already given to the Italians. I would just tell Barry that the Constitutional changes you have proposed- 'elimination of the Electoral College in favor of the popular vote' only; elimination of the 'lame duck' sessions; and the quick Inauguration Day after Election Day would require a 67% majority. By the way, what did Senator John McCall have to say about the 'extended summer sessions' of the House and Senate?"

"As I expected, a rather 'mixed bag' of compromises. They have passed the salary increases; have accepted the ban on direct cash contributions, and the responsibility for their personal staff costs and personal travel expenses.

"The crucial Tax Act and Trade Act have garnered a big majority of about 65%, which is close to the required Constitutional changes 'super majority' of 67%. The new salary for Chief Justice will be $30 million per year, plus $3 million a year to our Personal Pension Account, starting January 1, 2015, which leaves my personal staff costs- about $5 million per year, because I intend to recruit the best legal minds in America." Kathy squealed in delight:

"Good Lord, Jack! That's more than we have earned together in our entire working lives to date- including our *Credit Suisse* profits in Geneva. What else did John have to say?"

"Congress has compromised somewhat on the proposed Immigration Acts- and have chosen a flat 7 year period of continuous residency to apply for citizenship. They have also provided for a review of the tax revenue split every 2 years, beginning with the Congress elected in 2016, and effective as of the 2017 budget year, which has been changed from October 1st to January 1st – a new fiscal year which is also a calendar year.

"All in all Kathy, the outcome thus far during this Summer session has been somewhat better than I have hoped for. The only question remaining is whether or not they can complete the whole package before the new Congress is seated on November 15th. Congress has agreed to remain in session until Labor Day, at which time they will return home to campaign for the November 4th mid-term elections. Their campaign debates and town hall meetings with the voters should give us a pretty good idea of how Americans feel about my proposals, based upon the number of election winners backing my ideas- both Democrats and Republicans. This promises to be my 'moment of truth'."

Jack was on the phone early the next morning with Ambassador Rollie Giordano, to explain his meeting with the Italian Chief Justice, and to convey the likely outcome, which would be put to a Parliamentary vote before their traditional August 'shut-down'.

"One last thing I should tell you- we have tentatively set a meeting at the Prime Minister's *Palazzo Quirinale* for the last week in July, and I trust that you will attend- after you have discussed all these matters with our Secretary of State and he has discussed them with President O'Hara." Ambassador Giordano was quick to respond:

"Jack, this is like 'closing the barn door after the horse is stolen- you're going to catch hell about this from the 'powers- that-be' in Washington." To which Jack replied:

"You're right Rollie, but you must know better than I that Italy is a financial 'basket case', and that something drastic must be done to change their Napoleonic-based laws of the land, and their antiquated tax revenue system, which has never been completely enforced, because tax officials are much too easily bribed.

"I have also proposed that the Italians change their monetary system from Euros to American dollars, because I see a continuing future appreciation of our dollar versus all other foreign currencies. I also expect that very soon several other 'financially strapped' Euro Zone countries- Greece; Cyprus; Spain; Portugal; and Ireland- will follow Italy's example."

Jack had his evening single malt *Laphroig* Scotch in hand when the Presidential 'hot line' phone rang in his study- it was 6pm central European time and noon Washington time. "Yes Barry, I'm listening"

For the next few minutes, Jack remained silent as the President and Secretary of State vented their displeasure with his unorthodox actions, ending with the words 'Jack, this is definitely *not* in your job description'. To which Jack replied calmly:

"Gentlemen, I am fully aware that my actions yesterday were somewhat unusual. However, I am convinced that spur-of-the-moment opportunities require immediate response, providing that one already has the appropriate solutions. This is no time for humming and hawing with *Mickey Mouse* responses such as- 'I'll study the matter and get back to you'.

"Our close ally came to me, upon the request of Prime Minister Dino Cecchi with a Constitutional problem, and with a few exceptions, is already covered by our tried and proven American Constitution. For my part, that solution was a 'no brainer', but I also had to consider the changes our Congress is now debating.

"Contrary to our Congress, Italy already has a 78% Centrist coalition government, which I expect will confirm the entire legislative package and slightly amended Constitution by the end of this month, and go to the polls the first weekend in November.

"To sum up the situation, the Italian Parliament, with their 'super majority', is free to enact any legislation which will resolve their Constitutional and monetary crises- I just happened to be here to lend them a helping hand, and I would advise both of you to attend the late July meeting in Rome.

"One final observation- we have been given a unique opportunity to use Italy as a testing ground, and if it can work in this country, it can work anywhere in the world, because up 'til now they have had almost 50 new Administrations since the end of World War II- at times more than one in the same year.

Oddly enough for Italy, everything *did* go as planned during the month of July, and the conference took place the last week of the month, with the President; Secretary of State; Speaker of the House; Chief Justice; Treasury Secretary; and Senate Majority Leader; on the American side, and their counterparts on the Italian side. Prime Minister Cecchi opened the meeting, looking directly at the Americans across the table:

"Gentlemen, you honor Italy with your presence. Never before in our lifetimes have we Italians been so united in our purpose of bringing stability to our government, and economic prosperity to our people. We speak for our many political Parties, except for the Communist Party on the far left. We are all hopeful and optimistic that our future relations with America will only grow stronger, and that our successful implementation of these changes will be a guiding light for other nations now in political and economic turmoil.

"In conclusion, our time-table provides for a 3-week campaign before a National Referendum on adopting the American Constitution the first weekend in September, and a 6-week General Elections campaign ending on Friday, October 31st; voting to take place on Saturday and Sunday, November 1st and 2nd , followed by a two week period for any resulting election 'run-offs'. Inauguration Day is set for Monday November 17th, a new National Holiday, at which time the President, Vice President, and the new Congress will be sworn in, and then seated.

"Government business will commence on Tuesday morning, November 18th and the tax law; foreign trade law; and other new laws such as the conversion of Euros into dollars, will take effect as of January 1, 2015. There will be a 12-month period for dollar conversion, and for the conversion of all existing pension accounts and future liabilities into 30-year Italian Treasury Bonds denominated in dollars and tracking American 30-year

Bond yields. Are there any questions?" President O'Hara raised his hand:

"Why two-day weekend voting?"

"Because we want all Italian citizens to exercise their vote- Christians will probably vote on Saturdays, the Jewish/Muslim Sabbath, and others will vote on Sunday, the Christian Sabbath. I might add that all voters must show and have stamped their valid Italian passports, in order to assure that no one cheats the system by trying to vote twice. In this first Constitutional election, there will be no 'mail-in' ballots except for our elderly or disabled citizens, or for our overseas military and diplomatic personnel. We consider these to be necessary precautions against voter fraud.

"With regard to illegal immigration, we have already passed strict new laws to stem the overwhelming tide of illegal immigrants from North Africa. We have decided to make any illegal resident who has been in Italy for 7 or more years eligible for an Italian passport, assuming they have no criminal record. The remainder, which we estimate to be about 200,000 out of 300,000 *foreign invaders*, will be sent back to their country of origin to stand in line with everyone else seeking an Italian visa." President O'Hara commented:

"Why do you refer to these poor people as 'foreign invaders'?"

"For *clarity*, Mr. President, for *clarity*. They are indeed 'foreign' and they have invaded our country, simple as that. While we're on the subject of terminology, we will soon pass strict laws against *'Muslim Crazies'*, which again goes to the question of *clarity*- they are Muslim, and they have to be crazy to commit suicide bombings against anyone.

"Just before this meeting, I received word that a Muslim suicide bomber detonated himself and others at one of our sidewalk cafés on the *Via Veneto*, of *La Dolce Vita* fame. First reports indicate that more than two dozen tourists and café employees were killed by this explosion. As a result, I will go before the Italian people after our meeting and tell them that I have decided to declare war against all *'Islamic Terrorists'* including ISIS.

"These *'Islamic terrorists'* have declared war on the entire Western World, and now Italy will declare war on them. Henceforth, our government will not issue visas to anyone coming from warring areas in the Middle East or North Africa." President O'Hara responded:

"Dino, if I may call you by your first name, I admit that my approach to the issues you have raised is much softer than yours, perhaps because I view the American system of government as a compromise between various political factions.

"But Barry, you have been elected twice to take the leadership role, not only for America, but for the entire Western World. In this role, you cannot be viewed as 'mild'; soft; cautious, or indecisive in your approach, especially with regard to the *'Muslim Crazies'*.

"Tomorrow, I will order five thousand Italian Special Forces to take command of the Baghdad International Airport outside that city, and to guard our Italian Embassy. What are your plans to stop cold this terrorist invasion of independent Middle East countries?"

Barry suddenly realized that many changes in his foreign, as well as domestic policies, were being subtly engineered by his 'Chief Architect', Jack Fitzgerald. Barry begged Dino's question by responding:

> "Dino, I'll get back to you as soon as my Administration has had sufficient time to analyze the *ISIS* threat to Middle Eastern sovereign stability, but I doubt that America will need to declare outright war against *ISIS*. In closing, this meeting has been very instructive, and leads me to believe that Italy will soon become the lead nation in bringing true democracy to all Mediterranean nations."

Barry pulled Jack aside after the meeting, and in substance admonished him for exercising an inappropriate influence over foreign affairs. To which Jack replied:

> "All I can say Barry, is that the ball is now where it has belonged for the last 5 years- in your court. After the mid-terms, you will still have 2 years left for your *'legacy'*, and $50 million in salary for your efforts on behalf of the American people, but you'll need to take in a Republican partner from the Congress. For Bob Clanton, it was Newt Gingrich, and for you, I suggest you work hand-in-hand with Senior Senator John McCall and Speaker of the House Pat Rowan."

Chapter Seven

Upon his arrival back at the villa, Jack joined everyone for cocktails on the patio, and explained in general terms the purpose of his brief meeting in Rome. They had a number of questions, to which Jack replied simply that apart from several changes related to his proposed legislative 'package' now being debated by Congress, the American Constitution would soon replace Italy's Napoleonic parliamentary system, and that they would soon adopt the American dollar as their currency.

Jack and Kathy's twin boys Matt and Mark, recently graduated from St. John's Prep were now headed for Georgia Tech to study Astrophysics. They were particularly intrigued by the simple financial solutions their father had devised for a 2,500 year-old country that had worked its way into technical insolvency. Jack acknowledged their compliments, and changed the subject:

> "Getting back to Georgia Tech, what did your football Coach have to say when you visited the campus?"

Matt, the elder by 6 minutes, was distinguishable from his twin brother only by a small brown mark on his upper cheekbone below his right eye. Otherwise, both had flaming red, neatly trimmed hair, and green eyes; were 6 foot 6 and a lean 220 pounds, explained:

> "Dad, we told him that we had chosen Georgia Tech because their Astrophysics program was second only to MIT, and that they had not accepted a football scholarship for room, board, books and spending allowance, because their studies came first, and in any event, these two slots were best left to someone who needed the money.

"At first, Coach Phillips could hardly believe that in addition to playing wide receivers, special teams for kickoffs and punt returns, we also play safeties and linebackers on defense, when the opponents have the ball in our territory. In short dad, we let him know in no uncertain terms that we were 'free agents'; but that our first love was to play football at the level you played in your day. We also told him that we would be playing baseball in the Spring and would be trying out for the Olympic track team in the 100 and 200 meter dashes and the 4x100 relay team." Coach Phillips' response was predictable:

"I don't think you boys understand that we play the toughest teams in the country- however, I'll do this for you. I'll call a special practice and measure you against our starting team players. Perhaps then you'll understand what the ACC is all about. Didn't your dad tell you that football became a 'two-platoon game' more than half century ago? " To which Mark replied:

"Coach, all we want to do is to help Georgia Tech win the National Championship."

Later that afternoon, Coach Phillips started them out with the 40 yard dash. They lined up on the 40 yard line with the team's running backs; wide receivers; and punt returners, and proceeded to cross the goal line in 4 seconds flat, a full 10 yards ahead of the nearest runner, who was clocked at a very fast 4.3 seconds.

Next came a test of kick-off returns against the defensive team, and were taken either by Mark or Matt deep in the end zone. They immediately crossed paths near the goal line, sometimes exchanging the ball and sometimes not, thus confusing the defense as they sprinted up the field. The twin without the ball served as key blocker towards mid-field, while his brother sprinted towards the nearest sideline and up the field to the opposite end zone. Out of 10 tries each, Matt 'scored' 8 times, and Mark 7 times.

In their wide receiver trials, they easily outran the secondary, and caught every long ball thrown. On short passes, they again used their 'cross pattern' to confuse opposing line backers. Each catch was worth at least 15 yards before finally being tackled.

Their final test of the afternoon was to play dual linebackers against field goal attempts and punts, during which either one or the other brother managed to break through the line, leap two feet in the air, outstretch his long arms, and deflect more than half the kicks. Coach Phillips had finally seen enough, and called the entire squad for a sideline huddle.

> "Okay guys, you've all seen what I've seen- and seeing is believing. We won nine out of our twelve games last year, and this year I expect us to win them all! Matt and Mark, we all give you a heartfelt welcome to our varsity team, although I and my assistant coaches will have to spend the rest of the summer re-writing our 'play book'."

The next day Matt and Mark met with their baseball coach, Ty Cobb- a direct descendant of the one and only Hall of Fame 'Georgia Peach'. The boys repeated their Georgia Tech academic preferences and participation in other sports, concluding with a pledge to Coach Cobb's baseball program. Matt spoke for he and his brother:

> "Our goal for the team is to advance to the final round of the College World Series- whether we win the championship will not depend upon our hitting, base-

running, or defensive play in the outfield- it will depend upon our pitching staff." Coach Cobb broke in:

"Well boys, I'm going to give you the same kind of drill that Coach Phillips gave you yesterday. I've called in my best right-handed and left-handed varsity pitchers, to test your hitting powers, but first we'll start with clocking your times to first base, and then around the infield to home plate- so brush off your cleats and get ready to go from the batter's box, bat in hand in a simulated bunt when I say 'go'."

Mark went first, hitting lefty, held out his bat horizontally, then dropped it, and took off for first base from the right-hand batters box. As he hit the bag, Assistant Coach Scofield punched his timing watch and shouted back:

"Ty, I've got 2.92 seconds, what do you have?"

"Same time, Paul."

Matt repeated the trial in 2.91 seconds. From the right-hand hitter's box, to the left of home plate, their times were 0.5 seconds slower but still under 3 seconds flat. Lastly, they rounded all 4 bases in a clocked time of 12.4 seconds from either side of the plate. Coach Cobb called both of the boys into a huddle.

"Well boys, I think you should know that you've just beaten the Major League records set in 1951 by New York Yankee outfielder and Hall of Famer, Mickey Mantle. Speaking of the outfield, I understand that you play left field and right field, so I want to see if between the two of you, you can cover centerfield as well- Coach Scofield will test you with his fungo bat from home plate."

Try as he might, Scofield and his head coach witnessed an impeccable display of twin running speeds in the outfield- no fly ball escaped their gloves- up against the wall; in the corners; over the wall catches in the center field bullpen; and line drives, either diving one handed catches, or one bounce blocks and perfect throws all the way to home play on one bounce- no cutoffs needed.

Now it was time for Cobb and Scofield to learn how these freshmen could hit the ball, as delivered by the best pitchers on the varsity team. The coaches started out with their best right-hander, whose fast ball topped out at 98 mph. Batting as left handers, there was no need for infield defense, because the line drives they plastered inside the foul line; into the corners; or into the outfield alleys were clearly uncatchable- as were the one out of three pitches they put into the bleachers.

The coaches decided to bring in their 'crafty' left-hander, not realizing that Matt and Mark were ambidextrous switch hitters, who just stepped across the plate to the left side batter's box, where they repeated their prior hitting performance from the other side of the plate. Cobb and Scofeild looked at each other and smiled broadly before calling in 'the boys'. Coach Cobb spoke first:

> "Matt and Mark, that was quite a display of baseball prowess, and I am surprised that both of you have not as yet been drafted by a Major League team." Mark stepped forwarded to answer:

> "In case you fail to understand what we told you a few hours ago, we are here at Georgia Tech, rather than M.I.T, because they do not have a football team, nor a competitive baseball team, and we love to play both sports at the highest level, as did our father." Coach

100

Cobb called Coach Scofield aside:

"Paul, I want you to train both boys to play first base with the mitt on his right hand. The best of the two will play first, while the other plays center field. With these two guys we are not only *going* to the College World Series, we are going to *win* it."

Stephen, the youngest and perhaps the brightest of the brothers, had just finished his sophomore year at St. John's Prep, and would soon depart for Eton for his last 2 years, before transferring to Harvard for pre-law. Jack turned the conversation to his still growing, 6 foot 2, 190 pound boy who like himself, had wavy blonde hair and blue eyes with dark blue rings. Jack was prone to comment as a proud father:

"Well Steve, you've just led St. John's to a National High School Soccer Championship, and with your brothers, the National High School Baseball Championship. The sportswriters say that you are the best soccer center forward, and best young shortstop in the country. You already know that the Brits, at all levels, play perhaps the best soccer game anywhere, so you'll have a great opportunity to measure yourself at a higher level." Kathy then commented:

"Remember boys, we are leaving for Milan in a few days to see your sister Mary's debut at *La Scala* Opera House, where she will be singing the lead role of *Mimi* in Pucini's *La Boheme*. Your father is also buying me a brand new wardrobe at the fashion houses on Via Montenapoleone (Milan's 5th Avenue) as a belated anniversary present. My anniversary gift to him is a test drive in a *Ferrari* Formula One race car, at the track in nearby Monza, which will host the Italian Grand Prix early next month."

Jack couldn't contain himself- it was a complete surprise which prompted him to lean over and give Kathy a long, passionate kiss right in front of everyone. He was dumbfounded that Kathy had guessed his life-long dream to drive the fastest car in the world.

Their guests from Cissna Park, the Mauldins, left the next morning to pick up their European tour in Venice, and the boys were entertaining their local girlfriends at the swimming pool and tennis court complexes, armed with a hefty luncheon basket loaded with specialties prepared by Ursola. Jack and Kathy for the first time that Summer did absolutely nothing except plan for their trip to Milan, and chat with Mary on the phone about her upcoming debut, for which she was practicing daily, with her director and leading man.

"Oh mom, dad! Guess what?" she said, "his name is Nikolai Varenko from St. Petersburg, but I call him 'Nicky', and he seems to like it. He's blonde like me and about two inches taller- Mary was 5 foot 10 inches, gorgeous like her mother, and dubbed *The American Princess* by Italian opera critics and the public.

"He's very handsome, and has a beautiful tenor voice that is amazing on the mid and top ranges, but he's only 25 and still lean, so he has not yet developed the lowest range and bulging chest of a Luciano Pavarotti- but that will come when he puts on some more weight. We should be wonderful together, but you can judge for yourself when you hear us. Don't forget there's a big reception after the performance, courtesy of Italian multi-billionaire 'media king' Silvio Berlusconi." Kathy chimed in:

"Mary, please don't forget that you're only 21, and

Nicky is only 25, and both of you have your entire operatic careers still ahead of you. Are you romantically involved?"

"Mom, you can decide for yourself after you've seen the way we look at each other during our several love duets, but to answer your question, we're only at the very beginning. To answer your unasked question, he is Russian Orthodox and very religious, so why don't we just agree to let nature takes its course, and see what develops."

"Mary, I want you to come help me shop for my new wardrobe while I'm there, and your father wants you to pick out a pair of diamond earrings for yourself at *Cartier* to celebrate your debut. One more thing Mary, your crazy father is going to be test driving a *Ferrari* Formula One race car at the track in Monza the morning before your debut."

"Has dad gone mad!? Mom, Formula One cars go over 250 mph on the straightaways at Monza."

"I know dear, but he's going to receive heavy instructions before he ever puts his foot on the gas pedal, and will probably never go more than 150 mph, which is only slightly faster than he has driven his BMW Z8 roadster on rare occasions. Don't forget that men have this 'thing' about fast cars that we women can't even begin to understand- it has something to do with proving their masculinity."

They had barely finished their conversation with Mary when Jack received a phone call from Pope Luke's private secretary, Monsignor Casey.

"Mister Chief Justice, Pope Luke would like very much to visit with you and your family at his Summer residence at *Castel Gandolfo,* which is in the hills about 50 miles northeast of Rome. He says it's been much too long since he last saw you and the family at Bill O'Malley's funeral in Naperville, and thought perhaps you might stop for a day or so during your vacation."

"Monsignor, tell the Pope we would be absolutely delighted, and that we will let him know the exact date."

That evening at supper, the family discussed their itinerary and activities for the next few days. The boys in particular were surprised and somewhat nervous at the thought of seeing the new American Pope for the first time since their first communion some years earlier. Their local girlfriends, who would soon be attending the University of Florence, simply sat dumbfounded, inasmuch as they had little idea of the powerful positions and contacts of Jack and Kathy Fitzgerald.

The *Ferrari* garage on pit row at Monza was all quiet when Jack arrived for his big racing day. His instructor was one of the *Ferrari* test drivers, Carlo Bandini, a young lad of 19 who went through the routine of showing Jack where all the numerous controls were located, such as the gear shift on the steering wheel, the rear wing aerolon, and other unique features of all Formula One race cars.

Carlo continued with his tutorial by asking Jack to sit in the driver's seat, which was custom fit for each driver.

"Well Jack, this seat was obviously built for a much smaller driver, so let me get a bigger seat from the back room. But first, let me show you the track layout on this large flat screen used to follow the cars during the race."

Carlo led Jack to the race control booth, jam packed with TV monitors and instrumentation, which gave the race engineers real time data such as tire wear; brake wear; engine timing and just about every other piece of information the engineers would need to communicate with the drivers on their two-way radios. Jack tried to take all this mind-boggling information in, and was relieved to learn that none of it would apply to him for his short test drive.

Carlo then put on a demo film showing the Monza layout, as taken from the cockpit, and followed all of the twists and turns used in the actual race.

While Jack was fitted into his flame- proof driving suit and helmet, Carlo gave him final instructions:

> "Jack, I want you to take it easy on your first lap, and remember that the first *chicane* is only a half mile from the end of pit row, and should be taken no faster than 40 mph, which means that on your speedometer you should not be going over 100 mph as you brake down for the turn."

Jack squeezed into the cockpit and Carlo watched him depart down pit lane towards the front straightaway entrance. The roar of this 1,000 horsepower race car was deafening, as Jack eased onto the main track in second gear, then triggered into the third of seven gears. The tachometer read 15,000 rpm when he shifted down into forth gear towards the end of the first part of the front straightaway; then back to first gear for the upcoming *chicane,* which he navigated flawlessly; then back up through the gears to 7th gear for the long back part of the front straightaway; then geared down to third for the first big right-hander, which he took at 120mph before entering onto the long North straightaway. Jack looked at the speedometer, which read 220 mph, but he felt as if he was hardly moving.

He then approached the sharp right hand turn at the end of the straightaway; took it at 90 mph, and the following *chicane* at 60mph. The response of the car, which sat just 4 inches off the track, was amazing as he turned onto the long back straightaway, gearing up to 7th ; and keeping his speed at a steady 220 mph as he approached the final parabolic curve leading onto the front straightaway and the pit lane entrance.

Jack kept his speed at 220 mph as he passed Carlo, who was sitting atop the wall on pit lane. On his 3rd and last lap, Jack was determined to see just how fast his car could go, so coming out of the parabolic curve onto the front straightaway, he put his accelerator foot to the floor and waved to Carlo at 230 mph, while tapping his brakes as he brought the car to a stop and slowly backed up pit lane to the *Ferrari* garage.

Carlo was there to greet him.

> "Pretty good for an old man, Jack. In fact you drove this car as fast as any of we professional drivers during a real race, and set a new amateur track record!"

 The 43-year-old Chief Justice detached the steering wheel, extricated himself from the cockpit with some difficulty, removed his driving gear, and handed it to Carlo, who admonished him:

> "Jack, you didn't follow my orders. I told you not to try to navigate the *chicanes* above 40 mph."

> "Couldn't resist the temptation Carlo, but don't feel bad-I have never taken orders from anyone, and it's really a kick braking down to navigate those curves and *chicanes* without hitting any of the raised, ribbed concrete curb guides. All and all, quite an experience, and I can't thank you enough for letting me get a taste of the real thing". To which Carlo commented:

"Where did you learn how to drive so well, Jack. If you were 6 inches shorter, 50 pounds lighter, and 20 years younger, you could qualify for our driver program. I was following you all the way on my TV monitor, and will report to our President that you got our $10 million car back in one piece, and none the worse for wear."

Kathy and all the kids ran across the track from their seats opposite pit lane to congratulate Jack, and to thank Carlo for his brilliant instructions. Carlo did not mention that Jack had gone faster than instructed. Jack couldn't help announcing proudly that he had hit a personal high of 230 mph on his last run down the front straightaway. The fastest he had gone in his BMW Z8 had been 120mph.

"Kathy, this is the best present I've ever had. I just wish I could explain the feeling I had tooling around this world famous old race track."

The family decided to have lunch in the unique Milan stained glass domed *Galleria* fronting *Piazza del Duomo,* with its dozens of fancy shops and sidewalk restaurants.

After coffee and desert they proceeded through the *Galleria* into *Piazza alla Scala*, and made a quick right turn directly into the *Via Montenapoleone* boutique district. The next 3 hours were spent gazing at tall, long-legged fashion models display the very latest Fall fashions, which typically hit Fifth Avenue shops about 2 years later. Jack and the boys had the privilege of watching their mother and sister model the cocktail dresses, evening gowns, matching shoes and other garments they had chosen literally right off the models' back. By that time, a small crowd had gathered for this unusual display of tall, gorgeous American womanhood. At age 41, Kathy could still rival any of the models in stature, grace and beauty but Mary outshone them all.

At five o'clock the family returned to the *Grand Hotel Duomo* for tea time in the main lobby. Mary was recognized by many of the guests, so the Fitzgeralds were continually interrupted while opera fans solicited her autograph. The lobby clock struck 6'o clock when the Fitzgeralds departed for their family suite, which was the entire top floor penthouse, complete with private elevator and huge outdoor terrace overlooking the *Duomo* Cathedral and most of downtown Milan. The big night had finally come as Mary left early for *La Scala* opera house two blocks away. The rest of the family entered *La Scala* two hours later, and were shown to the royal box in the center of the first tier.

The opera critics would later report that this performance of *La Boheme* was undoubtedly the finest in many years and claimed that the combination of Mary "the American Princess", and Nicky "the Russian Prince" were truly the grandest young couple to hit the operatic stage in several generations- all and all, a glorious triumph. After a dozen curtain calls, Jack and family were escorted to Mary's dressing room, which was filled to the brim with floral arrays of every description.

The Champagne corks popped as Jack and Kathy embraced their daughter, and thought to themselves, 'a star is born'. Silvio Berlusconi, Nikolai Varenko in hand, was the last to squeeze his way through the crowd and to embrace Mary in typical Italian tradition with two cheek kisses, while Nicky amazed them all by kissing her passionately on the lips as he had done in the opera.

Silvio's reception an hour later at his town villa ballroom was on a grand scale, and was capped off by Mary and Nicky repeating their Act I *arias* and love duet.

The Fitzgerald family returned to their hotel and were greeted with cheers and applause by the entire hotel staff and several hundred guests, who had waited up patiently for several hours to get a first hand view of Mary.

Nicky arrived about a half hour later, and the scene was repeated, as the entire group drifted into the adjoining grand ballroom, where the hotel orchestra shifted from their waltz to the main theme music from *La Boheme*.

Nicky took Mary's hand and led her to a quiet alcove adjacent to the ballroom; bended to one knee, and asked her for her hand in marriage, which she quickly accepted, adding "Nicky, do you mind if I go find my father and mother and ask them to join us?" to which he replied "it is an old Russian tradition to ask permission- just find them quickly, I'm getting very nervous."

It didn't take Mary more than a few seconds to spot the tallest couple in the room, who were dancing together to the strains of Act II's mezzo-soprano aria, *Musetta's Waltz*; took them by the hand and led them to the side alcove where Nicky was waiting with trepidation to ask:

> "Jack, Kathy, I have the great honor to request your permission to marry your daughter Mary." Jack spoke for both parents:

> "Nicky, simply stated, welcome to the Fitzgerald family- it has been very easy for Kathy and I to witness young love in full bloom. We have been waiting for this moment, and the only thing we ask is that your marriage take place in Rome's St. Peter's *Basilica*, and performed jointly by Pope Luke and your Russian Orthodox Archbishop Mikhail later this summer, before we sail back to the States."

Nick then slowly removed the *Cartier* ring box from his jacket pocket; opened it to display a 5 carat emerald cut flawless diamond in a platinum setting; showed it to Mary and her family; removed it, and inserted it onto her ring finger, whereupon Mary broke into tears, exclaiming:

"Oh Nicky my love, this is truly exquisite! How could you ever afford it?"

"Mary, you are the most exquisite woman in the world-there is no such thing as any gift being too expensive for you, my darling." Nicky had never discussed money matters with Mary, nor had he told her that his aristocratic family had fled to Paris in 1917, and was now one of the richest in St. Petersburg." Jack broke in:

"Kathy, I think it's time we made an announcement to these wonderful folks." Jack led them to the orchestra platform microphone and raised his hands in the air asking for silence:

"Kind ladies and gentlemen, *Signori e Signore,* your attention please. My wife Kathy and I are honored to announce the engagement of our daughter, Mary Fitzgerald, to Nicholai Verenko. Their marriage will take place later this Summer in St. Peter's Basilica in Rome." When the applause subsided after many minutes, Jack continued: "In honor of this great occasion for my family, and also in honor of your warm welcome to all my family this evening, I now ask Mary and my future so-in-law Nicky, to repeat tonight's glorious Act I love duet from *La Boheme.*" Jack held out his arm prompting Mary and Nicky to step forward, while he took away the unneeded microphone to the side wings. The young couple proceeded to sing this song as it had never been sung before, after which the audience could only shout *bis! bis!* for an *encore.*

Chapter Eight

The hilly road from the main highway to *Castel Gandolfo* was typically winding and somewhat treacherous for the large SUV containing the Fitzgerald family, and the Medieval streets of the small town below the castle were not much wider than the vehicle itself. They wound their way curve by curve up to the front gate, which was manned by the Swiss Guards. Monsignor Casey was there to meet them and accompany them directly to Pope Luke's private study, where he greeted them as old friends:

"Jack, Kathy, children! It's been much too long since we last visited, and its so good to at last be talking with an American family."

Jack stepped forward and greeted The Pontiff by kissing his ring.

"It is quite an honor to be invited here Your Holiness, and I'm only sorry that Mary couldn't join us because of her schedule at *La Scala* this month. She is rehearsing for the lead role in Verdi's *Rigoletto*- a very demanding part. She and Nicky are now engaged to be married, and I would be greatly honored if you would perform the ceremony in *St. Peter's*, together with Russian Orthodox Archbishop Mikhail, who is very close to the Varenko family in St. Petersburg. Any date in late September will be convenient."

"But of course my dear friend, it would be my pleasure to marry your daughter and to renew my acquaintance with the Archbishop. We have been collaborating for some time on a very important project to reunite all Christian Churches.

"Mary has become quite the operatic celebrity, so you and Kathy must be very proud parents. It seems only yesterday that I baptized her at Sts. Peter and Paul in Naperville just one year after I married you and Kathy. We both have come a long way since then, with responsibilities now that neither of us could have imagined at the time. But why don't you tell me a bit about your Italian vacation?"

"Well, Your Holiness, it's been as much work as play, but not by design."

"So my spies tell me," The Pope said with a chuckle.

"Then you know about my original meeting with Chief Justice Zanussi, at the request of Prime Minister Cecchi, and our subsequent conference with the American President and a few of his Cabinet Secretaries late last month."

"Your proposals have apparently caused quite a stir within the government- I've never seen them move so fast in such a short period of time, especially on fundamentally important matters like adopting the American Constitution, and your simple new tax code, even before the American Congress has passed this new revenue law. Seems to me that this is as much a 'revolution' as my being elected Pope.

"You may have heard that I will soon be announcing the Vatican III council to continue the renewal of our Church, which began with Pope John XXIII, half a century ago. My plan is to lay the groundwork for reuniting all of the Christian Churches- Catholic, Protestant, and Eastern Orthodox, so we will be debating among other matters, the re-introduction of clerical marriage within our Church after almost a millennium of required celibacy. I believe that in this way we can bring our priesthood closer to Catholic families, and remove one of the main obstacles to a United Christian Church."

"That's a very tall order, Your Holiness."

"You're right, it will take me the rest of my natural life just to get started, but then I guess you've given a lot of thought to your lifetime job."

"I have, but I have nothing that even approaches the difficulty of the plan you just mentioned- difficult decisions regarding our Constitution no doubt, but I have a solid Supreme Court majority behind me."

"I'm not so sure it will prove to be that easy, Jack. Your tax plan and the return of social system power to the towns, and any other bright ideas you may have, sounds quite ambitious to me, especially when the Supreme Court becomes involved with creating legislation, which I believe is not part of your job description."

"Your Holiness, the President has asked me to come up with some new ideas on a number of subjects- the real job will be in the hands of the President and the Congress. Furthermore, there is nothing in our Constitution that precludes tight collaboration between the three branches of Federal government, especially in these times of domestic and international turmoil. If all goes well, my name will never be mentioned."

"Sounds a bit like your old *NSA* job, except that you have already been 'blown' by the President as 'The Architect' of all these proposed big changes. Yes Jack, I know all about it- my Vatican Secret Service is very efficient- perhaps the best in the world. Speaking of which, I would like to give you a personal tour of our information facilities before you leave Rome. Now why don't we go to my Chapel and allow me to give your family my Papal blessing in more appropriate surroundings."

Whereupon the Pope rose, and motioned for everyone to follow him. As was his custom, the Pope's blessing was short and to the point.

> "Dear Lord, we pray that you continue to look with favor upon our very dear friends, the Fitzgerald and O'Malley families, and to guide them in all of their future endeavors."

To which Jack and his family responded 'Amen'.

Two days before Mary's wedding, Jack's family was invited to a dinner party with the Prime Minister and his close advisors, which included key members of Parliament, after which the gentlemen retired to the PM's private study for cigars, espresso, and after-dinner drinks.

When the subject of tax revenues and the split between various governmental entities was brought up, Prime Minister Cecchi led off:

> "Jack, in this re-wording of the Tax Amendment of 1913, you have given most of Rome's powers, including health care; schooling; and guaranteed town employment to the local government. Why not leave these matters to the central government?"

> "Because Dino, I don't want your country to make the same mistakes we have made in the last century and a half, during which time Washington D.C has evolved into a giant octopus, which I call the 'D.C. Mafia', and which rules just about everything in our daily lives. This is *not* the America our Founders had in mind, which is why they created a Constitution which limits Federal

Government power to National Defense; Treasury Functions; Foreign representation; and regulation of free interstate commerce.

"Apart from the ensuing *Bill of Rights*, all the rest came later. The point is this- I firmly believe that if *'We The People'* cannot govern and provide for our own townspeople, then we are lost! There was not a word about healthcare; schooling; and many other Federal social services which we later adopted, because it was assumed that social problems would be resolved at the local level, as they had been since the days of the Pilgrims."

The Finance Minister, Gino Venturi, raised his hand and asked:

"Jack, why did you choose a 10% *'Tassa Unica'* (Single Tax) and not some other percentage? And, why is this tax collected locally, and why do you suggest a 50%; 10%; 10%; and 30% split of tax revenues between Towns; Counties; States, and Federal Government."

"To answer your questions- first, while the 10% tax rate is very low, I think the Italian people will strongly object to *collectively* paying higher taxes, unless there is a compensating 'pay-off'. On the other hand, the 10% tax also applies to many more financial transactions than your current tax code- including illegal activities.

"Paying the 10% Single Tax is *prima facea* evidence of a felony, and not paying the tax means a 2-10 year prison term. My solution to this is a nondescript category called 'Other Transactions', which includes 10% of prices paid, and another 10% of wages for employees' Personal Pension Accounts.

"In this regard, you may find that your jail and prison capacity is severely inadequate, but I have a proposal.

You might consider using your offshore volcanic islands, such as the *Lipari's,* off the north coast of Sicily, for the very worst of the 'bad guys'- convicted murderers; child molesters; rapists; child drug pushers and others, thus freeing up space in mainland facilities to house new tax evaders. You won't need any fences in the Lipari's, because there's no place to swim to.

"Secondly, the main reason for giving towns and counties the 'lion's share' of tax revenues is that in the future they will be paying for free family healthcare; free school tuition from age 3 through Ph.D.; and providing town jobs of $100 per day to those otherwise unemployed, from age 16 through retirement age 70.

"I would expect the lower levels of government to generate small yearly surpluses, and the Federal Government to receive hundreds of billions of dollars in 10% employer- paid Private Pension Accounts, which will result in substantial positive cash flow from the automatic purchase of 30-year T-bonds for these accounts.

"You may all wonder why this *Tassa Unica* provides for no other governmental revenues of any kind, and that includes tolls; fees; licenses; earnings and profits; property tax; and customs duties on imported goods from 'reciprocating' countries which agree to remove all tariffs and other restrictions on Italian goods and services.

"This is Global Free Trade on Italy's part, and the penalty for 'non-reciprocation' will be total exclusion from the Italian market. I realize that Italy has survived economically on foreign trade since before the time of the Roman Empire, and although you have little precious resources such as oil, you do have perhaps the

116

greatest artistic treasures ever conceived by mankind, and a thriving 'Silicon Valley', just outside Milan, which is also your national financial center.

"Returning to the issue of "no taxes on earnings and profits", you will recall that all revenues are collected at the time of transaction. I think you will find that foreign and domestic investments in Italy will increase substantially, providing fresh private capital of more than $1 trillion in year one, to fund a second "Italian Miracle", such as that of the 1960's.

"I also believe that 'town employment' will gradually disappear over the first two years, because the fresh investments I have mentioned will have to be put to work, and that takes lots of people, and in turn brings up the question of Italy's declining birth rate of the past few decades. Under my plan, just about everything of personal importance will be provided by the towns, and I believe that families will grow from 1 or 2 children to 4 or 5 children, as was the case a century ago. Parents will not have to worry about jobs; healthcare; or school tuition. With these basic economic worries gone, I would expect your birthrate to double or triple." Gino followed up his initial inquiry:

"Assuming that America adopts these same measures, I would foresee a substantial appreciation in the value of the U.S dollar."

"Very astute of you Gino, and yes I have. I would expect that in time, our dollar would increase in value from $1.15 per Euro to about 80 cents per Euro. There are a couple reasons for this. First, America would expect to receive about $10 trillion in new investments during the first year alone, because there would be no tax on earnings and profits.

"This money has to be put to work in areas such as exploration for our oil, gas, and precious metals in the Rocky Mountains and Alaska, which 'till now have been relatively untapped. I also foresee substantial new investments in our technology, and foreign-owned manufacturing facilities coming to many of our American cities- because the cost of labor tax and benefits would be 20%, rather than Europe's 50% or more. All this would mean substantial strengthening of the American dollar.

"Lastly, a good portion of American and Italian foreign debts will be paid off from the sale of Federal lands, and from a new National Daily Debt Reduction Lottery, whereby a $1 ticket can win $1 million for several dozen ticket holders- a lottery more popular than your current weekly soccer lottery. I expect that all of our foreign debt bonds will be redeemed within the first 5 years.

"Now if you gentlemen will excuse me, it's after midnight, and I have a wedding rehearsal early tomorrow morning. I wouldn't want to keep the Pope waiting."

The rehearsal, beginning with the bride and groom's *Ave Maria* duet, with the full Vatican Choir, went as planned. Early the following wedding day, several hundred thousand people gathered in St. Peter's Square, along with several dozen television networks from around the globe, who had been given special permission by the Pope to televise this event. A number of *Jumbotron* screens had been set up around the *Piazza,* and adjoining avenues, and by noontime there was not a square foot of standing room to be found within a quarter mile of the *Basilica.*

The public would not be disappointed- the 'American Princess' and her 'Russian Prince' were exactly as advertised, while

118

Pope Luke and Archbishop Mikhail conducted this unique Mass- it was the first time in history that a non-Catholic prelate had stood at the alter of St. Peter's during the administration of a Holy Sacrament- in this case the sacrament of marriage. By prior agreement, the ceremony was conducted in the English language, but the crowds were there the for 'Pomp and Circumstance'.

At the conclusion of their marriage ceremony Mary and Nicky walked down the center isle and greeted their friends and families but did not proceed beyond the vestibule- the front doors had been blocked hours earlier by the Pope's Swiss Guards. The couple took a sharp left turn and exited through the *Basilica's* rear entrance to a waiting limo, which then escorted them by a circuitous route to their bridal suite at the world-renowned *Grand Hotel Excelsior* on the *Via Veneto.* They were immediately spotted by those in the lobby, who on the chance that the newlyweds would be spending their wedding night in this establishment, were well into their third glass of champagne and were shouting greetings of *'auguri'; 'viva gli sposi';* and *'cent'anni'* as the newlyweds proceeded to the main ballroom for their formal wedding reception, which was selectively restricted to less than 200 guests.

Jack and Kathy had spared no expense in honoring their first child, nor their newly-adopted son-in-law, whose aristocratic grandparents had somehow survived the Russian Revolution and the darkest days of several Communist regimes, after spending 30 years in Parisian exile before returning to St. Petersburg, where Nicky was born to their daughter Sofia, and her husband Demitri shortly after the collapse of Communism. Towards the end of the reception, Mary and Nicky were obliged once again to sing their now famous Act I love duet from Puccini's *La Boheme.*

The following morning, they would depart for London and Covent Garden to sing in *Verdi's Rigoletto,* and *Pucini's*

Turandot before sailing to New York and the *Metropolitan Opera House*, where Nicky would mature enough to rival Luciano Pavarotti's 'workhorse' *aria, 'Nessun' Dorma',* from *Turandot.*

Jack and Kathy sailed from Naples to New York on an Italian cruise liner, and thoroughly enjoyed a six-day honeymoon, and a week in New York City's *Plaza Hotel* to take in the most popular Broadway plays and musicals.

Chapter Nine

Jack and Kathy had no sooner arrived at their Georgetown home when the President's secretary called to request a meeting in the Oval Office at Jack's earliest convenience. It was early Wednesday evening, so Jack suggested Friday morning at 10am-giving him the rest of the weekend to study possible cases to be proposed for the Court's Fall calendar, beginning the following Monday.

"Kathy, let me make us a couple of double *vodka Martinis* before dinner. That was Barry's Secretary, asking for a meeting, probably Friday morning. I don't have the foggiest idea what he wants to talk about. Most of the Congress are out campaigning for the mid-term elections in five weeks, and I doubt that anything will be done during the 'lame duck session' in December."

"The only thing I can think of Jack, is Immigration Reform, which Barry said he would take up right after the mid-terms. You don't think he will try to go around the Congress, do you?"

"I wouldn't be at all surprised Kathy- for a former Constitutional Law teacher, he has some pretty funny ideas about the powers of the Presidency as it relates to the separation of powers between the Executive; Legislative; and Judicial branches of Government."

Barry greeted Jack warmly; congratulated him upon his daughter's wedding; and asked about the rest of his family. The two men exchanged pleasantries for the next 10 minutes before Barry observed:

"It seems as though you have been much more successful with the Italian Parliament than I have with the American Congress. I still don't know how you pulled it off, and for that matter, why you did what you did."

"Barry, it was strictly personal, because Kathy and I have purchased the villa we leased this Summer- complete with *Chianti* vineyards; olive groves; and surrounding farmlands. *Villa Americana*, which is the name we have chosen, will become our vacation home, and some day our 'fair weather' retirement residence from April through October, when all my *Chianti* grapes will be ageing in their vats.

"The second reason is also personal. Their government came to me for help, and as a good Christian, I could not turn them down. My hope is that after their elections, and the new government seatings next month, we will have the first member of what I call the *American Commonwealth*- common Constitution; common currency; and a common prosperity.

"Thirdly, Italy will provide practical proof that the 'Legislative package' you have proposed to the Congress actually works. The only thing you need to do before the mid-terms is to get Congressional approval for the Global Free Trade Act- otherwise, Italy will be left standing alone come January 1st. I suggest that you call the Congress back from their campaigning for just one week to get this job done- and it certainly can't hurt your Democrat Party in the mid-term elections, because it will show bold leadership."

"Jack, I had already decided to make Immigration Reform my first priority *after* the elections, so if we can't get campaigners back *before* the elections, I will make the Global Trade Act my first priority afterwards."

"Barry, I strongly advise you *not* to try and go around the Congress on these matters of Immigration Reform and Free Trade. These issues are strictly legislative, *not* 'Executive Order' material. If you should decide to attempt a Presidential 'end run' around the Legislative Branch of Government, you would cause an *immediate* Constitutional crisis, which my Court would act upon very quickly.

"Look at it this way Barry, during the next two years you will be making $100 million, plus $10 million in your Personal Pension Account- and no campaign cost to worry about. This should be more than enough to take care of any and all projects you and Nichole may have in mind after leaving office. In the meantime, I suggest that you make peace with the Republican Party, and collaborate with them on the task of Immigration Reform and Global Free Trade."

"Jack, I have found it impossible to collaborate with anyone in the Leadership of the Republican Party." Jack was quick to respond:

"If you were a Baptist preacher, I could understand your reluctance to sacrifice ideology for the common good of the American people, but you are *not* a preacher, but rather the Leader of the Free World. As such, you have no inherit right to put the welfare of the vast majority of Americans beneath the ideology of your personal beliefs. This is the main issue behind the entire 'Legislative package' you have presented to The Congress for consent, and the only reason I have agreed to collaborate with you in designing a revolutionary 21st century solution to domestic American policy. Barry, this will be your *legacy*."

After stopping by his office to check on Monday's agenda, Jack arrived home to find Kathy waiting for him in the library. He poured himself a stiff single malt Scotch, sat down in his favorite lounge chair, took a long swig, and related his meeting with Barry to her, then added:

> "The first thing I will discuss with my colleagues is what I call the '90 day rule' for all lower level Federal cases. I'm looking at my Fall calendar and some of these cases are more than 5 years old. This is *not* what I call 'timely justice', especially for fundamental issues such as *'Separation of Church and State'*, and *'Affirmative Action'*, assuming of course that Barry does not attempt to go around Congress with an Executive Order on the question of immigration, in which case all bets are off. We would have a full-blown Constitutional crisis for my Court to act upon immediately." To which Kathy, now a Board member of the Georgetown University Law School, commented:

> "What in the world could Barry's arguments be- that he was frustrated by Congressional inaction?" Jack took another swallow and replied:

> "Probably, but he won't get too far with that argument. Speaking for the Court, I will quickly remind him that he had a Democrat Senate and House during his first two years in office, and failed to put immigration among his top priorities.

> "Next, he will probably argue that many Presidents during the past century have issued Executive Orders. Again, speaking for the Court, I will remind him that all prior Executive Orders

124

were given to hasten the *implementation* of new Congressional legislation- not to *bypass* the Congress. I will then acknowledge that implementation of all legislation is indeed the responsibility of the Executive Branch, but *only after* Congress has enacted the law, even in cases of declaring war.

"At that point in the proceedings, I will order an hour lunch break to confer with my Associate Justices, to determine if any of them have changed their mind since our previous unanimous decision in private conference. I believe that none of them will."

The following morning at 10am, President Barry O'Hara, his Attorney General, and his lawyers sat directly in front of the nine Supreme Justices, and presented his arguments, much as Jack had predicted to Kathy the prior evening:

"Your Honors, in my opinion The Congress has failed in its duty to provide acceptable immigration reform legislation, and I have determined that immediate action is now necessary- thus my decision to in effect, 'force' Congressional legislation on this matter." Jack responded quickly and decisively:

"Mr. President, you do not have Constitutional authority to *'force'* Congress to do *anything*. It is your job to enforce the laws passed by the House and Senate- nothing more. Furthermore, you have failed to enforce existing immigration laws regarding the protection of our country's borders- which is a Federal responsibility- and have challenged through your Justice Department various attempts by some border States to stem the flow of what might very well be called *'foreign invaders'*, because they are foreign, and they have invaded our country. Thus, it would seem to this Court that the only *dereliction of duty* falls directly on your shoulders, and *not* upon The Congress. We will now take a one hour lunch break."

When the Court returned, Jack read their collective decision, which on this rare occasion was unanimous:

"Mr. President, this Court would like to remind you that at this moment in time *We are* the Constitution, and like yourself, have taken a solemn oath to 'preserve and protect' this *only written contract between the people and their government*. By your actions, you have broken that solemn oath, and you are hereby judged guilty of 'dereliction of duty', and 'unlawful sedition' against the United States. While this Court has no authority to issue sentence upon *any* elected Federal Official, we *do condemn* your actions and declare *'null and void'* your Executive Order regarding immigration. This Court is now adjourned."

As the Justices filed out, the President arose and followed Jack down the corridor to his nearby chambers. Jack shut the door behind the two men and sat down in front of Barry, who was as angry as Jack had ever seen him.

"Jack, that was a lot harsher than it needed to be- I thought we were friends."

"Barry, this has absolutely nothing to do with you personally, and in any event it beats the hell out of impeachment, which is where this whole case was headed. It was indeed a strong statement and was made to deter any *future* President from trying to pull off a stunt like you just did. I believe the time has come for you to join forces with a powerful Congressional Republican, and I suggest to you that the man to deal with is Senator John McCall, whom I trust more than any other person on 'The Hill'- and, you could not find a truer American patriot.

"I am sure that together you could get immigration, or any other legislation we have talked about during the past year through both Houses in very short order- including some of the good ideas contained in the recently adopted Italian version of our Constitution. Assuming you still feel as strongly as ever about your 'legacy', this is the way to get it all done- everything we've discussed all year, and everything that was debated by The Congress last Summer, and it can be done before January 1st. All you have to do is to call both Houses back into session for tomorrow afternoon.

"That will give you all morning to talk things over with John McCall. I don't expect you to have any problems reaching agreement, but if you do, just give me a call. This evening I'll give John McCall a 'heads-up'. This will be the most active and productive 'lame duck' Congress in history, because it will fundamentally change our country into the 'town hall' nation our Founding Fathers envisioned."

"Jack, I've never had your kind of 'pressure' put on me before now. What do I tell the media about my change of position regarding the role of central government?"

"Barry, you've changed your position many times during the past six years, and gotten away with it, because the media, except for *FOX*, love you; Hollywood loves you; and believe it or not, I respect you for your unswerving dedication to left- wing Socialist ideology.

"That's why I have included Socialist solutions for healthcare; extensive schooling; and guaranteed employment- but all of them administered by our villages, towns, and cities- *not* by the incompetent Washington bureaucracy. Furthermore, I firmly believe that over the past two centuries *We The People* have more than earned these basic rights, and I'm sure our Founding Fathers would agree with me that this is where our nation *should be* in this 21st century."

"You've become quite the politician Jack, whether you know it or not. You've learned that delicate balance required to satisfy the great majority of American voters."

"Barry, along the way I've had a great teacher. Now, it's time to make all the political compromises you haven't made in your first six years, and to make your last two years worthy of a *'Roman Triumph'*."

When Jack returned home, he at first said nothing to Kathy, who had attended the proceedings in the back row, facing the 'Big Bench'.

"Jack, why did you 'crucify' Barry today?"

"I felt it necessary in order to protect the Office of the Presidency- and to alert future Presidents that as long as I am Chief Justice, don't even *think about* asserting any powers not granted by our Constitution. Personally, it saddens me to use Barry in order to remind American generations to come that the Supreme Court has, and will always have, the power to determine the ultimate legality of all actions taken by Presidents, The Congress, or anyone else."

"Jack, what's going to happen to Barry now?"

"Well, he's had his ego rightfully bruised, but he needs the $100 million salary, and the $10 million Personal Pension Account contributions that he will receive over the next two years. And Congress will not impeach him, because numerous legislative acts he says he supports still need to be enacted this year.

"However, the Democrat Party will be hard pressed to do anything but assent to Republican Party legislation, as of the first week of January. That will be the complete 'legislative package' that Barry and I put together last Spring, plus the changes in Constitutional dates for elections; inauguration; and Congressional seating before Thanksgiving- in other words, the end of 'lame duck' sessions. If Barry accepts, as Bob Clanton did in his day, a true collaboration between Democrats and Republicans, I am convinced that much can be accomplished."

As history would later note, President O'Hara and Senator John McCall would get the entire 'Legislative package' through Congress before January 1, 2015, with a 'super majority' of 69%.

It would not be a 'Happy New Year' for the more than one-half million Federal bureaucrats; administrators, and lobbyists, who would leave Washington before the end of January- and to another one-half million tax accountants, and attorneys, and IRS personnel who would find themselves temporarily out of work by the end of 'tax season' for the tax year 2014- the last year for tax returns.

Most would soon find productive employment with State and Local governments; some would retire; and the rest would spend a relatively short time in 'town work' at $100 per day, before being absorbed by the largest private industrial boom in American history.

On January 2, 2015, the first $100 billion of the year's total of $10 trillion in new foreign and domestic investments would hit the floor of the New York Stock Exchange, causing traders and the NYSE to extend hours from 4pm to 9pm in order to handle the vast number of stock transactions resulting from the new tax code's provision for 'no tax on earnings and profits'.

Also on January 2nd, the first daily tax revenues were distributed to the four levels of government, and although admittedly this would be a peak day, the Treasurer of the City and County of New York would report later that evening to the Mayor that New York's share of the day's financial transactions totaled $6 billion from Stock Exchange purchases alone (NYSE, NASDAQ and OTC), and another $2 billion from merchants involved in New Year's Eve celebrations in The City- a total of $8 billion in one day- a sum equal to New York City's entire first quarter expense budget for healthcare; free tuition; and guaranteed daily employment.

Jack and Kathy received the news while sipping after dinner Cognac beside the fire place in their living room. They were both in shock as Jack turned to Kathy:

> "Have I created a revenue monster? This is unbelievable! How could I have been so far short on the effects of 'no tax on earnings and profits'?" Kathy tried to soothe him:

> "Jack, it's not unusual for we Americans to underestimate the potential power of our industrial machine. In WWII we went from 500 planes per month, to 5,000 planes per month in order to win the war. Of course, it took millions of *'Rosie the Riveter'* housewives; secretaries; and sales ladies to make that happen, along with $80 billion of war bonds and stamps. It all depends upon the faith *'We The People'* have in

our National leadership, and FDR projected that image in spades."

In mid-January, 2015, Jack had a meeting with Senior Senator John McCall regarding the State Department's involvement in the 'Benghazi Affair' of September 11th, 2012. John came quickly to the point:

> "Jack, our Senate Foreign Relations Committees has so far been continually 'stone-walled' by ex-Secretary Eleanor Clanton, the State Department, and the Administration. As a result, after 2 years we still have no clear idea about exactly what happened when our Consulate was attacked, and our Ambassador and three other military personnel killed by terrorists. Furthermore, many of our *subpoenas* for documentation on the event have either been grossly incomplete or ignored entirely.
>
> "I view this as a Constitutional question of Legislative Oversight of the Executive Branch, and our Committee lawyers have submitted a lawsuit *demanding* that all written documents and emails be handed over immediately, including those contained on personal computers and servers, especially those housed in Eleanor's New York residence, since we have reason to believe that she uses her personal computer for governmental, as well as personal business." Jack was quick to respond:
>
> "John, why don't you give me a copy of your subpoena and lawsuit files? I'll review them this morning and if what you say is true, I'll call a special meeting of The Court this afternoon, and have an answer for you by this evening. How does that sound?"
>
> "Sounds like you mean business, Jack."

"John, in my mind there is no more serious business before this Court than the national security as provided for by our Constitution, and if all goes well with my Associates this afternoon, we'll be hearing arguments within the next 48 hours, possibly early tomorrow morning."

As soon as McCall had departed, Jack tackled the documentation; completed his review by 11 o'clock, and called in his Chief Clerk, Ed Woods.

"Ed, it looks like we have the makings of a Constitutional crisis on our hands. I want you to make a copy of these documents for each of my Associates; personally deliver them before lunch time; and asked them to review the case before our special meeting in the conference room at 2pm this afternoon. Also make a copy for yourself because I'd like to hear your thoughts by 1pm."

As Ed exited his chambers, Jack picked up the phone and called his long time NSA 'handler' Mike McMahon, who had foregone early retirement to accept the position of Deputy Director of Operations.

"Mike, Jack Fitzgerald speaking. I know it's been a long while since we've gotten together, and that this is very short notice, but I'd like to meet with you this evening at my home in Georgetown. I have a special job that should be just up your alley- say 7 o'clock? Fine, I'll see you then and explain everything."

The afternoon meeting between the Associate Justices went just as Jack imagined, although several Justices expressed concerns about the Supreme Court's 'preemptive strike'. Jack explained:

"This is our Court's first case involving national security and the Constitutional separation of powers- but knowing the President as well as I do- I doubt that it will be the last. The reason for such urgency is that the documents and e-mails involved in Congress's lawsuit must be obtained before they conveniently 'disappear'. Lastly, I have taken the liberty of advising the State Department that there will be a hearing on this matter tomorrow morning at 10 o'clock, with ½ hour granted to each side for their arguments. However, we are all aware that the basic question of Constitutional interpretation is in our hands."

That evening at home Jack, Mike and Kathy renewed old acquaintance over Mike's favorite single malt Scotch for about an hour before Jack brought him up to date on the day's happenings and gave him his marching orders:

"Mike, by noon tomorrow I would like you to have 2 teams in place, and be ready to seize all State Department documents related to the 'Benghazi Affair' 2 years ago, while your second team seizes the Clanton's server at their New York residence. I'd like you to attend the hearing tomorrow morning and be ready to move right after the Court has reached a decision, and after I have signed the Court Orders and Search Warrants. I'd also like you to have a special computer team ready to recover every file that may have been erased."

"This is pretty heavy stuff Jack, but I can see where it is definitely a question of National Security, which is what I get paid to do, regardless of who is involved."

The following day, the Supreme Court's unanimous decisions in favor of the Congressional inquiry came as a shock and a surprise to everyone except Jack and his Associate Justices, who had exercised their Constitutional powers more than any

Court in recent memory, and in so doing, shook the Washington establishment to its very foundation.

While it took several months to uncover the scandals ensuing the reconstruction of the Benghazi documents, a sinister 'cover-up' not seen since the days leading to President Nixon's resignation following 'Watergate', was clearly revealed.

Eleanor Clanton and the State Department were justifiably 'crucified' for incompetency, and subterfuge by most of the media, and President O'Hara came very close to being impeached by the House. Any number of high State and White House officials were forced to resign before the 'Benghazi Affair' was finally put to bed.

In late 2015 Jack and his Court once again acted in a preemptory fashion, this time to prevent another Constitutional crisis over the Iran nuclear weapons treaty. The Court quickly stepped in to announce that all documents, including any 'side' agreements- such as the IAEA inspection agreement- *must* be submitted to the Senate for their consent.

After having resolved this latest Constitutional crisis, Jack, Kathy and the boys attended Mary's opening night at *The Met*. As usual, she was glorious, and her husband Nicky gave the best performance of his life as *Rodolfo* in *La Boheme*- eliciting spontaneous standing applause from the entire audience and especially in the upper galleries- *bravo! (Nicky) brava! (Mary) bravi! (both)* they shouted from every corner of this grand opera house after the first act love duet.

Matthew, Mark, and Stephen had flown in for this special occasion, and *The Met's* management had arranged a reception in the Grand Ballroom of the Waldorf-Astoria. After several of rounds of vintage *Dom Perignon* champagne and *Beluga* caviar, they retired to their penthouse suite of rooms for a family reunion.

Matt and Mark had both been selected for the All-American Team, and Georgia Tech would be playing for the National Championship in several weeks.

Stephen was another matter. At Eton he had become the best *striker* that ancient school had ever seen. His rare athletic talent did not go unnoticed by professional football clubs throughout Europe, but at 17, he had let it be known that he was not interested in a professional soccer career, no matter how many millions they offered him, because he had chosen to follow in his father's footsteps at *Harvard University,* and then *The Law School.*

Upon his return to Washington, Jack once again met with O'Hara in the Oval Office. The President shooked his hand warmly, and said:

> "Congratulations on Mary's triumph at *The Met.* You must be very proud of her becoming the most famous American soprano since Maria Callas, half a century ago."

> "Thank you Barry, I had no idea you followed Grand Opera."

> "Jack, what do you think Washington is all about, except the grandest of all operas- and I'm supposed to be *Maestro Toscanini*, the greatest conductor of the last century. I only wish it were so, but as always, politics is the 'art of the possible', and I will have to make many compromises to get our plan through Congress.

> "To give you one example, both Parties feel that the 'private sector' salary levels we proposed for top elected offices would be viewed as self-serving, and unpopular with the people. So, we compromised by having all elected officials be responsible for their staffs' salaries and personal travel expenses, which in my case will take

a chunk out of my $50 million/year, because I will have more than 350 people on my payroll come January 1st.

"The second financially important compromise, which does not affect me, is that elected officials at every level will be required to pay for their own political campaigns, since they may not accept direct cash (or equivalent) contributions, nor contributions from Party National Committees.

"Regarding the Single 10% tax on transactions, as we both suspected, there have been many calls for tax exemptions, such as charitable institutions and other not-for-profit organizations. It will be my job to convince them that once we open the door to exemptions, there will be no end to it. I will make it very clear to them that it is all or nothing." Jack then commented:

"Barry, we have both done our research, and come to similar conclusions- millionaires; billionaires, and corporations will end up paying more than 80% of total tax revenues, because they have all that money to spend; to donate to charity; and to leave to their heirs- and one way or another, sooner or later, every dollar they possess will eventually be taxed at the standard 10%, because they will either spend it all during their lifetimes or leave it all to their Foundations and family heirs.

"This is not exactly your preferred 'redistribution of wealth', but it comes fairly close, and is as fair and equitable as we can get with any form of taxation, while maintaining maximum incentive for *all* the people to have an opportunity to get rich."

The last question resolved by the Congress was that of immigration. They would decide on a 7-year 'previous residency' requirement for 7 million illegal immigrants to apply for American passports, provided they have a clean criminal record; good command of the English language; plus a basic understanding of the Constitution.

Under the new immigration law, more than 10 million 'foreign invaders' and their families would be deported to their home towns, and given a $500 'start-up capital' allowance to stand in line with every other immigrant seeking a resident visa. In the meantime, the 'border States' would be responsible for the 'airtight' sealing of their confines with Mexico, Canada and both oceans.

The Congress also decided that, like foreign diplomats, America would follow international law, which provides that the children of foreign nationals follow the passports and nationalities of their fathers (if alive), or otherwise the passport of their mother or legal guardian- and therefore are *not* automatically American citizens just because they were born in this country- thus, families were *not* to be broken up. The new updated Immigration Act also provided that all official documents would henceforth be in 'English only'.

The new Immigration Act also opened the 'flood gates' for English-speaking, skilled workers to satisfy the requirements of private industry expansion- 10% of whom were experienced doctors and nurses for the optional *'Housecall Docs'* program, which most families with children chose- most senior 'singles' chose to keep their *'Office Docs'*.

The next bill introduced by the Congress was named the 'Federal Land Sale Act'- more than 600 million acres of it (excluding the District of Columbia, the National Parks and Monuments).

Federal lands were auctioned to the highest bidder, and would bring to the U.S. Treasury more than $2 trillion, for the purpose of reducing our current foreign debt of $6 trillion. Future reductions in foreign debts were also provided for by the authorization to initiate a new *Federal National Daily Debt Reduction Lottery*, whereby a $1 ticket could make the buyer an 'instant millionaire'. Each day there were several dozen winners of this 'patriotic' lottery, which in year one yielded the U.S. Treasury more than $1 trillion- and would eventually eliminate our foreign debt in 3 years.

American holders of the remaining $15 trillion in Federal debt were given the opportunity of contributing their T-Bonds, tax-free, into their Personal Pension Accounts, if they so chose. The next question was, how does America put to work $10 trillion in new foreign and domestic investments? The first big answer came quickly.

A privately-owned International Consortium, headed by *Pittsburgh Steel*; *DuPont*; *General Electric*; and *FIAT/Chrysler*, formed a new company, funded with $2 trillion, to create *American Super Bullet Railways*, boasting 400 mph top speed trains capable of transporting passengers and freight from New York to Los Angles in 10 hours or less, in *Orient Express* comfort and luxury .

Their first move was to purchase *Amtrak,* to secure railroads rights-of-way for their planned Trans- Continental network, and relieve the Federal government of their yearly operating deficits of $50 billion. *General Electric,* which already makes locomotives and jet engines, opened a new division to combine both technologies. *Pittsburgh Steel* also opened a new mill dedicated entirely to the production of their half weight, double strength steel alloy for the rails, wheels, and carriage sheet metal which would be used by a new *FIAT/Chrysler* facility in Detroit to manufacture rail cars and assemble the final product. *DuPont* opened a new facility for the manufacturing of resin-composite rail ties.

Altogether, more than 125,000 manufacturing jobs were created for the *American Super Bullet*, plus 600,000 track workers to modernize existing *Amtrak* railroad beds, bridges, and tunnels. The consortium began with three separate railroad express lines- New York to LA in 9 hours; Boston to Miami in 4 hours; and San Diego to Seattle in 5 hours.

The first *American Super Bullet Express* departed New York's Pennsylvania Station at 9am et for Los Angeles's Union Station on June 1st, 2016, with 1,200 pioneering passengers, who had paid $800 each to ride in eerily- quiet, super deluxe reclining lounge chairs; glass observation ceilings; a bar in each of the 24 passenger cars, plus four dining/ bar cars with different menus and live band musical themes.

Some of the 'old-timers' remarked to their neighbors that they missed the swaying, 'clacity-clack' they were accustomed to 'back in the day'. Nor was there any noise from the muffled jet-assisted front and back diesel locomotives. Their journey ended at 3 o' clock pm pt- a total record-setting, coast-to-coast time of 9 hours.

The search for American natural resource riches was more successful than anyone could have imagined- 200 years worth of oil for domestic use and foreign exports; 500 years of natural gas; enough gold to fill Fort Knox several times over; enough silver to mint 1-ounce pure silver $10 coins; enough diamonds to break the *DeBeers* cartel; and a host of other precious metals for the special steel alloys required to make Pittsburgh's Super Steel for the *Super Bullet* and other general construction applications.

These discoveries enriched the America economy enormously, and the U.S dollar rose accordingly, thus giving China, Japan and other foreign and domestic T-bond holders an unexpected 'windfall' when they were redeemed by the Treasury

Department. The same 'windfall' benefits would accrue to Personal Pension Accounts.

Our Gross Domestic Product would begin to grow at the average rate of 10% per year, with inflation held in check by the increasing value of the dollar, and the sound fiscal management of Treasury Secretary Johnnie Diamond.

There are growing operating surpluses at every level of government, especially city/counties like New York and San Francisco, whose revenues are 60% of tax receipts, including those from their respective stock exchanges.

Inflation remains at a low 2-3%, while 30-year T-bond rates rise slightly to 4-5%, because the only new T-Bonds being issued are for Personal Pension Accounts. The population growth rate increases by almost 50%, plus 2 million or more English-speaking skilled immigrants every year, to satisfy the demands of the Private Sector.

Since January 1, 2015, when the new domestic policy became law, Barry and Jack got together from time to time to review the progress of what is now the world's dominant economic Super-Power.

> "Jack, I don't know how you did it, but your economic predictions have so far proved to be, if anything, on the conservative side. We should both live to see the repayment of our entire national debt, except for T-bond pension accounts, but that program has a very large positive cash flow." To which Jack replied:

> "It seems that we have both underestimated the inventiveness, entrepreneurship, and productivity of the American people when left unleashed in a free enterprise economy devoid of either government regulations or taxation based upon earnings and profits."

"Jack, the State Department tells me that more than a dozen foreign countries have asked for our assistance in following the Italian model, including conversion to the American dollar and the adoption of our Constitution, with its revised taxation amendment. What are your thoughts?"

"From an international economics standpoint Barry, it shouldn't prove too difficult, since most all worldwide foreign trade is now conducted in American dollars. With regard to their currency requirements, it seems to me that this is a problem for our Treasury Secretary to figure out on a country-by-country basis.

"The foreign political ramifications I'll leave to you and your Secretary of State. I don't envy you having to deal with all the international problems of what is fast becoming a new *American Commonwealth* created by our enormous success in changing the way we do business, both at home and abroad. Starting with Italy, we have asked no nation to join the 'Commonwealth', neither do I think we should in the future- it's strictly their choice and they must make the first move."

Chapter Ten

Now that Jack and his Associate Justices had resolved another major Constitutional crisis, they turned to cases of domestic importance.

The first of these was the San Francisco Board of Education and the ACLU vs. St. Ignatius Preparatory School (S.I, the best college prep school on the West coast). The plaintiffs argued that S.I. was not sufficiently diversified in their admissions policy, to the detriment of minority ethnic groups- in other words lacking in 'affirmative action' as practiced by other San Francisco high schools.

S.I. argued that their admissions policy was based 95% upon academic excellence in passing their oral and written entrance examinations. They also argued that every freshman year applicant had the same opportunity, regardless of religion; race; ethic group; gender, or athletic ability. Of the 400 Freshman Class positions available each year, 5% (20 students) were admitted on the basis of 'special circumstances' which ran the full gamut of exceptions to the rule, and that all had passed the 75% minimum level for entrance, but not the 80% plus level of other chosen applicants.

Jack and his colleagues took just one day to reach their conclusion by a 7-2 vote, which the Chief Justice delivered the following morning:

> "This Court has decided in favor of St. Ignatius for the following reasons: Firstly, there is nothing in the Constitution regarding affirmative action; 'ethnic balancing'; 'gender balancing'; or any other form a 'preferential treatment' for any one person over another. There is however, much of our Constitution related to equal opportunity, and this Court finds that there is

nothing in the entrance requirements for S.I. that is not equal for all examinees- it is almost entirely based upon the academic talents of applicants gained during their elementary school years, whether public or private. Further, although this is a Jesuit school, there is no requirement to take religious classes- in fact, the student body is predominately non-Catholic.

"This Court has also found that these same Constitutional principles will, in future cases brought before us, be applied. In short, there are no 'selective preferences' embodied in our Constitution, and none shall be acknowledged by this Court."

Earlier in the year, Jack, Kathy and the rest of the family had decided to open up their villa in early June, when the Court went into Summer recess. Mary and Nicky's *Met* season would conclude with Puccini's *Tourandot,* in which Nicky would come into his own and be recognized as the world's number one tenor for his rendition of perhaps the most dramatic of operatic male *arias, 'Nessun' Dorma',* the late Luciano Pavarotti's hallmark 'crowd pleaser'.

Nicky had gained 10 pounds, mostly in his torso, and had finally developed the low end of his range. Mary had also gained a few pounds, and was in her 7th month of pregnancy, a baby daughter to be named Caterina. She and Nicky would set their Fall calendar to allow for as much time as possible with their new baby- no European tours during the next year, much to the dismay of *Covent Garden; La Scala*; the *Berlin* and the *Vienna Opera Houses*, and other venues- they would perform only for the *Met* season.

When the Fitzgerald family arrived at the villa in mid-June, the *Chianti* grapes and fruit orchards were growing at an encouraging clip- just the right amount of rain and sunshine had prevailed during the Spring.

Both President Cecchi and Chief Justice Zanussi paid weekend visits to update Jack on the Italian 'transition', which continued to proceed better than expected, both politically and economically- it was now just a question of time before Italy became the shining example of the benefits associated with being a member of the *American Commonwealth.*

Pope Luke was visiting Britain and the Archbishop of Canterbury for the first time in history, and was greeted enthusiastically by Protestants, as well as the minority Catholics of that Realm. He sent Monsignor Casey to inform Jack that the Greek Orthodox Church and the Egyptian Christian Coptic Church had both agreed to join the Christian Council, and that the Pope was now trying to convince The Church of England. His last stop would be in Dublin, Ireland, again the first time a Pope had ever set foot on the *'Emerald Isle'*, the birthplace of his forefathers, and those of Jack Fitzgerald. Predictably, his reception in that Catholic country was overwhelming.

In addition to a grand reunion with his family in County Cork, the Pope met privately with the Prime Minister, who informed him that Ireland was contemplating a move to follow Italy in joining the *'American Commonwealth'.*

During their Spring session, Jack and his Associate Justices had decided to take on several cases related to recent legislation- most of which had been brought through District Courts by the ACLU.

They challenged the Immigration Act because both written and oral examinations for resident visas were given only in English, and therefore discriminatory in favor of European; Scandinavian; and Asian Indian applicants, where the English language was required course material in every school, as was a basic understanding of the American Constitution. As the Justices had done the year before when voting on *'English*

144

Only' for official documents, voting ballots, and in all schools, their decision was to dismiss this case, by a vote of 7-2.

In a related case, the ACLU challenged a number of Southwest border states from Texas to California for sending their National Guards to protect their Southern borders, and 'deputizing' all border landowners and their employees to assist the National Guard in completely closing the Southern border to anyone without an American visa.

These Federal powers had been previously returned to the States as part of the new Immigration Act passed earlier by a veto-proof majority. As a result, illegal immigration came to a roaring halt.

The ACLU also challenged the *'Aleutian Solution'*, an Executive Order given by President O'Hara earlier in the year, and later confirmed by a Congressional bill. Their basis for suing the U.S Government hinged upon the Constitutional meaning of the term *'cruel and unusual punishment'*, and the transportation difficulties of attorneys meeting with clients during the 'appeal' process after conviction.

The Justice Department's rebuttal was based upon the dramatic effect the law had on decreasing the number of cases leading to exile in the Aleutian Islands. Apparently the 'solution' had produced a fearsome affect on would-be perpetrators of heinous crimes. The Court was quite divided on the issue, but voted to dismiss the case.

The issue of American passports as proof of citizenship was once again challenged on the basis that the administrative procedures for obtaining and renewing passports was unfairly burdensome, and that employers were not qualified to judge the authenticity of these documents- especially for teenagers 16-19 seeking after-school and Summer jobs. The ACLU further asserted that the real purpose of the law was to exclude

Mexican; Latin American; Caribbean, and other foreign seasonal farm workers, who would otherwise have an opportunity to earn the minimum wage of $100 per day.

The Immigration Department's rebuttal was twofold. Firstly, there was no need for foreign seasonal laborers because these jobs were now filled quite readily by legal citizens and visa residents; and secondly, it was nearly impossible to keep track of seasonal foreign workers, the great majority of whom in the past had remained in the United States as illegal immigrants, and who constituted a significant burden on social services such as free schools and healthcare, and on law enforcement agencies for those engaged in illegal activities. In its 8-1 decision to dismiss the case, the Justices noted that not all foreign workers were excluded from seasonal employment if they were 'sponsored' by employers, or other persons having American passports, and who would personally guarantee their post-season return to their native countries.

The next case on The Court's Spring calendar went to the very heart of the *Patriot Act* passed by Congress some years earlier. The main issue was the methodologies used by Homeland Security, and other government agencies, to prevent acts of terrorism on American soil, especially through the interception of telephone and internet communications, without prior approval by judges' warrants, or by the citizens involved. This matter went once again to the Constitution's guarantee of personal privacy.

The Justice Department claimed that prior approval procedures were much too cumbersome for them to perform a thorough job of intercepting incriminating communications- thus potentially endangering domestic security. In a quick 9-0 decision, The Court reiterated that the Constitutional guarantees given to citizens and legal residents take precedence over any and all governmental regulations to the contrary.

The next case on The Court's Spring calendar was a challenge to a recent law providing that all bearers of firearms, including law enforcement agency personnel, be required to obtain a license, which subjects them to two competency tests- an examination of mental soundness by a licensed psychologist, and the second, an ability test by a licensed 'target-range' officer.

The NRA had sued on the basis of the Constitution's Second Amendment rights for citizens *'to keep and bear arms'*. The government's position was that mental and physical competencies were also required to operate a vehicle, and that the new law was specifically designed to prevent the mass killings by mentally unstable persons, experienced in recent years.

It took The Court a full two weeks of internal discussion to arrive at a majority decision of 7-2 in favor of the government. The majority concluded that a citizen's right to bear arms was not 'infringed upon', anymore than a driver's operating license, which requires both a written test and a road test.

The famous *'free abortion'* case of Roe vs. Wade was once again challenged by The National Organization for Women and Planned Parenthood vs. the Catholic Archdiocese of New York, for not providing free contraceptives nor abortions in Catholic medical facilities, because they were contrary to that Church's fundamental beliefs.

Jack and his Associates debated for a full week before deciding to rule on this case, and another full week to hear arguments from both sides. After another week of private discussions, The Court rendered its decision, given by the Chief Justice:

> "This case involves several aspects of our Constitution. Firstly, with regard to 'free contraceptives', this Court finds this to be a personal decision by the parties

involved, and thus not subject to the laws governing free healthcare.

"With regard to conception, this Court is convinced that the recent scientific studies regarding DNA and the beginning of life have proven beyond a reasonable doubt that human life does indeed begin with the fertilization of the female egg with the male sperm. This goes directly to the Constitutional guarantee of 'protection of every human life', including the life of a fetus in the womb. We also recognize the *Oath* taken by every medical professional to save lives.

"At the same time, this Court recognizes the 'special circumstances' which led to the Roe vs. Wade decision several decades ago, and in our decision we include these. Henceforth, petitions for an abortion are to be determined by local Municipal Medical Councils, with the presence of the prospective mother and biological father in secret, closed sessions. That Council will decide based upon the facts and circumstances whether to grant permission for a procedure, and whether it is to be paid for by the town or by the applicants.

"Finally, the medical facility to be provided for this abortion may decline to do so based upon religious convictions."

Jack and Barry met again before the Court's Summer recess, and Jack brought up the matter of the Irish request to join the *'American Commonwealth'*.

"I guess by now you have been informed of Ireland's desire to adopt the solution that has been very successful thus far in Italy. I believe that we should give them top priority, and not just because of my Irish ancestry. In my view, it would be politically advantageous for your

Party, since there are more Irish-American Democrat voters in this country than in the entire country of Ireland today. More importantly, Ireland is in worse shape than Italy was a year ago, so their need is very real and immediate."

"Jack, I am well aware that the general elections are only 17 months away, and that the polls have my Democrat Party in a dead heat with the Republicans in both the House and the Senate, although my personal popularity has risen since the dramatic changes made on January 1st of this year.

"I'll try my best to get this through the Congress in the next couple of weeks, and since Ireland is in the 'Euro-Zone', we will be taking another big financial problem off the hands of the European Economic Council- leaving them with only four countries in need of governmental reform- Greece; Cyprus; Spain, and Portugal- all of which have requested membership in the *'American Commonwealth'*.

"Barry, I'll be leaving for Tuscany in a few days for summer vacation with my family, but let's plan on staying in touch by telephone."

"Jack, you've had a number of tough cases this Spring, and it looks like you can use a very long vacation."

"Maybe its just because I'm just getting older, Barry."

"Don't tell me that at age 45 you're falling apart- you're only 3 years older than I am, and I don't feel tired at all. If it weren't for the two-term limit, I'd probably run again, even though I have no new ideas on what kind of a domestic platform would be convincing, because we've done just about everything that should be done. This leaves only foreign policy enigmas to resolve-

'rogue nations' like Iran and North Korea, and rogue terrorists you call the *'Muslim Crazies'*. Got any bright ideas on the subject, Jack?"

"I can only speak as a well-informed American who would play this international 'game' the same way I played football 25 years ago- to win decisively!" Jack went on:

"If you'll pardon my saying so, it seems as though your efforts at never-ending negotiations and continuing appeasements with the 'mavericks' you mentioned have been a failure, considering our overwhelming military and economic power. The only thing missing in our arsenal is a fleet of 'laser-zapping satellites', which would minimize 'collateral damage' when we will inevitably be forced to take out their nuclear and missile delivery capabilities. In this future scenario, the United Nations, and most of our close military allies, would prove to be useless."

"Let me quickly clarify this for you, Jack. Our *'Star Wars'* program, begun during the Reagan administration, is now complete, albeit as yet untested for obvious reasons- it would break every 'Arms Treaty' we have made during the past 40 years, and has therefore been held under the tightest security blanket since our development of the A-bomb during WWII.

"My whole foreign policy thus far has been based upon our country being the world's 'Peace-Maker', but not the world's 'Peace-Enforcer'. I will not change that policy for the rest of my administration- even though the *'Muslim Crazies'* have long since declared *Jihad* war upon us and the rest of the Western nations.

"For example, if I were to use our *'Star Wars'* satellites to take out all of their known training camps, it would negate all of our peaceful negotiations with Russia; China, and Iran. In other words, my peace-making efforts to date would have been all for naught, and we would also be obliged to leave the United Nations."

"Barry, you've just described the toughest decision a President has had to make since Harry Truman wiped out Hiroshima and Nagasaki to end the Pacific War 70 years ago. Although I disagree with your decision, on the basis of our Constitution's mandate to protect our country against all enemies, I am honored that you have shared your thoughts with me- and no, I have no 'bright ideas' that would not involve the risks you have mentioned. Furthermore, I don't blame you for remaining cautious and leaving this problem to the person who will sit in your chair after next year's general elections. I wish I could somehow share your burden Barry, but our country has only one *Commander-In-Chief*, and that's you.

"However, I'll leave you with one last troubling thought. We Americans have been a 'warrior nation' since day one at Lexington, Concord, and Bunker Hill. With rare exceptions, we have defeated every nation who has opposed us, including, disgracefully, our native American Indians in order to fulfill our *'Manifest Destiny'*. We cannot at this time turn back the clock- what is done is done, and our vision must be one that looks to the future, and not the past, except for that one founding document called *"The Constitution of the United States of America*, and the creativeness of the men who invented it."

For the first time in several years, Jack and Kathy enjoyed a relatively quiet, uneventful three-month Summer vacation- it was 'all play and no work'. The family played tennis every morning before the sun got too hot; spent an hour or two swimming and sunbathing; and were served lunch by Ursola under the roof of the out door pool lanai. Afternoons were dedicated to reading, dozing off, and taking afternoon trips to the surrounding Tuscan areas of interest.

When Greve's Church bells rang to announce 6 o'clock evening Vespers, the family piled into the SUV, and drove down the narrow dirt road to the center of town. After services, they walked past all of the quaint little shops and seated themselves under the awning outside the town café at the opposite end of the main *Piazza,* and ordered *Negroni apperativi* before returning to the villa.

Before anyone realized it, mid-September had arrived, the grapes had been harvested and put to age in recently purchased used *Jack Daniels* Bourbon casks.

By the end of 2015, every American family, politician, and company, had experienced, and adjusted to, Jack Fitzgerald's *'Peaceful Revolution'.* Independent Polls consistently showed a growing approval rating of 90% or higher by late Fall. Almost every magazine had run extensive articles on Jack and his family, but not one could find any family 'skeletons in the closet', nor indiscretions by his children.

The leading magazine selected him as their *'Man of the Year'*- naming him *"The Founding Father of 21st century America"*- and suggesting that he would likely be elected President by a large majority in 2016 should he decide to seek the office. "Our next President?" was the title line on their front cover.

Barry O'Hara's popularity also rose somewhat, only to sink again after his 'nuclear deal' with Iran, and refusal to ask the Senate for its consent. Jack and his Court stepped in within hours to once again declare the President's Executive Order

Unconstitutional, thus avoiding another Constitutional Crisis. This, along with O'Hara Care and illegal immigrant amnesty, was 'strike three' for 'Executive overreach', and effectively ended Barry's Presidential authority for the rest of his second term.

Jack and Barry once again got together on the Friday before the first Monday in October, when the Supreme Court would begin its Fall/Winter session. The President began:

> "Jack, the Middle East has turned out to be my worst nightmare. We're not even close to bringing ISIS to heel, and the Pentagon now estimates that it would require about 100,000 troops to completely wipe out what you've termed the *'Muslim Crazies'*. Have you got any ideas for me?"

> "Nothing that will fit in with your traditional 'appeasement' stance on foreign policy. You'd have to go back to Teddy Roosevelt's approach, that is, 'walk softly, and carry a big stick'."

> "You know I can't do that Jack, it would estrange the entire left wing of my Democrat Party, no matter who our candidate might be next year. To now ask the Congress to declare war on these Islamic extremists is unthinkable. Isn't there any way around this?"

> "Barry, the only other thing I can think of is for you to try playing Commander-In-Chief of our Armed Forces with the same conviction you have shown in promoting your 'Socialist ideology'."

> "Stern advice Jack, and I will give it serious thought."

Jack was chauffeured home in the presidential limousine, and was greeted by Kathy at the front door.

"*Amore mio*, you look exhausted. Let's go into the living room and I'll fix you a drink."

"*Tesoro*, make mine a double vodka *Martini*, and I'll tell you everything."

Jack related his conversation with Barry, and observed:

"Kathy, I've never seen any President so afraid of losing his Democrat Party and the next general elections- which is probably why he called me to give him a 'magic bullet' for his failed foreign policy. It was pathetic. He will never change his ideology about American non- leadership around the globe. In substance, a man like Barry cannot, and will not, change his foregone strategy, even though it has lost him both Houses of Congress. Something tells me that we won't be seeing very much of each other in the future."

"Perhaps it's just as well, Jack. You've got the biggest case load in Supreme Court history- your '90-day rule'- giving each level of Justice below you just three months to process their case backlog before your Court takes them away, in the interest of 'timely justice', has put tremendous pressure on you and your Associate Justices to decide these cases within a 90 day period. How do you expect to do this?"

"The old-fashioned way Kathy, by everyone working twice as hard and by doubling the number of Senior Clerks on our Staff. There will be no days off except for Thanksgiving, Christmas, and New Years day. If I'm correct, we'll be able to eliminate our backlog by Easter time."

The entire Fitzgerald and O'Malley families got together for Thanksgiving at the farm because 'Big Jack', now 85, was semi-crippled and could not travel. He and Jack had lengthy discussions about the future of the farmland after the elder man was gone.

"Son, I've already questioned your brothers and sisters about taking over this land of ours, but they and their families have all planted deep roots elsewhere, as have you and Kathy. And, all of my grandchildren are well on their way to becoming career professionals- none has the slightest interest in farming. What do you think?"

"Dad, why don't you let me come up with a sensible solution that can benefit Cissna Park as well as our small, but growing Catholic community."

"Sounds like you've taken a walk downtown, and I bet you ended up at *Loeber's Café* to chat with the locals. Lots of new names on the store fronts- mostly Italian, Irish, and Polish 'immigrants' from the ethnic ghettos of Chicago, seeking a better life- *Franco's* barber shop; *Kelly's* Irish Pub; and *Polaki's* laundry and dry cleaners. Thus far, we have accepted them, but not enough newcomers to support a Catholic Church, much less a Catholic school."

"Dad, let me work on that- I think I just may have a solution, and I want you to be at my side when we put it into action. Remember, each of our family's four generations has added to the original quarter section of 160 acres and we now have a full section of 640 acres to develop into something unique."

Jack and Kathy had invited Senator John McCall and his wife over for Christmas morning greetings. Jack and John later retired to the library, a mug of warm Christmas rum grog in hand. They gazed out of the windows onto the snow-topped back lawn, sipped their drinks, and enjoyed the scene. McCall spoke first:

"Jack, I'll give it to you straight- the Republican Congress has been stymied, because too few conservative Democrats have given us the 2/3rds majority needed to override Presidential vetos.

"In short, only a Republican victory in next year's Presidential elections can break up this logjam. I and my Party are convinced that you are the only man of sufficient national stature and vision to win the Presidency in November." To which Jack replied:

"John, I'm surprised and overwhelmed by your 'draft' offer, and will certainly consider it, but I'm not a politician, and never have been, even though I've spent many years as Barry O'Hara's Chief of Staff, and lately as his 'Architect'. My main passion during my professional life thus far has been, and will continue to be, our Constitution.

"However, if I decide to run, you must be the Vice Presidential candidate at my side. Thus far, we have proven to be a very productive team, and ever since my football and baseball 'glory days', I have learned that teamwork has always been the essential key to winning.

"When I come to your house on New Years Eve, you'll have my answer, and I expect to have yours. In the meantime, when you talk to other Republican Party leaders, keep in mind that I will *not* resign my position as Chief Justice, just as you did not resign your position as Senator in 2008. Secondly, I will *not* campaign while the Supreme Court is in session, much less debate with other Republican candidates for the nomination. My first personal appearance will be at the Republican National Convention in mid-August.

"Furthermore, I will have one 2 hour debate with the Democrat Presidential nominee sometime between Labor Day and the first Monday in October. This Summer I will personally write the Party's platform, subject to the National Committee's advice and consent.

"One last thing John, apart from my Harvard professorship days in International Economics, the only direct foreign policy experience I have been personally involved with, is the transformation of Italy into a 21st century Constitutional and financial success, and the first member of the *American Commonwealth.* This concept will be the main subject of my convention acceptance speech, and the principal theme of my campaign speeches thereafter. The Democrat foreign policy to date has been an utter disaster for the President; Eleanor Clanton; and now James Carney. In other words, I'm going to hit their Party where they hurt most-failed foreign policy.

Jack Fitzgerald and John McCall sealed their pact with a solemn handshake at the stoke of midnight, January 1, 2016. It would prove to be a successful and lasting partnership.

The Republican convention in Atlanta was strictly *proforma,* and since the Electoral College had been eliminated in favor of election by popular vote only, the Party Chairman simply called for a standing vote by the delegates, who promptly rose from their seats in near unanimity on the first ballot.

Jack and John quickly moved to the podium and gave their acceptance speeches. McCall spoke about the domestic economic progress during the past 18 months, and Jack discussed his plans for an expansive *American Commonwealth,* as the best road to world stability and peace. John, the consummate politician, would spend the next 6 weeks campaigning, while Jack took the next plane for Italy to rejoin his family at *Villa Americana,* to prepare the Party platform and his debate with the Democrat presidential nominee.

The lone Presidential debate was held to a packed house in Madison Square Garden, and viewed by more than one hundred million American households- the largest American television audience in history- plus an estimated 500 million foreign viewers, all of whom were focused on Jack's vision of an expanded *American Commonwealth-* common Constitution; common currency; common prosperity; and common defense.

> "Firstly," Jack began, "we shall never attempt to assist any nation that does not formally request our help, nor shall we assist any nation ruled by a dictatorship. In other words, there must be in place, at the very least, an existing Parliamentary system of government. This was the case in Italy, and shall the blueprint for every future nation requesting admission to the *American Commonwealth.*" His Democrat opponent broke in, against the debate rules for a question:
>
> "How do you plan to handle deteriorating domestic racial relations, and why did your Supreme Court vote in favor of *St. Ignatius* on the question of racial diversity and 'affirmative action'?"
>
> "Since you are bold enough to bring up the question of race, I shall disregard our debate rules and answer. Constitutional law provides for *equal opportunity.* How would you feel if every American football and basketball team was required by law to play with 85% white athletes?" To which the Democrat nominee shot back:
>
> "That's completely different! Teams are put together on the basis of athletic talent only."

"This is precisely my point! You're admitting that natural talent is the sole basis of selection for team membership. Therefore, it follows that academic talent should be the main basis for scholastic selection." The now flustered Democrat nominee was trapped and he knew it! Jack graciously saved his opponent's butt by announcing to the debate moderating panel:

"Ladies and gentlemen, as far as I'm concerned this racial debate is concluded."

Needless to say, the morning newspapers, even those to the far left, overwhelmingly came out in favor of Jack Fitzgerald as the undisputed debate winner, and even criticized the Democrat nominee for ever bringing up the question of race.

III

Mister President

Chapter Eleven

Fitzgerald and McCall were elected by a decisive popular vote of 72% on the Saturday and Sunday voting weekend of November 5th and 6th, 2016, and the handful of 'run-offs' and 'recounts' were completed by the following weekend. They were sworn in by the new 'interim' Chief Justice on Tuesday, November 15th at 10am, and the new 'veto-proof' Republican Congress at noon. Jack made only a brief statement:

> "I realize that it is traditional for a new President to give an 'Inaugural Address', and lead a Victory Parade down Pennsylvania Ave to the White House. My Inaugural Address will be combined with my 'State of The Union Address' on New Year's Eve to a joint session of The Congress. Right now, I must attend to more urgent matters without delay."

At 1pm Jack and John headed directly to the underground White House 'War Room' bunker, where they joined the newly-appointed Secretary of State; Chairman of the Joint Chiefs; Secretary of Defense; Director of the C.I.A, and the leaders of the House and Senate.

> "Gentlemen, I have called you here to discuss the disarmament of North Korea and Iran, both of which I consider to be 'rogue' nuclear nations.
>
> "First, let's take North Korea, where my proposed solution is to entice them to advance South into the DMZ with their million-man army, once we have unilaterally withdrawn all of our troops and handed over

161

our military positions and ordnance to the South Koreans.

"This should be the irresistible 'bait' for our 'hook', because their ground forces greatly outnumber those to the South. I expect them to March directly on Seoul. At the same time, Admiral Brown, I want you to position our Pacific Fleet in international waters off their coast. Lastly, how long will it take you to get our laser satellites operational?"

"About 24 hours Mr. President, which is about the time it will take to transport our troops out of the area, and to move our Fleet into position."

Turning to his new Secretary of State, Rollie Giordano, he asked:

"Rollie, how many years have we been negotiating with the North Koreans about their nuclear weapons build up?" The Secretary replied:

"Including the Bush Administration, I'd say more than 10 years."

"Do you think that they will fall into our trap, and cross the line?"

"I can't say for sure, but they may be just crazy enough to start another Korean War, especially with our Pacific Fleet and submarines parked at their front doorstep. They did it in 1950, with no provocation at all, and without their 'nukes', or the missiles to deliver them."

"Admiral, how far away are our 'bunker busting' bombers?"

"Our bombers in Japan and Alaska are about 2 hours away and are on constant alert." Jack proceeded to sum up the situation.

"Broadly speaking, once they make their move to either cross the DMZ, or fire one shot at our 7th Fleet, our plan will be to attack his army with satellite lasers; fleet missiles, and our carrier-based war planes, while our battleships, cruiser, and destroyer cruise missiles take out their East coast Navy and coastal military installations. Should any North Korean fighter aircraft ever get off the ground, I want them destroyed.

"Now, I'd like to hear everyone's 'downside' views on this plan. Rollie, let's start with you."

"Mr. President, I believe that most nations, including North Korea and their friends the Chinese, would view our fleet movements alone as an act of aggression, and would be horrified by our use of military satellite lasers. I'm not so sure they won't preemptively declare war as they move into the DMZ towards Seoul. On the other hand, in 1950 they pulled off a Korean *'Pearl Harbor'*, and today most countries view North Korea as a dangerous nuclear 'rogue nation', especially Japan."

"I agree Rollie, and after this meeting I would like you to leave on a special mission to Beijing, and hold their hands when the shooting starts. Of course, we may be pleasantly surprised by their attitude, because North

Korea has been a continual economic drain on Chinese resources. I also want you to send your best Korean man to Seoul, and keep their government fully informed as events develop." Jack then turned to his Vice President:

"John, I want you to fly to Moscow on the same kind of mission, and try to keep them calm, because at the same time, we will be moving our Persian Gulf Fleet into positions off the coast of Iran, and our Mediterranean Fleet into positions off the coasts of Turkey, Lebanon and Israel.

"Admiral, I want you to alert our bomber bases in Turkey to be armed with "bunker-busting" ordnance, for the purpose of taking out Iran's underground nuclear and missile facilities, while our fleet blockades their Southern coast, including the Straits of Hormuz. I believe that Tehran will attack our fleet in the Persian Gulf, and declare war.

"Rollie, I want you to send your Assistants for Middle East affairs to Ankara, Turkey; Riyadh, Saudi Arabia; Beirut, Lebanon, and your best Israeli man to Jerusalem, to tell Netanyahu to sit tight while we do our job- eliminate the threat of nuclear warfare in the Middle East. Are there any last questions?"

The new Secretary of Defense, General Jim Patton spoke up:

"Mr. President, from where do you plan to conduct these wars?"

"For the duration Jim, I will be spending most of my time in the Pentagon 'War Room', with you; Admiral

164

Brown; the Air Force Chief of Staff; and the Chief of Naval Operations. Gentlemen, I believe we all understand, as I do from my college football days, that the 'best defense is a good offense'- we are going to war with the 'bad guys'. Lastly, I want everyone close to me like yourselves to call me 'Jack', because from now on we are teammates." The Commander-in- Chief had given his orders, and it was 4pm when Jack returned to the Oval Office.

"Marsha, anything important that I should be taking care of?"

"No, Mr. President. This afternoon had been set aside for your Inaugural Address and Victory Parade."

"Sounds like we need to bring the press up to date, so please send in my Press Secretary, Fred Whittington, and my Chief of Staff, Dick Westerhoff." When they arrived in the Oval Office Jack spoke:

"Guys, I think the public deserves a few explanations, so Fred I want you to call a televised press conference for 8pm this evening." That evening, the President spoke to the nation:

"At dawn this morning, Korean time, our Pacific Fleet was attacked without warning or provocation by warships of the North Korean Navy, while they maneuvered in international waters off the coast of North Korea- thus constituting an act of war against the United States. At the same time the North Korean Army invaded the DMZ, and began its march on the South

Korean capital city of Seoul. As a result of these actions, I have requested the Congress to declare that a State of War now exists between the United States and North Korea. That confirmation has just been handed to me by the Leaders of both Houses of Congress.

"To prevent a possible intercontinental nuclear war, I immediately ordered the destruction of every North Korean nuclear and missile facility by our bombers in Alaska and Japan. I also ordered the first use of our laser satellites to raze the entire DMZ to prevent the North Korean million- man army from invading the smaller South Korean army protecting Seoul.

"I can now report to you that the nuclear and missile facilities in North Korea have been eliminated, along with every other North Korean military facility- and that the invading North Korean army has been substantially destroyed in the DMZ by our laser satellites.

"The South Korean army is now marching North, and will occupy Pyongyang within the next 48 hours, thus reuniting the entire Korean peninsula for the first time since before WWII.

"In closing, today we have won a great victory over an evil nation, which for all intents and purposes, no longer exists. Good evening, and may God continue to bless America" Jack then buzzed his family quarters. "Kathy, I'm on my way up right now, so you can start making us a couple of strong cocktails."

Kathy answered the door, kissed her husband passionately, led him to his fireside recliner, and served him a large *Laphroigh* single malt Scotch over ice.

"You look like you've had a tough day, Jack."

"Not as tough as tomorrow will be, honey. We will take out Iran tomorrow morning at dawn, local time, with the same provocative strategy- Persian Gulf Fleet off their Southern coast; blockade off the Straits of Hormuz; 6th Mediterranean Fleet off the coast of Lebanon; bombers from our Air Force base in Turkey; laser satellites on their other military bases; and 50,000 Marine 1st Division combat troops landing on Iranian beaches, once the Persian Gulf Fleet has destroyed the Iranian Navy.

"Jack, what laser satellites? We're not supposed to have any of those!"

"It's the latest version of Ronnie Reagan's *"Star Wars"* defense system from the 1980's; is non-nuclear; embedded in our commercial communications satellites, and I'll be using them when necessary in the future."

"So Jack, your initial move as President is to entice both countries into attacking first, to give us an excuse to wipe out their nuclear and missile facilities with our bombers and their other military targets with our laser satellites. Very gutsy Jack, and quite brilliant if you can pull it off without some form of retaliation from the Russians and Chinese. I'd dearly love to be a 'fly on the wall' this weekend at Camp David when Varishnikov and Chang give you an earful about 'American aggression'."

"That's only part of it, Kathy. We will be condemned by the United Nations for the use of 'space-based-weapons', but I intend to withdraw America from the United Nations this coming January 1st in any event. This institution has been a great disappointment, just like the former League of Nations, after WWI.

"As I see it, the only way to prevent a nuclear war is to take out rogue nations like North Korea and Iran before they can wreak havoc in the Middle East and the Far East. My selling job this weekend will be to convince Varishnikov and Chang that my military actions are in the best interests of our three countries."

It was perhaps foolish of Jack to think that he could sleep at all that night, so after trying for a couple of hours, he gave it up and buzzed for his personal security team to take him directly to the Pentagon War Room.

"I couldn't sleep, so I thought I'd join you. Admiral, why don't you begin by giving us an update."

"Jack, thus far everything is proceeding as planned. Our satellite lasers will be in position above Iran by dawn, their time, and are all fully operational." The President turned to his new CIA Director, Mike McMahon, and asked:

"Mike, what are your spies telling us?"

"Lots of 'com traffic' Jack, but as yet no one is about to make a military move. It's now a waiting game to see who blinks first, but needless to say, everyone is on high alert." The President turned to the officer manning the communications center across the room, and ordered:

"Captain Kelly, put us through on the speaker phone to Vice President McCall in Moscow.

"John, what's the reaction from the Russians?"

"Jack, so far they're taking it calmly. I'm not so sure about the Iranians, because the Russians don't appear to have as much influence as they once had. In short, the Russians seem to be somewhat limited in their ability to hold back Iran's ambition to dominate the entire Middle East." Jack responded:

"Thanks John, and continue to keep these guys informed about what's going on here, as we pass it along to you."

"In short, so far they're playing it cool. They have a big investment in Iran, but not enough control over the Muslim extremist Government to sway any military decisions." To which Jack replied:

"Captain, I'd like you to get us our Ambassador to Israel, Sam Cohen, and ask him to include Giordano's Chief Middle East analyst, Bill Hastings, in on these calls."

"Sam, this is the President speaking from the Pentagon 'War Room', and I want you to inform the Israeli Prime Minister, Mordechai Mensch, that there has been no military activity thus far in Iran, and that we will keep him posted immediately when the situation changes. Now give me an update on his reaction to our plan."

"Mr. President, I think he understands the situation completely, but has one suggestion to make, which is to leave the commercial shipping lanes in the Persian Gulf open, and to not blockade the Straits of Hormuz until the shooting starts."

"Tell the PM that I will follow his suggestion."

For the next 4 hours, the War Room leaders could only stare at the 'Big Screen' for signs of military activities, and it came later that evening, Washington time, dawn Iranian time, when the Persian Gulf fleet was attacked by the Iranian Navy with their short- range missiles.

"Captain, I want you to put in a conference call to our men in Beijing and Moscow.

"Gentlemen, Iran has made its move, and they're throwing everything they have at us, including their short-range missiles. We will retaliate immediately, so stay on the line.

"Admiral, I want you to concentrate your Air Force bunker-busting bombers on Iran's missile silos and nuclear installations. I also want you to launch our carrier aircraft on their fighter jets and coastal vessels, and to land our 1st Marine Division on the beaches outside their port city of Bandare, and their 500 tanks behind them."

All eyes were now fixed upon the 'Big Screen', while Admiral Brown commented on satellite laser attacks, which were the first weapons to strike communications centers; military airfields, and Iranian armored divisions moving South from the Tehran area.

> "As you can see, our bombers have just taken out all of Iran's bunkered nuclear and missile installations before they could launch. That part of our job has been successfully completed as planned."

The Chairman of the Joint Chiefs continued:

> "Gentlemen, our Marines and their tanks have just completed their landings and will soon engage Iranian ground forces and tanks in about 1 hour, after our satellite lasers have annihilated as many Iranian ground forces as possible. While some ground troops will get through to fight our Marines, in my mind there is no question of the outcome.

> "While we are waiting for this decisive ground battle, we are dropping 10,000 paratroopers of the 82nd Airborne Division on and around the Tehran airport. At the same time, we are dropping another 10,000 paratroopers of the 101st Airborne Division North of Tehran in a 'pincer' movement which should occupy Tehran sometime this evening their time; about noon our time."

For Jack, running a war was much like leading his *Illini* football team many years earlier to the National Championship, although he was not personally a combatant on the field as he once was, but rather a winning Head Coach leading his team, headed by his Chairman of the Joint Chiefs, Admiral Brown who reported:

"During the first 3 hours, the Marines have thoroughly destroyed the laser-torn remnants of the Iranian Armored Divisions, and the Airborne troops have wiped out Iran's Elite Guard protecting the capital city. They have taken over control of all government facilities, including utilities.

"The American Flag once again waves proudly over the American Embassy, and every other government building. Most all of the original 50,000 Marines in their fast armored troop carriers will enter Tehran later this evening, followed by most all their original 500 tanks, which will park in the main city square, and all other principal avenues in the city." Jack listened and then commented:

"Guys, we have just won a tremendous victory for our country. I sincerely congratulate the combat troops who serve under American banners. Admiral, I want you and the commanding generals of your Army; Navy; Marine Corps; and Air Force combatants in yesterday's and today's military actions to personally decorate each conquering warrior.

"I would like these Commanding Generals to fly to Tehran and Seoul for these decoration ceremonies, and for each officer pinning these decorations to say aloud to each soldier, sailor, and airman that their President and

Commander-In-Chief, as well as their nation, glorifies their outstanding contribution to our victories."

Later that evening, Jack spoke directly to the American people:

"My fellow citizens, as was the case at dawn yesterday morning in Korea, when elements of the North Korean Navy fired upon American warships of the Pacific Fleet maneuvering in international waters in the Sea of Japan, this morning at dawn, the Iranian Navy attacked our Persian Gulf Fleet maneuvering in international waters.

"Our reaction to this unprovoked attack was swift-we have since destroyed Iranian nuclear and missile facilities with our bombers; our Persian Gulf Fleet and their aircraft have destroyed their Navy and their Air Force; and our laser satellites have destroyed all other military bases in Iran.

"As I speak, both nuclear 'rogue nations', are no longer in a position to threaten *anyone*, much less the United States. Within the next 48 hours, I expect both Iran, to be renamed '*Persia*', and a unified Korea to form civilian coalition 'interim' governments, followed by new general elections. In the meantime, Tehran will be a city occupied by our 82nd and 101st Airborne Divisions. Pyongyang will likewise be occupied by the South Korean Army.

"During yesterday's and today's hostilities, which the media will no doubt call '*The One-Day Wars*', I was represented in Moscow by Secretary of State Giordano; in Beijing by Vice President McCall; and in Jerusalem by Ambassador Cohen. Their mission was to 'hold hands' with Russian President Varishnakov; Chinese Chairman Chang and Israel Prime Minister Mordechai Mensch.

"I should also mention that President Varishnakov and Chairman Chang will join me this weekend at Camp David, to discuss my solutions to the Middle East terrorist crisis caused by ISIS.

"In closing, I wish to inform you that America will be resigning from the *United Nations* as of the first of January. Sadly, like the *League of Nations* after WWI, this organization, after 70 years, has failed in its mission to establish lasting world peace among nations. The answer I have at this moment is that America must 'go it alone'. We cannot look elsewhere, because there is no elsewhere, elsewhere.

"In the future, our foreign policy will be based upon world peace through economic prosperity, brought about by *Global Free Trade*, and the establishment of a new *American Commonwealth,* which today includes only Italy, but in the near future will include such economically troubled nations as Ireland; Israel; Greece; Cyprus; Spain; Portugal; Malta, and Crete.

"Our new *American Commonwealth* simply means this- common Constitution; common currency; common prosperity, and of course common defense. Goodnight to all, and may God continue to bless America."

After the TV broadcast, Kathy greeted Jack at their front door:

"Darling, you look beat."

"You're right honey, this has got to be the toughest job in the world." He flopped into his fireside lounge chair and asked her for a large *Laphroaig* single-malt Scotch on ice.

"I must have looked like hell on television tonight."

"Not at all dearest, your make-up man did a fantastic job. What's on your agenda for tomorrow?"

"A lot easier than today, that's for sure! I plan to 'laser-zap' over 100 terrorist training camps and supply depots supporting the "Muslim Crazies"- the first step in our continuing war against them.

"I also expect to learn that a new Persian secular 'interim' government will be formed quickly, and that we will resume diplomatic relations and lift our embargo. We will also establish several very large military bases from which we will attack ISIS. They won't need any economic aid from us, because they are sitting on a couple of hundred years worth of oil.

Upon Jack's arrival in the Pentagon War Room he addressed his military commanders and government advisors:

"Gentlemen, let's discuss the best ways to destroy the terrorists, after our laser satellites wipe out their known training camps and supply depots."

Jack turned to his CIA Director, Mike McMahon.

"Mike, how many terrorist militia fighters are we talking about."

"I'd say about 50,000 Jack, less those we wipe out today with our laser satellites."

"How many mercenary bounty-hunters could you recruit if we offered a $1/2 million per kill, and $1 million if taken alive for interrogation?"

"I'd say about 10,000 to start with within 30 days and a few thousand more within 90 days. Plus, I would need another 500 experienced CIA 'handlers' to verify the bounties- but could probably find these among our younger field agents."

"What do you guys think of this idea, as an alternative to using our own ground troops?"

After 2 hours of further discussions- mostly about the details- the consensus of opinion for the terrorist 'wipeout' operation was unanimous, including the use of American Special Forces; air support, and helicopter gunships.

The following morning Jack assembled his first full Cabinet meeting, including his 'inner circle' of Presidential advisors. With the exception of Vice President John McCall; House Speaker Pat Rowan; Senate Majority Leader Matt McGowan, and Secretary of State Rollie Giodarno, they were all new faces, and non- 'career politicians'.

Jack started on his right by introducing the new Secretary of the Treasury Johnnie Diamond.

"Johnnie has left Wall Street to serve as our 'national money manager' including responsibility for all functions previously handled by our Federal Reserve Bank. On his right is Dennis Powell, who has left as Dean of the Harvard Law School to become my Attorney General."

As Jack proceeded one by one around the conference table, it became clear that he had selected a preponderance of highly successful academic and business leaders, some of whom had once been either his fraternity brother, or his teammate on his National Championship football and baseball squads. When he had concluded the introductions, Jack observed:

"Gentlemen, as you can see, there is an array of extraordinary talent assembled around this table to help me govern our country. You may have also correctly surmised that I believe that 'the business of America is business'. We must create a domestic prosperity that will entice other nations to apply for membership in the *American Commonwealth*- which will lead to world stability and peace.

"During my Administration, this will be the theme and the formula for great success in American foreign policy. Today, we have just one member, and that is Italy, which has become the guiding light for the whole Mediterranean area by creating a prosperity which has allowed them to reduce their foreign debt by 50% in just 2 years.

"In the coming days I will submit new membership applications to the Congress for Ireland; Portugal; Spain;

Greece; Turkey; Cyprus; Israel; Jordan; Lebanon; and Egypt. As for the remainder of the Muslim countries in the Middle East and North Africa, they must first renounce *Sharia Laws*, because it is incompatible with our *American Constitution*.

"Our immediate problem of course, is to kill or capture all of the *'Muslim Crazies'* in the Middle East and elsewhere. I'll first let Mike McMahon summarize our game plan, after which Admiral Brown will summarize the tactical support to be employed in cleaning out Iraq and Northern Syria, thus wiping out ISIS on the Arabian Peninsula and other terrorist groups in North Africa."

Mike took the hand-off from Jack, and proceeded to explain the general strategy of using mercenary bounty-hunters as the primary 'boots on the ground', and retired CIA field agents as their 'handlers'. Mike also mentioned that his Deputy Director of Operations would be in charge, working out of the CIA's Jerusalem home base.

Admiral Brown then explained American military support for "Operation Terrorist Wipe-out". This would include both the Persian Gulf and the Mediterranean Fleet's carrier-based aircraft; helicopter gunships; field rocketry; Army Armored Divisions, and 20,000 U.S Marines for occupation of captured territories, once the mercenary bounty-hunters have cleared the area. Jack then concluded:

"There's one last formality- I'd like Pat and Mike to assemble the House and the Senate to confirm the Declaration of War against ISIS and all other terrorist groups in the Middle East and Africa, including the use of foreign mercenary bounty hunters. Gentlemen, I think that's enough for this morning. We'll meet again next week at the same time."

Ten minutes later Jack was in his living room relaxing with Kathy, who was preparing their cocktails.

"That's enough for today," Jack observed as he took a large sip of his vodka *Martini* , "I need to save some energy for this weekend with Varishnakov and Chang, who'll probably have a lot to say about the military action I've taken during the past few days. I'll try to make them my good buddies, because I need them badly to begin the painfully slow process of bringing about global peace through prosperity.

Chapter Twelve

Woodland- enshrouded Camp David was the perfect setting for informality, congeniality, and frank discussion, and by the end of Saturday morning all three leaders would discuss major world affairs on a first name basis- it would be Jack; Mikhail and Chang.

Mikhail and Chang were quite insistent upon knowing first hand why Jack had broken every international arms treaty by creating and using a space-based *Armada* of laser satellites, and why America was resigning from the United Nations. Jack responded earnestly:

> "Gentlemen, I used the lasers because I had them, thanks to former President Ronald Reagan, who never gave up on his '*Star Wars*' national defense system. However, I assure you that we have no nuclear missiles or other weapons in outer space, and are only concerned about minimizing civilian casualties.

> "My reason for leaving the United Nations is because it doesn't work, and never has since its founding in 1944. The building on Manhattan's East River may be impressive, but the organization has been fatally flawed since day one, including the concept of a Security Council with single nation veto power, and the constraints placed upon NATO 'peace-keeping' troops in the field, who have 'rules of engagement' which render them nothing more than 'glorified beat-cops'.

"Furthermore, I am convinced that my solution for peace through prosperity on this planet can bring about world stability, especially with regard to '*rogue nuclear nations*', such as North Korea and Iran, both of which will soon be under democratic civilian law based upon the American Constitution.

"My use of laser satellites to obliterate known terrorist training camps and supply depots is in the best interest of every country, not just my own. I suggest that we now combine our forces to eliminate individual terrorists wherever we may find them, and to this end, I will share our intelligence with yours to make it happen. Perhaps we can begin by discussing the toughest problem for us all, and that is, the Middle East.".

Jack proceeded to lay out his travel plans for Lebanon; Israel; Syria; Gaza; Egypt, Libya, and Tunisia, for which he would take personal responsibility, while Varishnikov would meet with Persia's new interim leaders, and Chang would meet with nuclear powers Pakistan and India. Jack then added:

"With specific regard to the Palestinian question, I plan to give them 3 choices- remain a completely independent nation in the Gaza Strip; join hands with Egypt; or, join ranks with Israel, which will soon become a member of the *American Commonwealth* - and in so doing, will become the fastest growing economy in the region, even though they don't have a drop of oil."

"With respect to the *'Muslim Crazies'*, there's no other solution than to wipe them out before they kill any more people. I have already given my overseas CIA operatives the command to search for them; find them; and either kill them or capture them for interrogation." Chang then spoke up for China:

"Jack, how will your foreign policy affect my country?" Jack replied in an even voice:

"Chang, after thousands of years of recorded Chinese history, you have somehow begun to find your way into the 21st century and its basic capitalism all on your own, so I don't think you will need much help from outsiders like myself, with the possible exception of how to honor free and fair global trade; acknowledgement of your neighboring unified Korea; and acknowledgement of the new Democratic Republic of Persia, with my guarantee that their oil will continue to flow to your country, and if you need anymore, I have dozens of billions of barrels in my Strategic Oil Reserve- which is now open for export." Varishnikov followed up Chang:

"Jack, Persia was our close ally, and only the efforts of your Vice President John McCall prevented me from destroying your Persian Gulf Fleet with my missiles. It came quite close, and I don't want to ever find myself in that position again."

"Mikhail, your wish is my wish. By tomorrow afternoon, we must come to a complete agreement with the regard to the stability of all lesser nations, starting with diffusing the Middle East tension. I further suggest that we meet here again in three months to review our progress in bringing about world stability- because instability, to put it capitalistically, is 'bad for business', and my country is a nation of businessmen, from international conglomerates to 'mom and pop' town shops.

"I don't know about you gentlemen, but I'm starved, so let's all go enjoy my chef Alferedo's offerings, and the wine from my vineyard in Tuscany, which is labeled *Villa Americana/Chianti Riserva Speciale/2010*. It won the Italian Gold Medal for the Chianti class, and at dinner tonight we will be serving my 2015 vintage for comparison."

Alfredo proceeded to serve a light luncheon, consisting of a fresh mixed garden salad, topped with his special dressing, made from Jack's barrel- aged *Balsamic* vinegar, and his orchard's 'first cold press' extra virgin olive oil. This was followed by a grilled veal cutlet topped with a creamy *Valdostana* cheese sauce, and white northern Italian *Tartuffi* shavings, with its unmistakable aroma. Alfredo finished by flaming his *Grand Marnier Crêpe Suzettes* at the table. The group then retired to Jack's study for *Havana* cigars, and 20-year-old *Remy Martin* Cognac. When everyone was seated comfortably in their leather lounge chairs around the roaring fireplace, the conversations turned to their wives; children; and grandchildren. The stories they each offered were confined to light- hearted personal anecdotes. When the mantle clock chimed 3pm, Jack suggested they return to work.

The long afternoon session was concerned with the individual missions for which each leader would be responsible in the coming weeks. It was agreed that Jack would tour the Eastern

Mediterranean and North African capitals of Beirut; Jerusalem; Cairo; Tripoli; and Tunis.

It was late afternoon the following day when Jack was helicoptered back to the White House lawn by *Marine One*, where he was greeted by his senior staff, none of whom were surprised by his success.

> "Not so fast, people- I've just laid the cornerstone, but the building has not yet been built. Let's go to the Oval Office and break out a few bottles of *Dom Perignon.*"

When their glasses were filled, Jack raised his, and suggested a toast for his closest collaborators with these words:

> "There must be a beginning to any global enterprise such as the one I have embarked our country upon, and I must say that thus far I am greatly encouraged. I am also certain that this will be a very long and bumpy road which will extend well beyond my Presidency."

Back in his family quarters, it didn't take Jack very long to put together the key elements of his New Year's Eve combined *Inaugural* and *State of the Union address* to the Congress and the nation:

> "Members of the Congress; my former colleagues in the Supreme Court; honored guests; ladies and gentlemen; and all of you townspeople who make our country the greatest nation on Earth- it is 8pm et, so you will have the rest of the evening to celebrate the coming year of 2017. As President, I am here to tell you that there is much to celebrate about.

"We have welcomed with great enthusiasm the changes adopted 2 years ago, when our former President and the Congress transferred most Federal powers back to our villages, towns, and cities. Today, no one in our society remains uncared for, or forgotten. Everyone between the ages of 16 and 70 who is able to work is guaranteed employment; everyone has family healthcare, and our economy will save $500 billion per year by employing 'house- call Doc's' to nip diseases in the bud during their bi-monthly visits.

"Your children are now tuition-free at *any* school- public, private or parochial, from age 3 through Ph.D, and all adults are encouraged to participate in *continuing education*.

"Some have claimed that this new educational system favors the brightest amongst us, and there is some truth in this, because God did not bless us all with exactly the same talents. Our Constitution *commands* that we give every citizen the '*same opportunity*' for success in life- and this has been accomplished- but it has never guaranteed the '*same outcome*'.

"In foreign policy, America has once again assumed world leadership, because there is no one else that can do this job. Our *American Commonwealth* now involves more than a dozen nations with a common Constitution; common currency; common defense; and a common prosperity.

"This invitation remains open to all nations with a stable democratic form of government, and where appropriate, we will assist you when requested to bring about this required stability by eliminating every terrorist element we can find with whatever means necessary, including 'mercenary bounty hunters'.

"During the coming year, our objective will be to destroy ISIS, now that the Persian Gulf is under our control. During the coming months, this Persian nation will be conducting a national *referendum* on joining the *American Commonwealth*, followed by general elections. In the meantime, they will be shipping record quantities of petroleum around the world to re-establish their economy.

"I trust that all of you understand our new position as a nation with worldwide responsibilities, and the enormous wealth we have created to back up our domestic and foreign policies.

"In closing, my family and I wish each of you an evermore prosperous New Year in 2017."

The day after New Year's, Jack assembled his 'inner circle', and addressed them:

"Gentlemen, before you get too carried away with the brunette beauty at my side, allow me to introduce the newest member of our team- Senator Cynthia Adams of Montana, Chairwoman of the Senate Foreign Relations Committee, and tell you some things about her that perhaps has not already been reported in the press.

"Beginning at age 10, Cynthia spent the next dozen Spring and Summer vacations living in foreign countries, from Japan, India, and China, to Israel; Egypt; Saudi Arabia; Italy, and several other Western European countries. She learned their languages; their customs; and their politics. This continued throughout her undergraduate years at Stanford, where she graduated *Summa Cum Laude*, before going on to the Harvard Business School, where she graduated at age 22, again as *Summa Cum Laude*.

"Her father decided during her teens that she was destined to lead the Adams pioneer empire in Montana, which had been built during the previous two centuries-wheat; cattle; horses; oil; gas; silver; gold and uranium-along with the processing, manufacturing facilities, and refineries to convert these resources into commercial products.

"After graduation, she took over *Adams Industries* as CEO, following the untimely death of her father, and grew it during the next 6 years from $8 billion to $15 billion, making it one of the largest family-owned private companies in America.

"Within her conglomerate, Cynthia promoted or hired the best Division Managers available, and left her company to serve as Congresswoman from Helena, and two years later as Senator from that State in 2014. In short, she knows how to 'run things' as well or better than any man or woman in this country.

"I have now asked her to allow me to 'pick her brains' in matters of foreign policy, and in return I have offered her to 'pick my brains' on matters of 'Presidential

Powers', and the limitations thereon imposed by our Constitution.

"In the future, we will be working together quite closely, and specifically, on managing the growing *American Commonwealth*, which is at the very heart of my Administration's foreign policy. Now, let's hear from our CIA Director regarding the elimination of the *'Muslim Crazies'*." Mike McMahon gave a brief recap:

"In the past few weeks we have enlisted over 10,000 foreign 'mercenary bounty-hunters', all of whom speak Arabic. To date, we have killed about 2,000 terrorists, and have captured another 300 for interrogation at 'Gitmo'. By this time next month, I expect to recruit another 5,000 mercenaries, which should be an ample force for the job in the Middle East and North Africa." Jack then turned to Admiral Brown, and asked:

"Where are we in wiping out ISIS military forces?"

"Jack, I have dropped our 82nd and 101st Airborne Divisions, which now surround Damascus, and redeployed our Second Armored Division from Persia to Northern Iraq in a classic 'pincer' movement. I expect the war against ISIS in Iraq and Syria will be over quite soon. Do you want to tackle Yemen after that?"

"I don't think that will be necessary, Eddie. Let's leave that job to our mercenaries and the Saudi Army. I think that Yemen will soon be cleaned up, and if Oman is smart, they'll stay the hell out of this operation- which leaves Libya next on our list, and they, along with ISIS, will have a lot to answer for when we hold War Crimes trials after the shooting stops- it will make the Nazi Nuremburg trials after WWII pale by comparison with the atrocities committed by these people during the past 5 years." Turning to his Treasury Secretary Diamond, the President asked:

"Johnnie, how are we doing in the money department?"

"We're running well ahead of last year, and the total national 'take' should be $5.5- 6.0 trillion by the end of this year, which means our Federal share will jump to at least $1.5 trillion.

"Our *Commonwealth* friends are also doing quite nicely, including Persia, which is now exporting about 50% more oil than last year. Thus far, none of the *Commonwealth* nations should require any further assistance, and all are on schedule with the pay down of their foreign debt, which our Treasury Department guaranteed when they joined the *Commonwealth*." Jack then added:

"We won't be meeting again for several weeks, because I will be making a tour- along with my new Foreign Affairs Advisor, Cynthia; our Secretary of State, and our Secretary of the Treasury. We will be taking a close look at our new *Commonwealth* members, and recent Middle East battlegrounds, and won't return until the week before Easter. Vice President McCall will handle all of my domestic administrative matters during my absence."

Air Force One made its first stop in Dublin, and Jack spent the afternoon and early evening with newly elected President Sean Maloney, while Cynthia and Rollie met with Ireland's Secretary of State and Johnnie caucused with Ireland's Treasury Secretary. They then all met for an exchange of ideas at dinner.

President Maloney led off:

> "Jack, you are the first American President to visit our *Emerald Isle* since President Reagan many years ago, and we shall all look forward to your next visit. As I mentioned to you in our meeting, the only political problem thus far has been the mass immigration of our brothers from Northern Ireland, where economic conditions cannot compare with ours. There will come a time later this year when we will no longer be in a position to absorb them." Jack thought for a moment, and responded:

> "Sean, it seems to me that the best solution would be to unite the two countries as soon as possible, before Northern Ireland becomes a financial 'basket case'. Why don't we start by you setting up a meeting in London between their Prime Minister, Britain's Prime Minister, and the two of us- I'll make a stopover on my way back to the States and let you know the exact date."

Next morning, Air Force One landed in Lisbon, where much the same routine was followed. When the groups got together for dinner, the discussion centered upon financial matters, especially the repayment of their heavy foreign debt and the increased level of domestic and foreign investments, which to date had absorbed more than half of the previously unemployed workforce. The largest foreign investment project was the *'Lisbon Super Bullet'*, which would soon connect with Paris, via Madrid, and then Barcelona.

The story in Madrid was somewhat different because of the separatist movements by the *Basques*, centered around the city of Bilbao in the Northwest, and *Catalonia,* centered around the metropolis of Barcelona to the Northeast. Otherwise, new foreign and domestic investments had doubled, and their foreign debt load now appeared to be manageable. The *Riviera Super Bullet* would begin in Barcelona then meet the new *Orient Super Bullet* in Venice, on its way to Istanbul.

The meetings in Rome the next day provided a pleasant atmosphere of good news. With a one-year head start, the Italian economy was booming as never before, especially in the hospitality industry, Italy's largest money-maker. Heavily controlled gambling had been recently legalized in almost every tourist resort, as had prostitution, for the first time in 65 years. Most of the dinner conversation centered around the tremendous problem of illegal immigration by 'boat people' from all areas of North Africa- the atrocities committed by the human traffickers were as bad or worse than in the days of slave trading. Jack had a suggestion:

> "For many years my country has had the same problem with *'foreign invaders'* from South of our borders. There seemed to be no humane way to deal with illegals who had settled in many parts of my country. But we finally compromised by giving legal resident status to those immediate family members who had been in our country

for 7 or more years; could pass our written English language test; and a test of fundamental understanding of our Constitution- about 7 million people who could then qualify for an American passport.

"We were then obliged to repatriate those foreigners who did not qualify for residency, or had committed another felony crime, in addition to illegal entry- about 10 million in all, including those born in America, who by law follow the passports of their father, or their legal guardian. So, we gave them a one way ticket back home; $500 'start up capital', and told them to stand in line at the nearest American Consulate just like everyone else if they wanted to re-enter our country legally. The best solution for Italy is to convince North African nations to enforce the illegal departure of these 'boat people'. In order to do that, they must have a stable government, which means wiping out all terrorists and their organizations- which my country plans to accomplish before the end of this Spring.

"I want to congratulate your Italian government, and the Italian people on becoming the shining example in the Mediterranean. My family and I will be spending a couple of weeks at our villa in Greve during Easter vacation, and I expect to report that American Armed Forces have completely destroyed ISIS in Syria; Iraq; and other terrorist groups in Northern Africa."

Jack and his group had much the same conversations with the new Greek President; his Secretary of State; his Treasury Secretary and his Secretary of Defense. Greek President

Aristotle 'Ari' Grigoris explained the awakening of his ancient nation:

> "Jack, as one of three major candidates, I had a tough time explaining why we should abandon Socialism, in favor of a somewhat social system based entirely upon individual and corporate capitalism for its future prosperity. The tide suddenly turned in my favor when the 'Euro Zone' finance committee refused to bail us out once again, and forced us into imminent default on our foreign debt.

> "At that point, we had no place to go but 'up' by becoming a member of the *American Commonwealth*. In short, our financial crisis is over, thanks to your government's guarantee of our foreign debt, and more importantly, the Greek people have bought into your American ideals."

At the dinner table that evening, the conversation quickly turned to the war against ISIS and other terrorist groups. All eyes then turned to Jack for comment:

> "Well, as we've all seen on the evening news, my 82nd and 101st Airborne Division parachuted into the outskirts of Damascus at dawn this morning. Initially, there was fierce resistance from Assad's forces, but anyone who has studied the history of our Airborne Divisions knows of their extraordinary fighting capabilities.

> "By noon today the American flag was raised over every Syrian government building in Damascus, and Assad was obliged to surrender unconditionally. He was then

flown to an undisclosed exile location and will eventually be tried for crimes against humanity, principally chemical genocide against his own people. I have as yet not received reports of military and civilian causalities, but I believe that they will prove to be minimal, all things considered during this 5-year Civil War.

"Also at dawn this morning, my 2nd Armored Division with 20,000 men and 1,000 tanks, now based in Southwest Persia, made a two-pronged attack against ISIS forces in Northern Syria and Northwest Iraq. They were supported by Kurdish troops in Syria, and by our Persian Gulf fleet with two aircraft carriers and their war planes. These carrier aircraft, including helicopter gunships, flew in to 'soften' the way for our tanks and ground troops, while Italian Special Forces parachuted onto the Baghdad airport and secured that important objective.

"Once again, enemy opposition initially fought fiercely, but soon realized what full American military power means in conventional warfare. At noon today, the American flag flew over all of the principal cities of Iraq and Syria, as well as the oil fields in both countries. This evening, both Iraq and Syria are American occupied countries. There are still at large many thousands of ISIS Forces who have fled our onslaught. They will be found, and either eliminated, or taken prisoner for interrogation."

There were many questions regarding this 'one day' war in the Middle East and why it took several years for the American Commander-In-Chief to take decisive action against the *Muslim Crazies*. Jack had this parting comment to make:

> "Every American President has his own philosophy about using warfare as a means of establishing stability, and each of us approaches America's dominant military power in different ways.

> "My philosophy is very different than that of my predecessor. I believe that any nation must first be stabilized in order to create a Democratic government based upon a tried and proven Constitution like ours, which promotes individual prosperity so that the individuals support their nation, rather than the nation trying to support the individual. During my time in office, I can only begin this process, nation-by-nation, and that is exactly why I am here."

Upon Jack's arrival in Ankara, Turkey, Jack's diplomatic group again split up to confer with their Turkish counterparts. Jack met with newly-elected President Ahmed Hamal; Johnnie Diamond met with the Treasury Secretary, and Cynthia and Rollie with the Secretary of State. Ahmed opened the conversation:

> "That was a very impressive display of military power you showed in Syria and Iraq." To which Jack replied:

> "Ahmed, if I have to spend more than one day on a small regional war, it means that the planning was not well thought out, and I consider Korea, Persia, and

Iraq/Syria to be a relatively small deal for America's conventional military might.

"I also believe that 3-4 months is sufficient time to establish a new civilian interim government; conduct a national *referendum* on becoming part of the *American Commonwealth*; and then holding national general elections, after which our troops will leave. By the way, I want to congratulate you on the job your Kurdish troops did in assisting us in Syria and Iraq, and trust that there will be no future disturbances in Eastern Turkey." Ahmed was prone to comment:

"Jack, I wish the Kurdish question could be resolved that simply, but there are centuries of historical animosities between my country's vast majority in the West and the eastern Kurdish provinces. Let's hope that our new American Constitution will serve to unify our people in the coming generations."

That evening, dinner conversation was very upbeat, mainly because of the improving financial position of Turkey, and the relatively smooth conversion to the American dollar currency. Foreign investments were up substantially, and GDP growth was up to almost 10%, as the country began transforming into a 'consumer economy'.

The conversation then turned to the on-going campaign against remaining Muslim terrorist groups. Jack proceeded to give his appraisal:

"The 'mercenary bounty-hunters' we have thus far recruited- which is now well over 15,000- have done an

196

admirable job to date, with relatively little civilian collateral damage, and our next phase of operations should eliminate North African groups well before the end of the Spring, now that Persia no longer provides them with economic or military support."

The next day in Beirut, Jack's conversation with newly- elected President Daniel Thomas, a coalition choice, and a Roman Catholic.

"Jack, now that the remaining *Hezbollah* are gradually 'disappearing', my main concern is the several hundred thousand refugees now living in temporary shelters in Lebanon. Our economy cannot possibly absorb more than a small fraction of these." To which Jack replied:

"Danny, there are more than 2 million refugees in the Middle East, especially in Jordan. I'll be talking with President Abdullah in Amman tomorrow on the same subject, and somehow we will come up with a solution. I think it's important that the refugees be given the opportunity to select their own country here in the Middle East, including Israel.

"I wish there was another Suez Canal to be built today, but the only thing that comes close is the American railroad system now being built in the States, which have put well over 6 million Americans to work. I have an idea that with a little prompting, they might contemplate an analogous *Beirut Bullet* as the focal point of a Middle East *Super Bullet System,* linking every capital from Istanbul throughout the entire Arabian Peninsula, including a direct route from

Istanbul through Beirut over a new Suez Canal bridge, and on to Cairo. Perhaps this project, coupled with a new adjacent super highway system throughout this entire Middle Eastern and North African area- might be grand enough to put everyone to work." Danny looked at Jack quizzically, and asked rhetorically:

"Jack, where do you come up with all this stuff?"

"Funny you should ask, because our former President once made the same remark when I laid out the new domestic plan for America. I'll tell you know what I told him then, and that is- the good Lord blessed me with the ability to find solutions to seemingly unsolvable problems." Jack continued:

"Danny, how can we make Beirut once again the *Paris of the East,* and to get all those cruise ships and airplanes to land on your shores? That project would probably absorb women, teenagers and 'middle-agers' who cannot perform tough manual labor."

That evening, the dinner conversation was all about Jack's off-the-cuff solution for the refugee and unemployment problem in the Middle East. Even Jack's companions were amazed at their leader's ability to resolve complex problems on the spot.

In Amman, Jack and President Abdullah spent the afternoon discussing the same subjects, and while the dinner conversation contained many different questions, the impact was equally reassuring to the Jordanian contingency. For his part, the former King had not only fought ISIS all on his own, but had relinquished his throne for a comfortable Presidential swivel chair behind an elaborate antique hand carved desk. He had one parting question the next morning, as Jack's *Air Force One* was about to depart for Jerusalem:

> "Jack, what makes you so sure that the Super Bullet *Consortium* will agree to gamble several trillion dollars on this enormous project to link North Africa and the Middle East by rail and road to the heart of Europe?"

> "It's very simple, 'I'll make them an offer they can't refuse'-it's called exceptional profits and right-of-way land."

In Jerusalem, Jack's discussion with newly-elected President Saul Steiner centered mainly upon the Palestinian question. Just before dinner break, Jack summed up the situation:

> "Saul, if you agree I would like to offer the Gaza government a choice of joining with either Egypt or Israel, or to 'go it alone'. I see no other options, now that we have effectively eliminated *Hamas* with our 'mercenary bounty- hunters'.

> "At the same time I will make it perfectly clear to them that if they 'go it alone' they will not have the support of my country, because they would become an economic basket case- with nothing to offer except now obsolete guns and rockets, and no support from any other Muslim Country. Should they decide to merge with Israel rather than Egypt, could Israel absorb this mass population of Palestinians?"

> "Jack, Jews and Arabs have lived here side by side for thousands of years, only to be set against each other by

reason of foreign dominance- from the Roman Caesars to the British Empire, until our full independence in 1948. We have the same great prophet, Abraham, and in these modern times there's no reason why we cannot live and prosper as one people. Should Gaza decide to annex itself to Egypt, as far as Israel is concerned we would have lost nothing but a very large migraine headache. Of course, apart from the Gaza Strip itself they would not take any land with them."

That evening's dinner conversation revolved around the economic possibilities of a combined Jewish- Arab nation, with or without the Gaza Strip, but including the *Consortium's* investment in a *'Super Bullet'* railway system connecting Jerusalem with Central Europe, North Africa, and the Arabian Peninsula.

Jack and party made a brief stop the next morning in Gaza City, where the entire Middle East future plan was laid before the Palestinian Gaza government, on a 'take-it or leave-it' basis. It took them just one hour to decide on annexing to the State of Israel, rather than Egypt. 'Going it alone' was not considered a viable option, because *Hamas* had been 'wiped out'.

When Jack landed in Cairo that afternoon, the Egyptian government was already aware of the American President's grand plan for the future of the Middle East and North Africa. The questions asked by the newly-elected Egyptian *interim* Administration were centered upon the role of that country in the economic development of their neighbors to the North (Israel to Istanbul); the West (Libya to Morocco); and eventually to the South (Sudan, Somalia and Kenya). Before the end of dinner, everyone had agreed upon the American President's ambitious plan for Egypt's future development, including the ambitious new bridge over the Suez Canal.

The final stop on the tour was in London, where the British Prime Minister Adam West had been meeting for several days with Irish President Sean Maloney to resolve the question of Irish unification. Jack joined the meeting in early afternoon:

"Well gentlemen, what's the verdict?" The PM summed up the situation:

"I've put the question to my Cabinet, and they agree that the only economic solution is to reunite Northern and Southern Ireland, in hopes that your American Constitution will assure the rights of our Protestant minority.

"There will be a referendum in three weeks in Northern Ireland, and in six weeks general elections held to elect Federal Representatives to the House and Senate, as well as Governors and other local offices." Jack was quick to respond:

"My heartiest congratulations on your joint successful efforts. It took America one hundred years to reunite our North and South, including the end of segregation." Irish Prime Minister Maloney, turned to the American:

"Jack, who would've guessed that after more than half a millennium, it would be an American to bring peace and prosperity to a united Ireland? I think it's time for a toast and I just happened to have a bottle of 30-year-old Irish Whiskey."

Chapter Thirteen

Jack and his 'foreign affairs team' flew overnight from London, and landed at Andrews early Friday morning. The group was then helicoptered directly to Camp David for a relaxing weekend, and to recap the events of the past ten hectic days. They all agreed that the trip was without question an historic triumph, and also agreed that many underlying religious problems and conflicts would take decades to resolve, as would the elimination of all terrorist groups now still operating in Africa and Asia. Everyone then waited for Jack to announce his future 'game plan'. Jack aired his thoughts:

> "Feel free to interrupt me, but I think that in the next few months we should take a breather and consolidate our victories, while planning similar operations for Central and South America, and the Caribbean Islands, beginning with Cuba, where entreaties have been made to our Ambassador in Havana by the Castro Regime, which has finally seen the 'handwriting on the wall'.

> "In this regard, I will accept no compromises to the successful formula we have developed for the *American Commonwealth*- nor shall we change anything for other dictatorships or *juntas* we may encounter in the future."
> Cynthia raised her hand and asked:

> "What about the rest of the African continent and Afghanistan?"

> "Cynthia, we need several months to let the dust settle in the Middle East, North Africa- and the rest of the

Arabian Peninsula will need to abandon *'Sharia Law'* if they wish to join the *American Commonwealth*, because these laws are absolutely incompatible with our Constitution. In the meantime, we must finish the job we began against the Afghani *Taliban*. That is, we must wipe them out once and for all.

"The Afghani government must convince the Afghani people of the great economic advantages to be gained as a potential member of the *American Commonwealth.* We have spent too many lives trying to bring this 'third-century country' into the modern world. At the same time, we need to qualify Syria and Iraq for membership and bring our troops home." Rollie then ventured his opinion:

"Jack, that's a very tall order." To which Jack replied:

"You're right Rollie, and that's why I'm sending Cynthia along with you, because she has the right smarts and knows all the languages you'll be faced with in Kabul; Islamabad; Damascus; and Baghdad. Secondly, this is exactly why I chose you for this job. Any man who can clean up New York City in a few years certainly has the ability to bring peace to the countries which desperately need it for their future prosperity- this is what my Administration's foreign policy is all about.

"Having expressed my position now, I suggest we all retire to the bar and ponder the problems in front of us. Sunday night, I will speak on television to the American people, and try my best to explain exactly why, after more than two centuries, America continues to be a 'warrior nation'. I'd like all of you to enjoy yourselves over the rest of the weekend- there's tennis; nine-hole golf; fishing; hiking; swimming; a fully stocked bar and a great chef. I'm going home now to prepare my Sunday evening telecast. *Marine One* will be back for you Monday morning and we'll have a full meeting on Tuesday morning at 10 o' clock."

Jack and Kathy spent the rest of Friday evening and all day Saturday getting 'reacquainted'- both in bed and out. After Sunday Mass, Jack retired to his private study and composed the talking points for that evening's telecast, which as always would be short and sweet:

> "A very good evening to my fellow citizens; immigrant citizens-to-be; new members of the *American* Commonwealth; other foreign viewers; and most importantly to the Commanders, men, and women of the victorious 2nd Armored Division; and the 82nd and 101st Airborne Divisions, who have raised our American Flag over Baghdad and Damascus in yet another 'one day war', which has demolished ISIS.

> "As your Commander-In-Chief, I decided it was absolutely necessary to bring stability to the Middle East in one quick and decisive stroke, using only conventional war weapons in order to minimize innocent civilian casualties. To you gallant warriors, I assure you that your nation will honor you when you return home.

> "For those of you who may think that America has become a 'warrior nation', I must remind you that we were forced to become a 'warrior nation' at the very

beginning of our Revolutionary War with the British, at Lexington; Concord; Bunker Hill; and Boston Harbor in 1775, and that *We The People* will never accept tyranny-either at home or abroad.

"Too many American lives have been spent defending our freedom at home, because of a lapse in guaranteed freedom in Europe and elsewhere. We have always accepted these missions with great reluctance, but I have come to the conclusion that there can be no global stability, peace, or prosperity without American leadership. Simply stated, there is no other nation, or combination of nations capable of doing this job the right way- and the right way is voluntary membership in our newly created *American Commonwealth*.

"In bidding you good evening, let me remind you that we Americans are always at our *very best* when things are at their *very worst*, as was the case when I took Office and implemented my design for 21st century American domestic policies, which former President O'Hara successfully guided through our Congress.

"I cannot say the same for the foreign policy I inherited upon my Inauguration- it was a disaster that has required immediate attention as your Commander-In-Chief, and has taken most of my time since then. I can now report to you that our Military Establishment has performed above and beyond the call of duty, with a string of victories unequaled since the final years of WWII."

"Jack, I surrender," admitted Cuban leader Raul Castro. "The revolution my brother Fidel and I brought about more than half a century ago has at last given way to the harsh realities of Communist ideological failure. My people now demand more from life than I can possibly deliver from a tight, centrally-controlled form of government, so I am prepared to apply for membership in the *American Commonwealth,* if you agree." Jack responded promptly:

"Raul, it takes courage to admit defeat, and I wish you the best of luck in explaining your reasons to your fellow Cubans. It has been a very bumpy road since our former President Teddy Roosevelt led his *'Rough Riders'* up San Juan Hill more than a century ago, to give your country its independence from Spain." Jack then continued:

"This unfortunately resulted in a series of bad dictators, including Batista, and after 1959, to your Communist regime, which came very close to provoking WWIII between ourselves and your Russian masters, when you allowed them to install medium-range nuclear missiles on your island. Now, you may consider your past sins forgiven, but I don't want to see any member of your current regime on the general election ballot, after your national *referendum* on membership in the *American Commonwealth.*

"You've got about two months before the national *referendum,* and 6 months before election weekend in November. This should give you ample time to explain the situation to your people, and to free all of your political prisoners upon your return to Havana.

"On the economic side, after the November elections you should see a substantial increase in foreign investments, especially in your resort hotels and casinos, which I suggest you sell to private investors, along with your nationalized airlines; railroads; and oil enterprises. You should also auction off your national lands, especially the tobacco and sugar plantations you confiscated. These measures should serve to substantially increase the trading value of the Cuban *peso*, and make the conversion to American dollar currency much less traumatic.

"I'd like to see you push the concept of new economic growth and prosperity through large influxes of foreign private capital to make it all happen. And don't forget to keep reminding them that the new $100 per day minimum wage will be phased in, and the new Personal Pension Accounts will provide economic security for their families.

"Apart from selling off or giving back your nationalized oil; tobacco; sugar; hotel/casino; and other industries, I think I could persuade the *Super Bullet Consortium* to build a trans-island rail line from Havana to the Eastern Province of Santiago and then Guantanamo Bay, which I am prepared to buy from Cuba, replacing our lease. Think of a price for 100,000 acres and get back to me.

"My plan is to greatly enlarge our Guantanamo Bay Naval facility into headquarters for my new Caribbean Fleet to protect Cuba; the other Caribbean Islands, and Northern South America. My proposed Havana-

Santiago- Guantanamo *Super Bullet* railway will provide work for about ½ million laborers, and the new Naval Headquarters will employ several hundred thousand workers for the next several years, and then permanent jobs for several thousand employees."

One by one, the remaining independent island nations in the Caribbean visited Camp David, and received the best economic advice Jack had to offer. Congressional approvals for membership would come after their *referendums* and November elections. Problem nations in Central and South America were told in no uncertain terms that they would not be accepted until they had rid their countries of 'drug lords' and the associated bribery of governmental officials at all levels. While each country's official representatives nodded his head in the affirmative, they were all lying through their teeth, because they knew full well that neither cartel nor bribed officials would ever willingly renounce their profits or payoffs.

Jack did not tell them that he had already made a plan to assist them with Hispanic military convict forces from the Aleutian Marine training camps.

Pope Luke's landing at New York's JFK Airport was reminiscent of Lindbergh's landing at Paris's *Le Bourget* ninety years previously. One million New Yorkers jammed the tarmac as his plane came to a stop. The six-foot Irish-American in a white double breasted suit and white skull cap stepped down and announced:

"It's good to be home, especially during this Holy Easter Season. My travel plans are somewhat fluid, but I will be conducting Palm Sunday Mass in *Yankee Stadium*;

renewing President Fitzgerald and his wife's wedding vows in St. Patrick's Cathedral the following day; visiting with my American Cardinals and Archbishops; visiting with my family, and then conducting Mass at Wrigley Field on Easter Sunday."

The Pope's visit was a great success, especially among America's 90 million Catholics. He also took time to confer with the leaders of many American Protestant religions regarding the unification of all Christian Faiths.

Jack and Kathy's renewal ceremony was attended by the Fitzgerald and 0'Malley families, who were greatly outnumbered by Secret Service and NYPD security forces, especially in the areas within 500 yards of the front entrance to St. Patrick's Cathedral, where thousands of well-wishers gathered to hail the President and First Lady.

There was also one lone gunman who had managed to edge his way to the front, while assembling the components of a two-shot pistol he had carved from a block of composite plastic, and which had passed through all of the metal detectors. As Jack and Kathy walked down the steps towards their waiting Limo, the assassin broke through the Security line and fired his two bullets directly into Jack's chest- which was protected by what he called his Tin foil T-shirt made from Pittsburgh *Super Steel*.

The would-be assassin, a Muslim terrorist, was immediately shot and killed by the Secret Service, while Jack was driven to nearby Doctor's Hospital, where he was quickly examined and pronounced substantially unhurt. Kathy and other close friends gathered beside him anxiously, but Jack made light of his brush with death, stating:

"Hey gang, this prototype vest really works well, but my chest hurts like hell." to which Doctor Epstein replied:

"Well Mr. President, you have some nasty bruises and a little skin blood that are going to keep you out of business for a few days, but there's no permanent physical damage. I suggest you take a few weeks' vacation to get your mind and body back to normal." Jack turned to his wife:

"Kathy my love, are you alright?"

"No my hero, I'm shaking like a leaf in a hurricane, and to think I always made fun of you for wearing a high-tech Medieval knight's' 'jousting' protector- but it saved your life."

Jack then called Vice President McCall to his side:

"John, I want you to draft an Executive Order stating that all military combat personnel; all law enforcement personnel, and other possible targets will henceforth be issued this same 'tin foil' T-shirt as standard equipment." Turning to his Chief of Staff, Dick Westerhoff, he added: "Inform the Congress and the Supreme Court, that they will be adjourned for the next 3 weeks, and that when I return from Italy, I will expect them to once again be at my side."

Halfway across the Atlantic to Florence, Jack turned to his Secret Service Captain, Jeff Donovan, and asked:

"Who the hell shot me?"

"Mr. President, it was an *Al Qaeda* operative we set free from 'Gitmo' 5 years ago. He was smuggled into Canada on an Iraqi tanker, and just walked across the border at Watertown, in upstate New York; took the train straight down to Grand Central; and went directly to a Mosque 'safe house' in lower Manhattan. That's all we know at this time- it will take several days to find the other people connected with your assassination attempt." Jack quickly replied:

"If and when you catch them, I want them all sent directly to 'Gitmo' for intense interrogations." It would take another three months to round up all the co-conspirators involved in the failed assassination plot.

Villa Americana was relatively easy for the American and Italian Secret Services to guard, as it was located on a steep hilltop, with one narrow dirt road leading to the premises. The townspeople below in *Greve* knew that the President was in residence, because the American flag waved high above his villa- and also knew that they were the first line of defense in identifying any suspicious characters they might come across in and around their town.

Atop the hillside with Jack and Kathy was their resident housekeeper, Ursola; their personal chef Alfredo; their Secret Service crew; and his personal physician, Navy Captain Brian Sullivan, all of whom lived in the ground level residence below.

It wasn't exactly the balmy Hawaii that they had originally planned, but the weather was mostly sunny and pleasant, and they made love morning, afternoon, and night as they had on their first honeymoon. They swam in the pool, played tennis, and took long walks with their vineyard keeper who assured them that the 2017 vintage would become the best *Vendemmia* to date. They also made many day trips to Florence and other historic locations throughout Tuscany- always ending up in the town's main square for evening Vespers, and a short stop at the square's principal sidewalk café to chat with their fellow villagers.

After three weeks of relaxing, Jack and Kathy were anxious to return to their White House home, their children, their granddaughter Caterina, and to hold their first grandson, which Mary and Nicky had named 'Jack'. Air Force One touched down at Andrews on a rainy Sunday afternoon, and one hour later Jack summoned his Chief of Staff to the Oval Office for a debriefing on pending matters for the following week.

> "Jack, we have a long list of countries wanting to sign up for the *American Commonwealth*- Canada; Mexico; Guatemala; Honduras; Belize; Costa Rica; Nicaragua; Panama; Venezuela; Columbia; Ecuador; Bolivia; Chile; Argentina; Paraguay; Uruguay; Brazil; Guyana; Suriname; and French Guiana. In addition, several Arabian Peninsula countries, including the Saudi Kingdom; the Persian Gulf Emirates; Oman and Yemen, all of which have been advised that to qualify, they must abandon *Sharia Law*- All have reluctantly agreed, given time, but somehow I have a feeling that they're just 'Whistlin' Dixie'."

> "Dick, that's one helluva long list, and I agree with you about the wishful thinking of the Arabian Peninsula

countries. I want to take all of them on one-by-one at Camp David, so let's begin with Canada for a half day and the same for all the rest. I'd like to finish this thing up before Summer recess."

Jack's discussion with the Canadian Prime Minister was short and to the point:

> "Jason, I believe that both our countries have been twins separated at birth. You have all the natural resources that we have to continue Canadian prosperity, so the only thing that changes in our relationship is that in the future, after your *referendum* and general elections, I will be calling you 'President' *in lieu* of 'Prime Minister'."

Jack's discussion with Mexican President Jose Jimenez was much more heated, as he laid out his terms for *American Commonwealth* membership:

> "Jose, your country has caused us more problems than I can possibly enumerate- from your *foreign invaders;* to your drug traffickers; human traffickers; and your drug cartels. Since money seems to be the only language you people understand down there, I'm going to make it easy for you to pay off, or get rid of, all these 'bad guys', including your bribed officials.

> "I will give your Treasury the same deal that I give to my foreign 'bounty hunters', and $50 million each for eliminating your drug cartels. This is an offer you cannot refuse, because if you do, I will *do it* for you, just as our Marines occupied Mexico City after the Mexican

American War in 1848." Jack and Joe came eyeball to eyeball, and Jose blinked first.

"Jack, you understand the way our country operates very well, so consider the deal done."

During the following weeks, Jack repeated the same offer to every problematic Central and South American country, especially Colombia, the heroin and cocaine center of the Western Hemisphere and Europe, after which the word went out- "Don't screw with Jack Fitzgerald, or he'll cut your testicles off."

Surprisingly, the few Caribbean island nations who had not applied for membership- the British, Dutch, and French *Antilles*- fell into line by dissolving their relationships with their former European colonial masters.

The remainder of South American discussions in Camp David presented little or no problems for Jack- all had ample natural resources for their national prosperity.

After Rollie Giodarno and Cynthia Adams had reported the results of their Middle East mission, the last group of nations to receive Jack's invitation were those on the Arabian Peninsula- Syria; Iraq; the Saudi Kingdom (now including Yemen); the Persian Gulf Emirates- all of which were blessed with several hundred years worth of petroleum, but devilishly conflicted by the various sects of their Islamic religion, and otherwise had a great domestic problem in the Constitution's ban on the establishment of *any* religion, and the guaranteed equality of women. Jack explained the rules to each country:

"One of the many reasons my country has become the greatest nation on the planet is because our laws guarantee that no religion; race; creed; skin color; or gender shall be discriminated against in any way whatsoever. You will find in time that this American concept will eventually bring prosperity to all your people, and to your nation. So for now, I ask you to return home and ponder this question before we meet again. At this time, I find that any form of *Sharia Law* is incompatible with our common American Constitution. It is up to you leaders to decide on these key issues."

The denunciations of the *Jihads* and *Sharia Law* portions of the *Koran* would prove to be as profound a change in Islam as the schisms caused by Martin Luther; John Calvin and King Henry VIII were to Catholic Church authority 800 years earlier. It would take only a year to abolish *Jihad*, and another 3 years to abolish *Sharia Law* – all against a backdrop of Muslim 'clerical rabble- rousing'.

In the end, Jack would win the battle, because *'prosperity talks and dogma walks'*.

Chapter Fourteen

Jack decided that he would once again break with tradition by giving the combined Congress a 'quarterly update' of his yearly *'State of the Union Address'*, because world events were moving at a pace never before witnessed.

"Ladies and Gentlemen of the Congress; Justices of the Supreme Court; and other invited guests, before we all adjourn for Summer recess, I want to tell you the first results of our new American foreign policy, which is as bold as the *Monroe Doctrine* nearly two centuries ago, when that President told all European powers to desist from further colonization in the Western Hemisphere.

"Well, the entire Western Hemisphere has now held *referendums* and agreed to adopt our Constitution and our dollar, thus creating a common law; a common currency; a common prosperity; and a common defense for all our nations, from the *Arctic Sea* to *Antarctica*.

"Their reasons for requesting membership in the *American Commonwealth* should be self-evident, since we Americans have prospered for the last 2 centuries greater than any nation in the history of mankind. The 'peaceful revolution' that you the Congress approved as of January 1, 2015, whereby all Federal powers except for National Defense, Foreign representation, and Treasury management, were returned to the Towns, Counties, and States has proved to be an unqualified success.

"On the issue of our several 'one-day wars', I have asked and received your concurrence that they were necessary actions in the interest of not only America, but also global peace and stability- which is always in America's best interest, because we thrive on foreign consumers of our goods and services.

"With regard to the remaining Islamic terrorists, my policy will continue to be that that of 'search and destroy', by whatever means I deem necessary. This, as well as our short wars are a bloody, nasty business for any President, because of the casualties involved when wiping out the 'bad guys'.

"Thus, the burden of establishing, and maintaining, world peace and stability has fallen upon our country, because we are the only nation strong enough and prosperous enough to get the job done.

"In bidding you all a pleasant remainder of the evening, I suggest that we pray that God continues to bless us, and guide us, in this noble endeavor."

Back in his residential quarters, Jack asked Kathy her opinion about his speech:

"Darling, I think you were right on target in telling our countrymen what lies ahead during your first term, but it took you several hours to write it yourself- time better spent figuring out how to deal with Russia and China. Why don't you hire a speech writer?" Jack sipped on his vodka *Martini* and replied:

"*Tesoro*, if I thought that professionals could put words in my mouth, I would have hired them long ago. Good, bad, or indifferent, what I have to say to the American people and the Congress can only come from my own thoughts and lips, and I don't use a teleprompter, because sometimes I change my mind in midstream, as I did this evening on two occasions. Just like my college football days, when carrying the ball downfield, I zig and zag many times before scoring a touchdown.

"After two years with Barry, you might think that I knew in advance that this job is damned near impossible- but doable. I thank the Lord that for now, the Congress and the American people are behind me, but cleaning up Barry's foreign affairs blunders is a full time job all in itself."

There was a momentary lull following Jack's Address to Congress and the nation, but it proved to be the proverbial calm before a foreign policy storm, beginning with those countries in the Middle East. At the next meeting of his 'inner circle' he put the question to them:

"Rollie, Cynthia, I've read your summary report on the Middle East, Afghanistan, and Pakistan. The bottom line is that no leader is willing to directly take on the problem of the *Taliban* or any other group of remaining terrorists, notwithstanding our recent military defeat of ISIS, so I have decided that we must do the job for them.

"Rollie, I want you to return to Kabul and tell the Prime Minister that we are about to destroy the *Taliban* safe havens in Northeast Afghanistan and Northwest

Pakistan, including the use of our laser satellites, if need be. Cynthia, I want you to make the same presentation to the Pakistan government leaders in Islamabad, and tell them to sit tight until this *operation safe havens* is completed. I'd like both you and Rollie to hold their hands when the shooting starts." Turning to his Chairman of the Joint Chiefs, Admiral Brown, Jack commented:

"Eddie, the military strategy you used in Syria and Iraq worked quite well, with minimum casualties on either our side, or the civilian side. As I understand it, your 2nd Armored Division is now back at their Persian base and is ready to proceed Northeast to '*Taliban* country', skirting the principal Afghan cities. Why don't you take it from there, Admiral?"

"As was the case with Syria and Iraq, we will be 'chuting in both our 101st and 82nd Airborne Divisions into Pakistani territory due East of the *Taliban* safe havens, and proceed with a 'pincer' movement from both East and West, thus trapping the *Taliban* forces as they flee from the 2nd Armored Division's 1,000 tanks and 20,000 ground troops, which together with the 20,000 men of the two Airborne Divisions, represents a total of 40,000 combat soldiers. We are prepared to fight them 'cave-to-cave', as we did during our Pacific Islands campaign in World War II against the Japanese.

"Overhead, we will have full air support, including 200 helicopter gunships, from our Air Force bases in Persia, and to the extent required in mountainous areas, once the enemy is located we will employ our laser satellites. Unless the enemy decides otherwise, we don't plan to touch the villages, so civilian casualties should be minimal.

"At the conclusion of this campaign we do not intend to occupy *Taliban* territory in either Afghanistan or Pakistan- it will be entirely up to those governments to deal with their own 'clean up' operations. We will launch this campaign at dawn, the day after tomorrow, and bring back our soldiers to their Persian bases within a week to 10 days." Jack then proceeded to wrap up the meeting:

"Thanks for giving us a preview of our next short war, Eddie. Now, let's all retire to my well-stocked bar for a much deserved pre-dinner cocktail, or if anyone prefers, a sampling of my *2012 Villa Americana Chianti Riserva,* which has just been released for public consumption, after four years of ageing in very old *Jack Daniels* Bourbon casks.

Jack, single-malt Scotch over ice in hand, made it a point to speak with each member of his inner circle, ending up with Mike McMahon, his CIA Director.

"Mike, why don't we step out on the veranda for some fresh air?", and guided him through the French doors looking out upon the White House rose garden. Mike spoke first:

"Jack, you seem to be holding up well under all this pressure. When we met years ago, I had no idea that you would be where you are, or that I would be where I am, but I was dead right about Barry O'Hara- he left all of the unfought wars to you."

"Mike, I should be asking you how you are holding up. I've given you more responsibilities than any CIA Director in history, and you're 15 years older than I. You should be sitting on the porch of your oceanfront beach house in the Bahamas, watching the sailfish fly. If nothing else, life has been unpredictable for the two of us. How do your operations agents feel about 'vetting' our mercenary bounty-hunters' claims for a half million, or a million bucks each for dead or captured terrorists?"

"To tell the truth Jack, they'd much rather be collecting that bounty themselves."

Three days into the '*Taliban War*', that terrorist organization no longer existed. American 'shock and awe' had rid both Pakistan and Afghanistan of the main threat to their governmental stability- the first necessary step in qualifying to become a member of the *American Commonwealth,* and the individual prosperity it brings.

Jack's next 'inner circle' meeting was held the morning before he and his family departed for their July/August vacation at *Villa Americana.*

"First, I want to congratulate Eddie and his staff on a well-conceived plan and superbly executed military operation. We should also recognize the diplomatic skills of Rollie and Cynthia in keeping the Afghani and Pakistani military out of our way.

"Our next military operation will be designed for our 1st Marine Division, who will hit the 'shores of Tripoli' in Libya, and occupy that nation's capital city, as well as Benghazi. They will then proceed to wipe out every terrorist element in that North African country. Yes, it's 'pay back time' for our murdered Ambassador and the *Navy Seals* who gave their lives defending him from the terrorist group that attacked our American Consulate and CIA Annex.

"As was the case with the Japanese sneak attack on Pearl Harbor, we have not forgotten the sneak attack on our Benghazi consulate on September 11, 2012. After Libya, our Marines will advance upon Tunis and occupy that capital city of Tunisia. Once again, it will be up to Rollie and Cynthia to form interim new governments, as they did in Damascus and Baghdad.

"With regard to the rest of North Africa- that is, Algeria and Morocco, I want Rollie to keep our Ambassadors in Algiers and Rabat fully informed, and assure those governments that we have no plans for any action in their countries- assuming that they maintain their governmental stability by keeping out the many Muslim terrorists fleeing westward towards them.

"That leaves us with the remaining Northern African terrorist trouble-spots, which are Egypt's neighbors to the Southeast-Sudan; Somalia; Eritrea; and Kenya- they will soon become 21st century 'hunting grounds' for our mercenary bounty hunters and CIA agents- except they will not be looking for elephant tusks or leopard skins, but rather renegade Muslim terrorists. These two major operations for July and August will be conducted by Mike, who will report to me daily at my villa. Any questions?" Vice President McCall raised his hand:

"Jack, why are we moving at such a fast pace?" To which Jack replied:

"Excellent question, John. Previous administrations, which shall go unnamed, have left my administration with the Herculean task of cleaning up their foreign policy blunders and inactions, and we are now burdened with cleaning up the mess they left behind. As Chief Justice of the Supreme Court, I was very fortunate in convincing former President O'Hara and the Congress to go along with my solutions to most major domestic policy problems with regard to taxation; employment; healthcare; retirement; and the *nexus* of political bribery, *aka* 'campaign contributions'. Otherwise, we would all be spending our valuable time trying to convince the Congress to adopt necessary domestic solutions, rather than concentrating as we have on a previously disastrous foreign policy of appeasement- which did not work at Munich in 1938, and will never work for America.

"Although we don't think of ourselves as a *warrior nation,* we have in fact been one since our inception. We love the sting of battle, because we have always won in the end. Our nation loves a winner, but does not tolerate a loser. This is why our military campaigns have been successful in Korea; Iran; Syria; Iraq; and 'Taliban country'- and must be so in future military campaigns," Treasury Secretary Johnnie Diamond queried:

"What about Russia and China?"

"Johnnie, undoubtedly they will continue to remain relatively silent while we wipe out every known terrorist in the markets all three of us compete for. I will meet with their country's leaders over the Labor Day weekend at Camp David, to confirm their neutrality in the matter of our growing *American Commonwealth*. It will be strictly *realpolitik* in the broadest worldwide sense, and in no way involve the divisionary compromises arrived at the infamous Yalta Conference between FDR, Churchill, and Stalin in early 1945.

"America is not going to 'divide up' anything with anyone ever again. Too many American lives have been spent liberating foreign countries, some of which cannot even be pronounced by the average American citizen. Never again!"

That evening, Jack spoke directly to the American people:

"My fellow Americans, I am pleased to announce yet another military victory against the *Taliban* terrorists in Northeast Afghanistan and Northwest Pakistan. This was not a 'one-day war', but rather a 'three- day war', which involved our 2nd Armored Division on the West and our 101st and 82nd Airborne Divisions on the East of that treacherous, cave-ridden mountain terrain. It proved to be a replay of the Iwo Jima assault on Mount Suribachi against the Japanese during the final days of

WWII- a bloody business that ended the same way-
Taliban cave- dweller suicides or napalm flame-
throwers. There were no *Taliban* survivors. However,
there were also no casualties in the hamlets and villages
on the plains below.

"I wish I could report to you that this military action will
be our last- but it will not, because the *'Muslim Crazies'*
who have vowed to destroy our country and all of
Western civilization, are still lurking in other areas, and
it is my job as Commander-In-Chief to protect you from
enemies at home and abroad.

"In closing, I should announce that I will be meeting
with the Russian and Chinese Presidents over the Labor
Day weekend at Camp David. We will discuss a broad
spectrum of world problems. In the meantime, good
night, and may God continue to shine his grace on our
deserving country."

Chapter Fifteen

During the days leading up to the 1st Marine Division's landing on the beaches just outside Tripoli, the Fitzgerald family returned to their familiar vacation routines. By late evening on the 3rd of July, the American 6th Fleet was 'parked' just offshore of the landing beaches, while Cynthia conversed calmly with the leaders of the Libyan government. At dawn's early light, 20,000 Marines boarded their landing craft, and went ashore, without a shot being fired. They were followed by 200 tanks, other auxiliary personnel, supplies, and equipment. By sunrise, military operations were ready to begin.

At the same time, 200 tanks and 5,000 Marines crossed the Egyptian border and headed West, in another 'pincer' movement designed to trap all mobile Muslim terrorists in traditional desert warfare.

As expected, not one terrorist was taken alive, preferring to explode their suicide bombs in hopes of killing the hated Americans, along with themselves.

By sunset July 4th, Admiral Eddie Brown reported to Jack 'mission accomplished'.

Half of the Marine landing forces had turned West towards Tunisia and their capital city of Tunis. Rollie held the hand of that country's leader, as Cynthia did in Tripoli. The only question was whether or not Algeria would defend their border, as promised, against the remaining Muslim terrorists fleeing West. The Algerians, who had fought the French Foreign Legion for many years to gain their independence, were not about to let in any terrorists- Muslim or otherwise. Again, there were only terrorist corpses left during their skirmishes with the Algerians.

That evening, as Jack had promised, he reported to the American people:

> "Once again, I am pleased to report that our 1st Marine Division has wiped out the Muslim terrorists in Libya and Tunisia, with very few casualties on our side, or the civilian side, as a result of terrorist suicide bombers, who chose death over capture as they ran from our Marines. There is no better way for us to celebrate our nation's birthday than with an important military victory over those who have sworn an Islamic religious oath to 'bury us'.

> "Americans take these challenges very seriously-as we did when then Russian premiere Khrushchev uttered these same words on the floor of the United Nation General Assembly more than half a century ago. It took many years thereafter to prove to the world that Communist ideology was not the answer to the world's lack of prosperity. In fact, it was not even the answer to prosperity for the Russian people.

> "I do not mean to imply that world prosperity is 'just around the corner'- because it is *not*. There will be several Presidents after myself left with this nation's 'Noble Cause'. It's a lot like our Forefathers' push westward towards the Pacific Ocean- in other words, a renewal of our *Manifest Destiny*- common Constitution;

common currency; common defense; common free trade; and then, common prosperity.

"My administration is dedicated to laying down the path. Future administrations who follow this path, build the roads, bridges, and tunnels required, and will complete the vision I have for our nation's 21st century foreign policy. Once again I remind you not to look elsewhere, because there *is* no elsewhere, elsewhere- just we Americans leading other nations in what I have named the *American Commonwealth.*

"In closing, I wish you all a very happy 4th of July and extend my congratulations to the families and friends of our brave warriors of the 1st Marine Division and its many living veterans, including my father, whom you may recall won the Congressional Medal of Honor at the battle of Iwo Jima in 1945."

There was a very different type of war brewing as the 'Big Three' met at Camp David over the Labor Day weekend. Russian President Mikhail Varishnakov and Chinese President Chang were clearly suspicious of the expanding *American Commonwealth*, so Jack repeated the policy as laid out to them by our American Ambassadors:

"Mikhail, Chang, you have already witnessed that my American foreign policy is based upon the economic advantages of democracy and capitalism over every other form of government. Except for minor purchases, we have not added one square meter to our territory, and have no plans for annexing any part of any other country in the future- which is more than I can say for your countries' clear intentions in the Ukraine, and the islands in the South China Sea.

"It is my belief that world prosperity is the key to world peace, and that the key to prosperity begins with governmental stability, which we have established on the Arabian Peninsula; and in Persia; Israel; Lebanon; and North Africa- and with the exception of North Korean and Persian first strikes at our Fleets, always at the *invitation* of those nations concerned. Our trade with these nations has more than doubled, as has your trade. I would like to think that our gradual 'extermination' of the *Muslim Crazies* has your full support, if for no other reason that it is good for our businesses.

"This brings me to the question of not only Global Free Trade, which you have both grudgingly accepted, but also Global Fair Trade- and specifically, our minimum wage of $100 per day, which I strongly suggest you move towards at a much faster pace. I'm certain that you'll find, as we Americans have, that national prosperity follows personal prosperity." The Russian President commented:

"Jack, what are your intentions with regard to Central, Northern, and Eastern Europe?" Jack responded quickly:

"I have received no request from any other European country to join the *American Commonwealth*, nor do I expect to in the future. We have already relieved the Euro Zone of their financially troubled countries from Ireland to Greece and Cyprus, which are all for the moment economically sound. I see no reason why any other nation in Europe would change their system of government- they are financially stable; have traditions, cultures and customs- and their peoples are relatively prosperous. In short, they appear to neither need nor want to be 'Americanized'. Should this situation change for any reason, I'll let you know immediately.

"Which brings me to the question of the Ukraine, which has indeed requested membership in the American Commonwealth. Look at it this way Mikhail, we have more Russians in Brooklyn than you claim to have in Eastern Ukraine, and I don't think you plan to stir up any problems for me in that part of New York City.

"So my suggestion to you is to leave those people alone and let them work out their own problems, without any American or Russian intervention. My policy has, and will continue to be, that all nations have minorities of one stripe or another, and that the best solution is to make them live together in peace- and refrain from trying to either absorb them, or create new nations.

"A good example are the Kurds, who continue to live in Turkey, Syria, and Iraq. All three nations will eventually be the stronger with them included. To sum it up, I believe that if anyone does not like the country they're living in, they should be able to 'vote with their feet' and move to another country. Mikhail, why not let this be the solution for every Russian living in Eastern Ukraine."

"I wouldn't ask any ethnic Russian to leave his home."

"I didn't say 'ask'- I said let them decide on their own whether it's more important for them to live in Russia."

"My country doesn't need 100,000 or more unemployed immigrants."

"Brooklyn didn't need 200,000 Ukrainian immigrants either, and I didn't suggest that they all come at once. I'll make you a friendly bet that not more than 10,000 Russian-Ukrainians would elect to change citizenship during the first year."

"What will this friendly bet consist of?"

"How about a case of my gold medal Chianti against a one kilo tin of your best Beluga caviar?"

"Done!" Mikhail responded.

Jack turned to the Chinese President:

"Chang, what can I offer you to stop 'hacking' into my computers and stealing technology from my Silicon Valley companies?"

"Not quite sure Jack, I haven't tasted your wine yet."

On that note, the three most powerful men in the world finished their afternoon session, and retired for pre-dinner cocktails, during which Yang tried every vintage of Jack's superb Chianti.

The best that can be said for that Labor Day weekend is that the three 'main men' on the planet became quite friendly- in a 'getting to know you better' kind of way. They failed to agree on anything new, but did agree on maintaining the *status quo,* and that Jack could proceed with his policies of the *American Commonwealth* and the destruction of all terrorist organizations, wherever they might be, because it was good for worldwide business, and the stability of 'third world' countries.

At the joint press conference Labor Day Monday morning, the three parties were all smiles, but it did not fool any of the 'Media's' astute analysts, nor did it alarm them.

That evening by the fireplace, Jack and Kathy discussed the non-confrontational approach that Jack had taken over the weekend.

"Jack darling, you expected nothing going into these meetings, and got no significant concessions, other than their handshake agreements to not challenge your foreign policy of expanding the *American Commonwealth.* This indicates to me that the other two world powers may believe that they are better off by letting you do all the 'grunt work' in order to open up new, prosperous markets."

"That's okay by me, *tesoro,* because before they know what hits them, I'll be 'rounding third base and heading for home plate' by the end of my first term."

Jack's late September 'quarterly report' to the Congress and the nation described the progress to date in stabilizing all of the countries which had either been subjected to American military intervention, or had recently joined the *American Commonwealth.*

"First, I wish to congratulate the Republic of Korea for not only stabilizing that peninsula, but for quickly instilling the basic principles of a constitutional democracy in less than one year. It appears that the North is fast becoming a new industrial 'powerhouse' by converting their technology and manpower from military products to industrial and consumer products. It's not hard to imagine that in the near future, Korea will become competitive with Japan, Taiwan and China itself in the manufacturing arena.

"Much the same can be said for Persia, which under civilian administration this year, has also converted its technology and manpower to industrial and consumer products, which together with their enormous oil reserves, will soon make them a leading nation in the Middle East.

"Ireland, Portugal and Northern and Eastern Mediterranean Sea countries have all survived their economic crises and in fact, have begun paying down their foreign debt. Much of this improvement is due to foreign investments including the *'Super Bullet Consortium'*, which has begun construction on this multi-year project, which will soon connect Istanbul with Cairo, and eventually pass through the other capital cities on the North African coast and terminate in Casablanca, Morocco. This huge project represents an investment by *Pittsburgh Steel; FIAT/Chrysler; GE; DuPont*, and a number of international bank holding companies, of more than $2 trillion, and the employment of more than 3 million railroad workers, many of whom had been living in refugee camps.

"The Eastern branch of the *Super Bullet* will connect Beirut with Jerusalem, Damascus, Amman and other Arabian Peninsula capital cities. The North African branch, initially terminating in Casablanca will be extended down the West African coast to Cape Town, South Africa, while the terminal in Cairo will extend its branch down the Eastern coastline of Africa, also terminating in Cape Town. The transcontinental Central African link will begin construction as soon as those nations involved become stabilized, and free from tribal and terrorist warfare. In return for the governmental land grants given the consortium by various nations, the rail lines will be accompanied by 'Super Freeways' for auto and truck traffic, providing employment for yet another 2 million workers.

"I have been asked about what will happen to the refugees and other nomadic workers, once their respective sections have been built? I always try to keep my solutions as simple as possible, so the answer is- they will all purchase new houses with the excellent wages they have earned. Like here in America, there will be an unprecedented 'housing boom'- new towns; new stores; new industries; and everything else that occurs in an entrepreneurial, free market society.

"Why Africa, you may ask? Again, I answer simply that the 'Western World' has historically ignored that Continent's plight in the wake of the previous colonial exploitation of their natural resources. There are 1 billion potential consumers waiting for the opportunity to become genuine middle class customers, instead of ghetto-dwellers. It's no mystery that America is the only nation on Earth that can make their dreams come true.

"With few exceptions, South America, Central America, and the Caribbean islands, with ½ billion potential consumers are well ahead of Africa, and almost every nation South of our borders has requested admission to our *American Commonwealth*. My administration is reviewing each of their applications thoroughly- especially with regards to dictatorships; juntas; drug cartels, and illegal drug production.

"I will recommend to the Congress that all of the Caribbean Islands be admitted by the end of this year. I have also advised our Ambassadors to tell every other nation South of our borders to 'clean up' their countries *before* we take any further steps towards their membership in the *American Commonwealth*. I have every reason to believe that their actions will be forthcoming by the middle of next year. The actions I refer to include national *referendums*; adoption of the United States Constitution as the rule of law; new general elections, and elimination by whatever means necessary of all drug cartels.

"I ask all Americans to remember the dominant role played by our military in the successes we have witnessed thus far. Therefore, before Veterans Day on November 11th, I will propose to the Congress a 'New Deal' for our military men and women. In broad terms, I will put forth substantial new benefits for those who have served or been killed in combat; our veterans; and particularly our disabled veterans.

"During the coming weeks, I will visit as many VA hospitals as I can, and will be asking one main question-would you prefer to continue physical/mental rehabilitation in this hospital, or would you prefer to be taken care of in your own hometown? I will make my proposal to the Congress based upon my personal investigation."

During the next several weeks, Jack spent almost all of his time at the bedside of disabled veterans, and it didn't take very long for him to discover first-hand that the VA was a bureaucratic disaster in almost every respect-except that their facilities were first class-once a disabled veteran was *finally* admitted after an unacceptably long wait.

In late October, Jack called together his Chief of Staff; Speaker of the House; and the Senate Majority Leader. Jack laid out the broad lines of the Veterans legislation he wanted:

"Gentlemen, first of all I propose that we bring home every American military body buried on foreign soil, and that they be re-buried in a place of their family's choosing. If they have no surviving family, they are to be re-buried in Arlington Cemetery with full military honors. Dick, do whatever you have to do to buy up the extra land we need to accommodate those Americans who gave their lives on foreign soil-enough for about ½ million new graves. I also propose that their families, or other beneficiaries have their PPAs increased to a total of $1.5 million.

"With regard to our disabled veterans currently recovering in our VA hospitals, I conclude that about 80% of them would rather be re-located to hospital facilities in or near their hometowns. Although we cannot compensate for the loss of limbs or minds, their Personal Pension Accounts should be increased to $1 million in recognition of their combat sacrifices. I further propose that all VA hospitals be turned over to the towns and counties, and that the VA bureaucracy be eliminated.

"As regards combat military personnel currently on active or inactive duty, their PPAs should be increased to $1/2 million, in recognition of their having risked their lives for their country.

"For those non-combat military personnel, active or inactive, their PPA should be increased to $1/4 million." The Speaker then asked:

"Jack, that's about ½ million men lost in combat more than ½ century ago. It'll take forever to track down their beneficiaries."

"Not really Bill, it goes to whoever he listed on his G.I $10,000 insurance policy at that time. I guess you'll have to put a special committee together to come up with the beneficiaries of our dead soldiers, and integrate that into the beneficiaries' PPAs.

"Look guys, we all know that there is no way to compensate surviving families for the ultimate sacrifice their loved ones have made for our country, but I believe

237

we should do something, and I will now leave it to the House and the Senate to decide what that something should be, apart from re-burial with full military honors for those we disinter from foreign cemeteries and bring back home. Should either of your Houses come up with something better, let me know before my speech on Veterans Day.

On November 11th, Jack spoke before an audience of several thousand military veterans at Arlington National Cemetery:

"Today, our entire nation joins us in honoring our living warriors- the unscathed, the wounded but fully recovered, like my father standing here at my side; and those in this representative group from each of our Armed Forces, who can never fully recover from loss of limbs; eyesight; hearing; or minds.

"At this point, I would like to introduce all of you to Marine Master Sergeant Jack Fitzgerald Senior, a former member of Easy Company, 1st Platoon, 1st Battalion, 1st Marine Division, who fought the Japanese from Guadalcanal Island in 1942, to the island of Iwo Jima in 1945. On his way to Japan he was shot twice and recovered from his wounds. He was finally stopped by yet another Jap bullet in his left leg, just as he led his platoon to the top of Mt. Suribachi, and watched his men hoist the American Flag to signal the Fleet below that the principal symbolic objective on that island had been taken. He was the highest ranking member of that now-famous flag raising group- all of his superior officers had been shot or killed on the way up the mountain. For his extraordinary heroism under heavy fire, he was awarded the Congressional Medal of Honor. Dad, why don't you say a few words to your fellow veterans."

Jack Senior stepped smartly forward ten paces; stopped; executed a perfect right face and a snappy salute to his Commander-in-Chief, who returned his salute equally as snappy. They both then executed a right face towards the American flag and the service flags draped at the rear of the podium, and executed the same snappy salute, followed by a military about face, as Jack the elder strode briskly to the front of the podium, withdrew his ceremonial sword; held the handle to his face; dropped it 90 degrees toward the assemblage, and to the wind-blown American flag waving proudly behind the thousands of lawn chairs.

Then he neatly sheathed his sword before stepping to the microphone. He looked much younger than his 88years- a lean 190 pounds, 6 foot 2 inches, white-haired warrior in his Marine 'dress blues'; white topped dress cap; white gloves; and white leather belt.

The left breast of his uniform was covered with 3 Purple Hearts; 2 Bronze Stars; 2 Silver Stars; 2 Navy Crosses, and around his neck he wore the light blue beribboned Medal of Honor. The right breast of his uniform was covered with more than two dozen campaign ribbons earned during General MacArthur's 'island hopping' military campaigns, from Guadalcanal, off the tip of Northern Australia, to Iwo Jima, near the Southern tip of the Japanese mainland. In short, this elderly gentleman represented the pride of the entire U.S. Marine Corps, and fit the part perfectly, as he began to speak:

"I think I see a few recognizable faces from *Easy Company*, and others from my 1ˢᵗ Regiment in the Marine 1ˢᵗ Division. Something tells me that my son the President had a lot to do with your presence here today, and I look forward to our reunion banquet at the White House this evening.

"It's been more than half a century since we last fought together. I'm sure we remember the many island battles, and have passed these stories on to our grandchildren.

"I'm also sure we remember the help we received upon returning home. For example, I was able to finish my college studies at the University of Illinois, and after 4 years more of post-graduate studies in veterinary medicine, became the 'Vet Doc' for my town and county. I also received a loan to buy an additional quarter section of farmland. But my son feels strongly that this is not nearly enough for combat veterans, nor for those who made the ultimate sacrifice to keep our country free.

"For those of you combat veterans who have returned from WWII; Korea; Vietnam; Afghanistan; Persia; the Middle East; and North Africa, our President has proposed to the Congress a series of measures which will assure your financial independence for the rest of our natural lives. You guys and gals have given your country quick victories, after so many years of military stalemates. As a senior veteran, I applaud your victories overseas, and applaud our President's bold actions- which should tell everyone on this planet that American victory in war is not *everything*- it is *the only thing* for the continued future freedom of our country, and the *American Commonwealth*."

After the applause died down, Jack once again addressed his audience:

"Over the years, our Federal Government's Veterans Administration has tried to take care of *all* our disabled veterans as best they could, but my personal inspection during recent weeks has convinced me that the V.A.'s best is not nearly good enough. I have therefore issued an *Executive Order* to dismantle the V.A. bureaucracy; turn over all VA hospitals to towns or counties; send these warriors; and equip their local hospitals with the best doctors and equipment that money can buy.

"I will also bring home every fallen warrior currently buried on foreign soil.

"While there can be no price put on the lives or limbs of our brave heroes, I have proposed to the Congress that American warriors, and their families, need never again worry about financial security.

"Good day, and may God Bless those who risk, and give, their lives to protect our freedom here at home. During my campaign last year, I promised everyone that National Defense would be my number one priority. I have kept, and will continue to keep, that promise."

During the following days, the Congress debated and passed the Veterans Security Act, which Jack signed into law the day before Thanksgiving. His telecast to the nation the next day, was as always brief and to the point.

"We have much to be thankful for on this Thanksgiving Day. God has looked upon us with favor, because our cause has been noble and humanitarian for every nation and their peoples.

"We have stabilized Northern Africa, and I propose that and we stabilize the remainder of the African continent and its 1 billion population- but only upon invitation from their respective governments.

"Now let's all enjoy our national day of feasting, and praise our Heavenly Father, who has given us this bountiful land."

Chapter Sixteen

In the weeks before Christmas, Jack met regularly with his 'inner circle':

> "First, I'd like to see where we are with 'stabilization' of
> the countries in which we have used military force.
> Rollie, why don't you and Cynthia bring us all up to
> date?" Secretary of State Giordano spoke first:

> "Except for the Kurds, who want their own Statehood,
> we believe that the Middle East has progressed about as
> we had expected- most have decided that the advantages
> of *American Commonwealth* status, especially the
> American dollar and American military protection, far
> outweighs the continuance of *Sharia Law*. Lebanon;
> Israel; Jordan; Syria; Iraq, and Egypt have all applied for
> membership in the *American Commonwealth* and are
> ready to go forward with Constitutional elections early
> next year. Saudi Arabia; the Emirates; Oman and Yemen
> are unable at this time to abandon *Sharia Law*. It's about
> the same story for the North African countries of Libya,
> Tunisia; Algeria, and Morocco. Cynthia, why don't you
> tell us about your meetings with the Ukrainians, since
> you spoke with them in their own language?"

> "Simply put, they want no part of the Russians, and
> want to join our *Commonwealth*. At the same time, they
> realize that the Russians are willing and able to take
> over their country at any moment they choose. So Jack,
> the ball is back in your court, because there is no way of

telling whether Varishnikov is prepared to go to war with us over this issue." Jack thought for a long moment before responding:

"Sooner or later, I will have to come eyeball-to-eyeball with Mikhail and see who blinks first. I don't believe that Russia has the economic strength to do battle with us, even in a limited 'area war'.

"In the last 2 years, we have taken away more than half their previous captive Western European market for oil and natural gas, their main source of foreign exchange. Don't get me wrong, Russia has enormous quantities of undiscovered natural resources, but that takes trillions of dollars of new foreign investment- and no investors will put money into a country that cannot meet next month's government payroll, or so my Treasury Secretary tells me. Johnnie, why don't you bring us up to date on the Russian money facts of life."

"Jack, you just hit the nail on the head- Russia is dangerously close to national bankruptcy- *Rubles* are fleeing the country like rats from a sinking ship, and have been for some time now. In fact, I would go as far as to say that America is the only country that can now save Russia from financial chaos. Even a limited area war in the Ukraine could not be sustained." Admiral Brown quickly cut in:

"On the other hand, Russia has more conventional and nuclear arms today than we do. But neither they nor the Chinese have laser satellite capability as yet." Jack returned front and center:

244

"Okay, this is what we're going to do. Rollie, I want you to go to Moscow and advise Mikhail that Ukraine will be holding a national *referendum* before the end of the year regarding membership in the *American Commonwealth*. If the answer is "yes", they will be holding general elections a few weeks later, which should give him plenty of time to withdraw all of his troops from that country. "

"For his cooperation, we pledge to postpone the creation of an American Black Sea Fleet, based in the Turkish port city of Zonduidak. On your way to Moscow, I would like you to drop Cynthia off in Kiev.

"Cynthia, you can fill in Ukrainian President Gregorov on the political and military moves, and give him the 'green light', once Rollie has reached an agreement with Mikhail. You can use Air Force One- I won't be needing it until you both get back." Jack then turned to Admiral Brown:

"Eddie, I'd like you to have one of our Mediterranean Fleet's Task Forces pay a friendly visit to Istanbul, and include two aircraft carriers in that group. This move will reinforce Rollie's hand in Moscow, by showing Mikhail that we mean business.

"In the unlikely event that Mikhail refuses to vacate the Ukraine, I want the Istanbul Carrier Task Force moved North to Yalta, and await my further instructions. This 'plan B' means that the Ukrainian *referendum* will have us face-to-face with the Russians. One more thing, you better plan on having that Task Force include our 1st

Marine Division. Unless there are further questions, I think that's enough for today."

Halfway over the Atlantic, Rollie telephoned Jack:

"I just talked with our Ambassador to Turkey, and he assures me that they will empty out their Istanbul harbor, if necessary, to accommodate our Black Sea Task Force and first Marine Division troop ships. I've also spoken with our Ambassador in Kiev, and he tells me that it'll take less than a day to resolve any Ukrainian election problems that may pop-up. With this in mind, I would like to wrap up the details of our plans, and have Cynthia accompany me to Moscow, since she is fluent in the Russian language."

At 10pm local time, Air Force One touched down at Kiev International Airport, to a city throng of ½ million people. If there was any doubt about Ukraine joining the *American Commonwealth*, it was dispelled on that festive evening.

At 8am the next morning, Rollie and Cynthia laid out Jack's Plan A and Plan B. It was agreed by both parties that 'come hell or high water' the Ukrainian national *referendum* would be held the following weekend, depending upon the Russian response to the Secretary's proposals. Should American Carrier Task Forces be obliged to move North to Yalta, it would be explained as a 'joint military exercise' with participation of Ukraine's Black Sea Navy. The presence of the US 1ST Marine Division would be explained as a 'joint exercise' with Ukrainian troops to assure a smooth *American Commonwealth referendum*. That drama was played out in Moscow over the next 3 days.

There were no crowds at Moscow's International Airport. The usual black limousines brought Rollie and Cynthia to the Kremlin at 3pm local time. The Russian President greeted the American Secretary of State and the Chairwoman of the Senate Foreign Relations Committee with the warmest outward show of friendship, but his eyes betrayed nothing but fear:

"My intelligence services tell me that you have reached agreement with the Ukrainian government regarding a national *referendum* next weekend to join the *American Commonwealth*. This is unacceptable to the Russian people in the Eastern Ukraine, and therefore unacceptable to the Russian government." Rollie shot back:

"We are quite aware that 'free elections' are disturbing to you and your followers, and since your Ukrainian Russians are outnumbered six to one, the outcome of this election is a foregone conclusion. However, we are prepared to give you certain guarantees to stay out of this coming election and let the people, including Russians, decide their own future.

"Firstly, if you decide to withdraw all of your military forces from the Ukraine, including Yalta, we will postpone the construction of a new American Black Sea naval base in Northern Turkey. Secondly, we will refrain from moving our Carrier Task Force and 1st Marine Division from Istanbul to Yalta.

"Mikhail, we and the Ukrainians want you out of their sovereign national territories, and are prepared to fight for it. This is an 'area war' you *cannot win.*" Mikhail blurted:

"This concession will ruin my credibility as the leader of *Mother Russia.* I'll be finished!"

"Not necessarily, Mikhail. You can be a 'hero' of Russia for avoiding unnecessary bloodshed in a 'area war' you cannot possibly win, no matter how many troops and tanks you may bring to battle. I suggest that we all think about this overnight and pick it up again tomorrow morning at 10am."

Mikhail spent the evening and most of the night consulting with his close government associates about the American proposal. Unfortunately his 'hard line' compatriots could not accept Rollie's offer on behalf of President Fitzgerald. There was no 'up side' for any of them- they would only be blamed for a Russian retreat.

Next morning, Mikhail presented his case to Rollie and Cynthia:

"Russia cannot accept any terms which block the expansion on our current territory, including the Ukraine, which is a vital base for our Russian Black Sea Fleet, and our entrance into the Mediterranean Sea." Rollie responded:

"Very well, Mikhail. Your decision has just triggered our Naval Task Force movement from Istanbul to Yalta by this evening. My only comment, on behalf of my President, is that you have proven to be a very foolish leader of your people. This evening, our 6th Fleet Task

Force, with 2 Aircraft carriers and 400 jet aircraft; and our 1st Marine Division of 20,000 troops will dock in Yalta and conduct joint military operations with the Ukrainian Navy and Army on Yalta. Your forces on Yalta will be eliminated within hours, and by this time tomorrow, there will be no Russian military forces left in the Sovereign nation of Ukraine." Mikhail was flabbergasted:

"Rollie, this means war between Russia and America!" to which the Secretary of State responded:

"Not really Mikhail, just a 'scrimmage' over non-Russian territorial integrity, on behalf of any *American Commonwealth* country that is threatened now, or in the future. It's your choice, and if you ever doubted the strength of our Fleet; their war planes; or our best Marines, you're welcome to test us.

"I suggest you back off, and spare us as all the embarrassment of a head-to-head combat in which your glorious Red Army and Black Sea Fleet will be humiliated. This is not the outcome America desires. We want stability among nations; new markets to compete in; and eventually, global prosperity, where everyone is a winner.

The *American Bald Eagle* looked the *Russian Bear* straight in his eyes, and the bear blinked. There would be no direct military confrontation between these two 'super powers', because in the final analysis, Mikhail had too much to loose, and too little to gain, because nuclear weapons were out of the question, and therefore meaningless.

Rollie explained the situation to Jack over his 'secure' phone line. Jack gave his orders:

> "I'll tell Admiral Brown to go ahead and bring the Task Force and the Marines into Yalta- might as well give everyone, including the Russians, a show for their money. The Fleet and the Marines will stay there until the last Russian has left the Ukraine- there will be no intimidation of voters next weekend. I think it best that we leave the Marines behind to guard the voting stations during the *referendum*, and remain there until the general elections are completed. Find out how many voting stations we're talking about and make sure there is an armed Marine in 'dress blues' posted at each station for both elections. Our Navy can leave next Tuesday and go back to the 'Med'. Otherwise, our non-duty military can enjoy shore leave for the next few days- after all, Yalta is a world-famous resort area.
>
> "You and Cynthia can return to Kiev and check all of this out with the Ukraine government, especially the part about leaving the 1st Marine Division behind until after their general elections. Also, I want to congratulate both of you for the great job you have done so far in Kiev and Moscow, and be sure to tell Mikhail that I congratulate him on making a very wise decision. Give me a call as soon as this plan has been confirmed in Kiev."

In their final meeting, Rollie and Cynthia conveyed Jack's compliments to Mikhail and reminded him of the 'friendly wager' regarding the Eastern Ukrainian ethnic Russian population. After the elections, only a few hundred Eastern

Ukrainians returned to Russia, primarily for family reasons, and for Christmas Jack did indeed received a 1 kilogram tin of prime Beluga caviar.

Jack's next staff meeting was held the Tuesday after the Ukraine general elections:

> "As expected, the Ukrainians have elected an overwhelmingly 'centrist' government, including their former Prime Minister as President. I believe that having an armed Marine at every voting station contributed to there not being a single incident of disturbance. Perhaps more importantly, other nation members of the *American Commonwealth* have seen what it means to be protected by our country. As promised, our Marine 1st Division will be leaving Yalta, and rejoining the Mediterranean Fleet, which will be anchored at Naples and other 6th Fleet 'ports of call' for the coming Holiday Season.

> "I and my family will be at the White House to light the Christmas tree on the South Lawn; receive calls from family and friends, and to give my 'Christmas Address' to the nation. However, I will not be giving my 'State of the Union Address' on New Year's Eve, because I will be spending the following weeks meeting with *We The People* in as many States as possible. When I return, I shall address the entire country, and report my first-hand findings. During my extended absence, Vice President McCall will be conducting 'ordinary business' in my stead.

"I will be travelling for the first time on my Presidential *Super Bullet*, a Christmas gift from Congress. I want to see what it feels like to travel earthbound at 400mph. My exact itinerary will be known only to the Secret Service, and there will be no ceremonial events, except for open Q&A Town Hall meetings."

After lighting the White House South Lawn Christmas tree, Jack addressed the nation on the eve of Christ's birthday:

"Although we have been obliged to conquer several rogue nations and terrorist organizations during my first two years as President, our nation can now look forward to a time of peace. I have decided to create new prosperities amongst so-called 'third word countries', beginning with the Continent of Africa.

"In this regard, we intend to 'stabilize' any country on that Continent which requests our help- in other words, we will *not* enter any African nation unless invited to do so by their government. This new foreign policy portends great things for many undeveloped nations around the world, and more particularly, new trading partners who will soon be able to buy our goods and services.

"I will be postponing my State of the Union year-end address until I return from visiting as many States as possible, and to speak with as many average citizens as I can in average towns.

"With this said, I shall borrow the Christmas words of author Clement Moore- "Merry Christmas to all, and to all a goodnight.""

At 8am December 27th, Jack whisked up to Boston in two hours, and then slowed to 100mph on the last leg to Waterville, Maine. His entourage consisted of his communications car; family car; Secret Service car; media car; two general purpose *Pullman* cars; a dining car, and lastly a double deck observation car, with full 'open bar' privileges, including a well- stocked assortment of Jack's *Villa Americana Chianti Riserva*.

So it was that Jack would just 'show up' and speak with his fellow citizens in diners; high schools; nursing homes; local hospitals; taverns; colleges; churches; and anywhere else that his instincts led him to learn the true feelings of *We The People*.

Jack would then cap off the day with an open forum at Town Halls, where he usually received a fair cross section of opinions, and specific questions such as "why are we fighting so many wars in foreign lands?" Jack would ask each person to state their name and occupation. He would then answer each question without hesitation, and in this particular case replied:

"Good question Harry, and my best answer is that there were in each case, many bad people that wanted to see us dead. Such threats to our country cannot go unanswered, and as your Commander-in-Chief, I have taken the actions necessary to assure the continuation of our American way of life- which is freedom and prosperity for all. Next question please"

"My name is Jane Withers, a housewife with three young teenagers, and I am not pleased with the competency of our mayor or our councilpersons. Our town has many people experienced in 'running things', but none chose to run for office. I don't think it has anything to do with money, because our mayor is paid $400,000 per year and our council people are paid $200,000, which is a lot more than any of them has made before."

"Jane, my answer is that a person must be a *patriot* to take two, four, or more years away from their profession to serve their fellow townspeople- and you're right, I don't think money has anything to do with it for a town of about 20,000 or so. These salaries seem quite appropriate, so the reason must lie elsewhere- perhaps it is the stigma of being classified as a 'career politician', rather than a 'citizen politician', which connotes a sense of public duty- just like our *Founding Fathers*.

"The men and women you need to run your town should possess this innate sense of duty to their community. This is an election year, and my advice is to seek out those who have demonstrated an ability to 'run things', and convince them, or even shame them, if necessary. Waterville needs the 'best and brightest' to step forward and serve their township. This is how I designed the transfer of power from the Federal Government, and how I have selected my own personal staff- none of whom are career politicians.

"You in this Town Hall have been responsible for taking care of your fellow townspeople for the past two years- not me; not Congress; not the Supreme Court, but you the townspeople of Waterville, Maine- just as your 'Colonial' ancestors did in the very beginning. In time, I believe that 'taking care' will then turn to *love*- just as God commanded, and just as Jesus Christ taught during his life amongst us."

This 'stump speech' response by Jack, in front of the people who elected him, would become his 'theme song'- repeated and added to again and again in every town he visited.

That afternoon, Jack and party arrived in the New Hampshire town of Exeter, pop. about 18,000, including Exeter Academy student residents. He wanted to learn, for personal reasons, the effect that a famous 'prep school' has on an otherwise ordinary American town, because he had already formulated a concept for his own hometown of Cissna Park, which he would discuss with his father.

Jack spent most of the afternoon strolling the Exeter Academy grounds, with particular attention to the facilities offered to its students. He also stopped at a local diner and the local pub for a *Sam Adams* draught beer and to converse with townspeople, especially the working class. His last stop was the Exeter Auditorium, where the Q&A session afforded him some new insights.

"My name Is Jamie Johnson, and I'm a freshman from Toledo, Ohio. Why does Exeter pay my tuition, and not my home town of Toledo? Secondly, why did your 'superstar' soccer son Stephen turn down multi-million dollar contracts offered by *Manchester United*, and other top European soccer teams?" Jack thought for a long moment before answering:

"Jamie, Exeter township pays your tuition because you live here 9 months a year, and most of your money is spent here- and most of your taxes are paid here. The same is true for very large college towns like Boston. With regard to my son Stephen, it's quite true that he is an exceptional goal scorer. But he has been taught for many years he that he is responsible for his own decisions- it's his life, not mine or his mother's- and he has chosen to pursue a career in law, with the goal of one day becoming a Justice on the Supreme Court. I can only hope that your parents- and this goes for everyone in this auditorium- will give you the same power of career decision-making, including the choice of your lifetime companion in marriage."

"My name is Sam Horowitz from Berkeley, California, and I'm a senior. Why don't you have more 'diversity' on your personal staff?"

"Sam, like most good leaders, I chose my personal staff from amongst the 'best and the brightest' because it's my own money, and if you would not do the same when your time comes to chose close associates, I would consider you to be a fool. 'Political correctness' has no place in my job, because fundamentally I am *not* a professional politician, but rather the *'leading servant'* of you, your schoolmates, and every other American citizen."

On the trip from New England, the train was routed to the central Illinois farm belt, so that Jack could visit his dad and his home town of Cissna Park, pop. 988, most of whom were at the station to greet their 'favorite son' and then follow him to the school auditorium. There were many familiar faces, and a number of new ones, since Jack's last visit during his presidential campaign in 2016. After shaking as many hands as he could following an open-ended Q&A period, which centered mainly on farming matters, Jack invited the town's Mayor, Bob Hoffman and his wife, old friends Tom and Berta Mauldin, and 'Big Jack' to lunch in his train's dining car. Jack opened the conversation by addressing the Mauldins:

"How long as it been since you visited with me at my villa?"

"Jack, I believe it was about four or five years ago, just after your appointment as Associate Justice, and your hospitality still remains the highlight of our European vacation." Jack then turned to the mayor:

"Bob, I couldn't help but notice there are a number of new faces in our town."

"You're right Jack, there are about four dozen new families out of the Chicago area, and we are adding an average of one family per month- mainly of Hispanic, Italian, Irish, or Polish ancestry- and just about all of them are Catholic, so there has been a lot of talk about the need for a Catholic Church. They are all hard-working folks- mainly manual laborers who mind their own business and stay out of trouble."

"Don't worry about the Catholic Church Bob, my family and I will be taking care of that very shortly. The Church will be part of an entire campus complex to be called *St. Luke Academy*, which will include a pre-school/ kindergarten; an elementary school; a College Prep Academy with student boarding facilities; and most importantly, a teaching faculty second to none. St. Luke Academy will be designed to attract the best scholars and athletes from every State in the Union.

"Finally, there will be a St. Luke Hospital, and behind the Church, a St. Luke Catholic cemetery. All these facilities will be open to everyone, and tuition will be kept in line with those charged by your k-12 public school.

"This entire enterprise will be managed by Kathy's cousin, Jesuit Priest Father Timothy O'Malley, currently a Professor of Math and Sciences at Loyola University in Chicago, who by the way, is a former college basketball star. He will be assisted by his wife, Dominican Sister Mary Elizabeth O'Malley, who is an Associate Professor of Arts and Languages at the same University, and also a Registered Nurse.

"They will be moving into our farmhouse next week, and will be opening one of the barns for religious services as soon as it can be renovated. The bigger barn was converted many years ago into a ten bedroom, ten bath annex for our joint family reunions. There will be plenty of room for our faculty housing, and plenty of land for expansion, including my Presidential Library when the time comes.

"Bob, a superior education for all youngsters is at the very top of my national priorities, and I plan to move America from 25th in the world to number 1 before I leave Office. The Fitzgerald family understands that an outstanding education is very expensive, and all we are doing is giving Cissna Park a much needed head start. Speaking of money, I'm asking you, as I've asked every other Mayor during my personal survey-how are the town's finances?"

"Well Jack, I'm happy to report that each year we have had a small budget surplus, and have retained all of our Federal T-bonds for a rainy day. What did the other town mayors tell you?"

"Bob, what has surprised me most is that practically no one has seriously challenged my domestic 'architectural design' for 21st century America."

"Why should they, Jack? You've got our American machine running like a Swiss watch- 10% annual growth rate; 10% annual appreciation in our dollar; zero unemployment; victorious short wars against North Korea, Iran, and ISIS; many new *American Commonwealth* countries in North Africa and the Middle East; the Caribbean Islands; Central and South America; a successful campaign against terrorists and drug cartels. If Cissna Park is indeed a typical example, why would anyone complain about your extraordinary leadership of our country?"

An hour later Jack visited his *Alma Mater* at the University of Illinois in nearby Champaign/Urbana. He stood at the podium for a two-hour question and answer period, and fielded every tough question thrown at him- especially those which challenged his decisions regarding the 'neutralization' of North Korea and Iran; his *American Commonwealth* with far-off countries; and his use of foreign mercenaries to kill or capture terrorists and drug traffickers. At the end of the session Jack summed up his position with regard to the broad meaning of national defense.

> "Defending our country can at times be a very nasty business, but that is part of my job as your Commander-in-Chief. There are no 'rules of war' in our fight against suicide bombers, or drug dealers who poison the bodies of our people. The best I can do for you young people in the audience, is to try to eliminate all of them by any means at my disposal."

Suddenly, Jack was interrupted by the Chief of his Secret Service, who whispered in his ear:

> "The Vice President just called and needs to speak to you immediately. Apparently, Somali terrorists and pirates are marching upon the capital city of Mogadishu, and threaten to overturn their government." Upon hearing this, Jack made a parting remark to his audience:

> "Sorry folks, I've just received word that there is an urgent problem in Northeast Africa, which I must attend to immediately. I am as disappointed as you, because I had been looking forward to re-visiting my campus, and speaking with many more of you students and faculty.

Alas, for the time being my visit must end now." Jack then promptly left the podium for his communications center on the train, where he picked up the direct line to the Vice President, and asked:

"What's going on John?"

"Jack, Admiral Brown is here with me. It looks like 'Yemen' all over again- the Prime Minister of Somalia has requested our help because 30,000 terrorists are marching upon the capital."

"Eddie, what forces do we have in the area, including our Persian Gulf Fleet?"

"Luckily Jack, we have a Fleet Task Force with one carrier anchored offshore Aden on the Southwest point of the Arabian Peninsula. They can be in Somalia in about 6 hours, which will be about 2am local time, but they only have an attachment of about 5,000 of the 1st Marine Division. The Mediterranean 6th Fleet will have to go across the Med, through the Suez Canal; down the Red Sea; around 'the horn', and then steam southward."

"Where is our 7th Fleet?"

"They're currently anchored in Pearl Harbor, Jack."

"One more question, Eddie. What's the status of our 'convict lifers' in the Aleutians- you know, those *desperados* our Marine D.I.'s have been training for the past 2 years- because we're going to need them right now. How many are there, and how many of the black guys do you think will volunteer for African combat, if offered a Presidential pardon?"

"Jack, these convicts have only been drilling to keep them busy- no live weapons, and no live ammo, but considering their backgrounds, I think most of them would know how to fight quite well once we put a live machine gun in their hands. My best guess is that at least half of the 300,000 black 'lifers' might take the bait and volunteer- and maybe more." It didn't take long for Jack to formulate a rough war plan:

"Ok guys, this is what we'll do for now, subject to corrections as we proceed. I want the 5th Fleet in Aden to get underweigh right now and beat the terrorists to Mogadishu with their 5,000 Marines. Next, I want either the 82nd or 101st Airborne Division to drop at the airport just south of Mogadishu and proceed towards the capital. Next, I want the Mediterranean Fleet to bring along another 10,000 Marines and land them just North of the terrorist army.

"Next, I want the 7th Fleet to send a squadron to the Aleutians and pick up the first 50,000 best qualified 'volunteer lifers', and then sail directly through the Indian Ocean to a point in Somalia near the Kenyan border. Next, I want a second squadron from Pearl Harbor to go the Aleutians and pick up another 100,000 'volunteers'; turn around, and transport them to a point just off the coast of Ethiopia, which like Kenya is to be considered in danger of attack by Somalian *Muslim Crazies*/pirates. I will advise the French government that tiny French Somaliland is also endangered, and that it will be up to them to safeguard their own colony with their own armed forces.

"To sum it up gentlemen, our planned Spring African Campaign has been moved forward by about 2 months, but we must always be prepared for the unexpected-world events govern our military actions, not our 'war room' calculations- we must always be ready to improvise. One last note, I want all black Officers, Sergeants, and Corporals with combat experience to be reassigned to this African Campaign, once we have secured Mogadishu, and killed all the 'bad guys'. In short, I expect the Central African Campaign to be won by African-Americans."

"Eddie, the same thing applies to our 'Latino Lifers'. How many volunteers do you think we can get out of these guys, just in case we need them 'South of the border'?" To which the Admiral replied quickly:

"Out of a total of about 120,000 I think we can expect about 50-75,000 to join the Latin American Campaign."

"Very good Eddie. I want you to transfer these men to the Camp Pendleton Marine Training Camp near San Diego, along with their Drill Instructors, and transfer Marine Latino Officers, Sergeants, and Corporals to provide the leadership. I'd like their training to be completed in about 3 months. We'll pick this up tomorrow in the White House War Room at 10am. And Eddie, please advise the others in our group." Jack's Presidential *Super Bullet* was back on the main transcontinental section of the railway in about 40 minutes, went into high gear and arrived in Washington well before midnight.

Chapter Seventeen

The 10am War Room meeting next morning began quietly enough, as Admiral Brown recapped the previous days military movements. Jack then turned to CIA Director Mike McMahon:

"Mike, how much advance notice did your people get before these Somali terrorists grouped together for their march on Mogadishu?"

"Jack, I admit that it was a complete surprise. Neither our satellites nor our group operatives- my guys and mercenary bounty hunters-saw this coming before the terrorists had already left Northeast Somalia, and started their march along the coastal road to the capital city. Once they were spotted, we advised our Ambassador, who immediately advised the Somalian Prime Minister, who was also ignorant of any pending terrorist attack to take over the government, just as the terrorists had done 4 years ago in Yemen. The Somali Prime Minister requested our help to support his 5,000 troops, stationed in the area just North of the capital." Admiral Brown then took the floor:

"Our 5,000 Marines landed at dawn this morning, and linked up with government troops at 9am. At the same time, our 82nd and 101st Airborne Divisions landed just South of Mogadishu, with orders to secure the airport and the capital, and to protect government buildings and public utilities.

"Our 5th Fleet carrier *Vinson* launched 100 Navy war planes and helicopter gunships at 10am local time, with the mission of destroying the 30,000 terrorists before they get within 50 miles of the capital, while our Marines and their Somali allies marched northwards towards the oncoming enemy. By noon, our Airborne troops had secured Mogadishu, and raised American flags over every principal building in the city. By sunset local time, we had completely destroyed the main body of the invading terrorists. Right now, we are leaving the fate of the terrorist escapees in the hands of our foreign mercenaries and their CIA 'handlers'." Jack then asked:

"Why would these *jihadists* think that they could take over Mogadishu in the first place?" Cynthia cut in:

"Jack, I don't think they realized that we would take on a military operation so far from home, and with a nation that 'till now has never shown any particular fondness for America. Also, we should remember that these *Muslim Crazies* are driven by religious fervor- not by common sense. They still remember the victory of Islamic terrorists in Yemen, before the Saudis intervened, and proceeded to wipe them out, and absorb Yemen into their Kingdom." Jack's Chief of Staff, Dick Westerhoff knocked politely, entered the War Room, and whispered into the President's ear. Jack cut him short, and told him to give this information to everyone present:

"We have a new crisis in Nigeria. *Boko Haram,* the Islamic terrorists in Northeast Nigeria, is forming up with 40 thousand *jihadists* to march Southwest towards the capital city of Abuja in the central part of the country. They will be moving out at dawn, local time tomorrow." Jack commented without showing any anxiety:

"It seems to me that the Somalian and Nigerian Islamic terrorist attacks were to have taken place simultaneously, figuring that any American military support could not take on uprisings in both the Northeast and Westcentral areas of Africa at the same time. Eddie, what would be your military strategy at this point?" Admiral Brown thought this over for several minutes before responding:

"Jack, it looks as though we are being forced into an East-West campaign on the Africa continent- call it an African "Belt". We have detailed plans for proceeding from North Africa to South Africa, but none for the East-West 'belt' campaign I just mentioned, which will involve a number of other African nations in the central part of the Continent. I'll have new plans in about 72 hours- which will give us about 6 weeks to be prepared for the landing of the first 50,000 'Aleutian volunteers'." Jack then spoke:

"I guess we'll just have to improvise as best we can. It may be that the 'belt' strategy will turn out to be a better one than the 'trickle down' strategy we have prepared for.

"First Eddie, I want you to drop the remainder of our Airborne Divisions outside the capital city of Abuja; secure the airport, and all government buildings.

"Next, I want the Atlantic Fleet to sail from Norfolk, Virginia to the Nigerian port city of Porto Novo.

"Next, I want the remainder of our Med Fleet to sail westwards through the Straits of Gibraltar; turn around the Moroccan coast; and head straight to the port city of Harcourt, at the mouth of the Southern Nigerian delta; disembark the remaining 15,000 troops of the 1st Marine Division; and then link up with Airborne troops protecting the capital city, because I presume that most of the Nigerian Army troops will be on their way to confront the *Boko Haram* troops coming down from the Northeast.

"Next, I want the remaining 100,000 African-American troops coming from Alaska, after their training at Camp Pendleton, to be transported out of San Diego by a Pacific Fleet Task Force; through the Panama Canal; across the Atlantic; and disembark on the Southern coast outside Lagos, then link up with the Airborne and Marine troops protecting Abuja and surrounding areas.

"Next, I want the Airborne troops defending the Abuja airport to be air lifted and dropped behind the *'Boko Haram'* troops marching from the Northeast, and execute another classic pincer movement.

"Next Rollie, I want you, your best African guy, and Cynthia to hop on Air Force One after this meeting and fly to Abuja. Leave your key guy to hold the Prime Minister's hand until the end of the war; then continue on to Mogadishu with Cynthia, who will hold that Prime Minister's hand until the end of that war.

"Next Rollie, I want you to get permission from the Nigerian Prime Minister to stop the terrorists on the road to their capital city; and also ask permission from the governments of Ethiopia, Sudan, Chad, Central African Republic, and Cameroon to use a strip of their land temporarily as part of the Central African 'belt' defense, until such time as we have ridden Central Africa of Islamic and other tribal terrorists.

"Tonight, I will address the American people directly, and let them know in broad terms what is going on in Africa, without revealing any of the campaign plans we have discussed here today. Eddie, as always, I leave the gory military details to you. Rollie, and Cynthia, you can pick up my telecast on *Air Force One*, and best of luck in smoothing the feathers of those African governments I have mentioned. Now, let's adjourn to my 'Hospitality Suite', and enjoy a well-earned pre-dinner cocktail or two, while I call my wife down to join us."

Ten minutes later, Kathy arrived on the scene, looking as glamorous as ever in her new cocktail dress. After embracing Jack and acknowledging the greetings of his 'inner circle' companions, she returned to Jack and asked:

"Jack *tesoro*, what's happening?"

"We've just gone to war in Central Africa, and have had to change our entire strategy for the African Campaign. I told you about Somalia last evening, but we have just learned that the same type of *Muslim Crazies* are threatening Nigeria. This is a complete African Campaign 'game-changer', but I've gone through this many times before during my college football days- it's *all* about winning- and if the Lord's willing, we shall prevail here as we have elsewhere. *Amore,* excuse me while I have a word with Eddie.

"Admiral, something tells me you have been waiting your whole career for this kind of opportunity to put your name into the history books, alongside those other successful Supreme Commanders. I've got one more wrinkle for you to ponder- I want you to get together with my Attorney General, and find a way to transfer the remainder of African-American *convicted* felons from all Federal and State prisons to your Marine Drill Instructors in the Aleutians. I also want you to transfer all convicted Latino-American felons to a separate island, because we will eventually be fighting the same kind of 'bad guys' in Central and South America, beginning with Mexico- especially those convicted of dealing in narcotics. When the day comes, we will probably need about 200,000 'convict volunteers' to take on Central and South America.

That same evening Jack gave his belated *State of the Union Address* to the Congress; the Supreme Court; and other American and foreign invited guests:

"Tonight, I want to talk to you about the Continent of Africa- perhaps the poorest populace on this planet, but blessed with enormous riches in the form of their natural resources, which can only be realized with an equally enormous investment by private enterprises around the globe.

"Two days ago, without warning, Somali Muslim terrorists and disenchanted Tribal Chieftains launched a combined effort of 30,000 men to attack their capital city of Mogadishu, in an attempt to overthrow Somalia's legitimate government, which then called upon the United States to intervene on their behalf.

"I decided to answer their call for help and six hours later, elements of our 1st Marine Division landed outside their capital city, and joined up with elements of the Somalian military, and proceeded to march Northeast to confront the terrorists.

"At the same time our Airborne Divisions landed at the Mogadishu airport and proceeded to secure Mogadishu by noon that same day.

"By sunset yesterday, local time, the entire Islamic invading force had been annihilated by our Navy carrier warplanes, helicopter gunships, and the Somali/U.S Marine ground forces. Those enemy forces fleeing into nearby jungles will be taken care of by our foreign mercenary bounty-hunters and CIA operations personnel on the ground.

"The next day, I received word that the terrorist *Boko Haram* organization had a similar force of about 40,000 men headed for the Nigerian capital city of Abuja.

"The Nigerian Prime Minister asked for our help, which I did *not* refuse. Overnight, our Med Fleet Task Force arrived at dawn in the Nigerian harbor city of Porto Novo; disembarked another 10,000 1st Division Marines; and sent 100 carrier warplanes and helicopter gunships to counter the *Boko Haram* terrorist coming from the Northeast on the road to the capital city. We then dropped another 10,000 troops from our Airborne Divisions behind enemy lines, in a classic 'pincer movement'. It is now 2am in Nigeria, and the American flag has been raised once again over every government building in Abuja.

"We Americans cannot praise our military enough- they have time and again proven to be the finest Army, Navy, Marine Corps, and Coast Guard on this planet.

"As you all know, my planned trip to visit average towns in all 50 States was interrupted by the war events I have just described. But from those few town hall meetings I did have, there was a common complaint. Apparently, those people who know best how to 'run things' have thus far declined to run for political office- perhaps because of the stigma of being labeled *'career politicians'*, rather than a *'citizen politicians'*, which is how I viewed them, and how our *Founding Fathers* viewed themselves.

"This is the most important election year in recent American history- 80% of this Congress will be leaving office on November 15th , either because of the two-term limit on all elected offices, or because they have chosen to retire and enjoy their *'golden years'*. I am therefore obliged to ask our 'best and brightest' leaders to come forth and serve two, four, or six years of their time and talents, for the benefit of their country. I also call upon all of our townspeople to *shame*, if necessary, your 'best and brightest' into serving the people who have made them so successful in their private enterprises.

"While there remains little room for *'career politicians'*, there will always be room for exceptional Councilpersons to climb their way up the political ladder to the White House, without having to risk their *lives*; their *fortunes*; or their *sacred honor*. That particular brand of *patriotic* selflessness shall forever remain with our Revolutionary War ancestors.

"Goodnight, and may God continue to bless America, and particularly those patriots who have stepped, or will step forward to serve our country- in either military uniform or civilian clothes."

Chapter Eighteen

As Easter Week approached, Jack decided to call Pope Luke:

"*Papa Flynn*, this is Jack. "I just wanted to let you know that we will be spending Easter at home, but the whole family will be at our villa by mid-June." Pope Luke responded:

"Then I insist that you bring everyone down to *Castel Gandolfo* for a weekend visit. There are many things I'd like to discuss with you face-to-face, and it's all good news."

"Your Holiness, thank you for the invitation, because I also have many things to discuss with you in person. In the meantime, the Congress has agreed to recognize *The Vatican* as a separate nation, so you will have to decide upon the person to be the first Vatican Ambassador to the United States. The rest can wait until we meet again in the next few months."

Jack then called Mexico's new President, José Jiminez.

"What's new, Jack?"

"Just checking in to see if you are still alive, after chasing all those cartel drug lords."

"Well Jack, I'm wearing one of your 'tin foil t-shirts' just in case, and so does my military and police. There are still lots of 'bad guys' out there, with their own small armies, and it's going to take a lot of dollars to get rid of them."

"*Amigo*, how would you like to sell us *Baja California?* Think of a price, and get back to me. We need a drastic clean-up of the Colorado River basin, and you don't have the money to even think about this massive project, so throw in the Colorado River delta land, and your half of the Gulf of California into your price tag."

Mexican President Jimenez offered *Baja California*; the Colorado River delta areas; and Mexico's half of the *Gulf of California* for $10 billion. Jack accepted this purchase price on the spot, and wished President Jimenez *'buena suerte'*, knowing full well that eliminating the drug cartels in Mexico would eventually require substantial American military help.

 He also knew that the offshore oil reserves in Baja California would someday be worth $500 billion. The Baja purchase also fit in nicely with his plans to split California into two States, North and South, and at same time bring in debt-laden Puerto Rico as the 52nd State.

Jack and Kathy were the *'Guests of Honor'* at the Italian Embassy Ball on Easter Sunday evening, celebrating the Resurrection of Jesus Christ. Jack was attired in *Armani* white tie and tails, while Kathy displayed a spectacular new creation by *Yves St. Laurent*. They descended the embassy steps just as the orchestra struck up *Hail To The Chief*, for the American President and the First Lady.

They went directly to the dance floor to signal the start of the evening's musical entertainment. Jack had requested the orchestra leader to mix Viennese Waltzes with classical slow dances for the first hour. The Presidential couple did their best during the first three numbers to imitate Fred Astaire and Ginger Rogers- they weren't even close, but no cigar. Nonetheless the audience, which included everyone who was anyone in Washington, gave them a sporting applause at the end of *'Dancing in the Dark'*. Jack and Kathy bowed and curtsied in acknowledgment, and promptly returned to their places at the head table for a well-earned rest, and a fresh glass of champagne.

> "Kathy, I must speak both privately and professionally with Cynthia about her near-term and long-term future, and I would like you to act as if nothing is happening for the next hour. We'll be sitting alone at a candlelit table for two on the outside patio."

> "Jack, it's quite obvious to me, but I hope to no one else, that she has an awful 'crush' on you. If she were not such a beautiful young lady in her early thirties, I might even call it a 'school girl fantasy'- but it's not."

> "I know *amore mia*, and that's one of the things I'm going to take care of right now."

Jack proceeded directly across the ballroom floor to the window table where the Italian Ambassador, Andrea Cecchi, eldest son of the Italian President, was hosting a group of six in lively conversation. Jack had witnessed Andrea and Cynthia during several dances earlier in the evening- he was a tall, handsome Italian gentlemen, but Jack had seen no signs of 'spark' between he and Cynthia.

"If I may interrupt, I'd like to invite Cynthia to dance with me." Andrea rose to his feet, took Cynthia's hand and led her to Jack and replied:

"Good evening Jack, how do you like our party so far? It was kind of you and Kathy to provide our spontaneous entertainment, even though you are almost a foot taller than 'Fred', and Kathy is four inches taller than 'Ginger'- with flaming red hair, rather than a 'natural blond'."

"Andrea, why don't you go over and ask Kathy to dance with you?"

Jack took Cynthia lightly into his arms to the classic Cole Porter hit *Night and Day,* and maneuvered to the edge of the dance floor.

"Cynthia, it will probably happen something like this-you will see a tall, handsome stranger, about your age, approach you from across a crowded ballroom. He will look deeply into your eyes and ask you politely "would you care to dance?" You will look him up and down, and a tiny 'spark' will ignite in your heart; you won't say another word, but rise and float together with him onto the dance floor.

"Before the end of your first dance, he will be holding you uncomfortably close, and you will find yourself with no resistance at all, because you will know instinctively that you are both made for each other. It may take as many as two dances, but certainly not more than that. It's kind of like 'love at first sight', but my theory is that it is 'love at first dance', which just happens to be the case with Kathy and me."

The Cole Porter tune ended, and Jack took Cynthia's hand and led her outside to the candlelit table, and poured out two glasses of vintage *Dom Perignon* champagne. Jack then explained:

> "Cynthia, I brought you out here to talk about your future. First of all, John McCall will be retiring as Vice President before the end of this year. He has spent his whole life serving his country, in combat and in politics, and now wishes to retire while he is still young enough to enjoy his final years. That means that I will need a new Vice President, and I have chosen you to take his place, and to run with me in the 2020 general elections."

Cynthia sat speechless for several moments, contemplating Jack's words before answering:

> "Why me, Jack?"

> "Because my dear, I became aware of your leadership skills, and linguistic abilities at our very first meeting several years ago, when you were a freshman Congresswoman on the House Judiciary Committee, and I was still Chief Justice.

> "When I became President in 2016, I again interviewed you a length, and came to the conclusion that your talents go well beyond your Northwest constituency- in short, you had then, and even more so today, a nationwide appeal to voters that surpasses your natural womanly beauty. So next, I made sure you were

appointed Chairman of the Senate Foreign Relations Committee, so that I might 'pick your brains', and use your ability to speak many foreign languages and dialects.

"Your ability to select key *Adams Industries* CEOs to take over your family company's business affairs proves to me that you also know how to delegate authority.

"At age 21, after *Harvard Business School*, your father's premature death obliged you to take over the family business, with 60% of the voting stock and a net asset value of $5 billion- dealing with everything from cattle ranching to uranium mining." Cynthia quickly interrupted:

"Jack, it was only $4 billion, and after 7 years I purchased an additional 2 million acres of Federal lands for $200 million in early 2015. Adams Industries now has a net asset value of $14 billion, and my extended family holds all of the Board seats, and the remaining 40% of our stock." Jack continued:

"When I became President in 2016, I selected you for my 'inner circle', representing the Senate's confirmation of all the wars we have fought abroad during the past 3 years. I also made sure that you would receive a 'night school' Doctorate in Constitutional Law from nearby Georgetown University, where Kathy is the Chairwoman of the Board of Trustees. Now, I have laid out my best plans for your future service to our country. What say you, Cynthia?"

"First of all Jack, I will be honored to be your Vice President. I realized tonight that you are my 'elder brother', and are 'joined at the hip' with Kathy forever.

"Secondly, I have been courted by several suitors since puberty, but never discovered that instant 'spark' you refer to. My feelings for you have simply grown over the years, and now we both agree that this door must be closed and sealed forever. On the other hand, I do want to have a husband and family, and then grandchildren to spoil shamelessly, so I will be on the lookout for that tall handsome stranger, across a crowded room.

"Thinking further ahead, I will *not* commit to run for President until I have become a wife and mother- I will then be obliged to balance the needs of my own family, and my company family, against the needs of my country.

"One last thing Jack, those 2 million acres of mountains and grasslands are about to be turned into a pioneer's dream come true after nearly two centuries of our branch of the Adams family moving West. During the last 3 years, we have found enough oil; natural gas; gold; silver; copper, and other precious metals and minerals to stagger the imagination- and I am sure that many other private enterprises will find the same fortunes just waiting to be tapped, especially in our Rocky Mountains. In short, you have seriously underestimated the natural gifts that God has given our country- they are beyond comprehension."

Jack escorted Cynthia back to her ballroom table where she sat down as if nothing had happened.

Tuesday morning's 'inner circle' meeting revealed no important new developments on the world front. It seemed that the only thing moving across the 'African Belt', apart from the jungle animals, were the camel caravans and the pick up trucks, which were thoroughly searched for arms, drugs, and slave trafficking by the 200,000 African- American troops now in place from Somalia to Nigeria. The 100,000 Hispanic-American troops had completed their Marine basic training at Camp Pendleton near San Diego, and were now stationed for advanced training at Army bases throughout Southern Texas, New Mexico, Arizona and California.

Almost all the natives in Baja California elected to remain, rather than transfer to the Mexican mainland. They would eventually receive a *green card*, and after 5 years would qualify for an American passport, assuming they kept their noses 'squeaky clean', learned to speak English; and had a fundamental understanding of the American Constitution.

This 'quiet period' would soon come to a roaring halt 3 days later, when more than 10,000 armed Kenyan *Muslim Crazies* began to march on the capital city of Nairobi. The Prime Minister reacted quickly by calling upon the United States to assist the Kenyan Army, which was predominantly Muslim. Jack called a special meeting and asked CIA Director, Mike McMahon:

> "Don't we have any spies in Kenya, or did these guys just spontaneously march out of the Kenyan highlands? And what about the other countries in Central Africa? I

suggest that you reinforce your agents in Africa immediately, by reassigning anyone sitting at a desk in Langley who has any African experience. I don't like getting 'blind sided'. Eddie, what's your game plan?"

"Nothing much new in the way of tactics, Jack. I'll order 30,000 troops in armored personnel carriers, and 300 tanks to travel overnight and be in Nairobi sometime early tomorrow. Next, I'll drop our Airborne Divisions behind enemy lines, and assault their rear guard. Next, I'll move the Persian Gulf Fleet Task Force from Aden, and station it just off the Kenyan East coast. This may sound like 'overkill', but my objective will be to end this conflict by sundown tomorrow."

"Very well, Admiral. Rollie, I want you and Cynthia to take *Air Force One* to Nairobi; keep everyone in government calm; and then send Cynthia on to Mogadishu to explain to the Somalis what's going on with their Southern neighbor. On second thought, let's extend your presence in Central Africa to include all of the capital cities in Central Africa who have an airport large enough to accommodate *Air Force One.*

"Your joint mission is to get a full understanding of how these countries truly feel about American military intervention on the 'Dark Continent', and what their future plans might be with regard to joining the *American Commonwealth.* Remember, we are not selling a damn thing, and quite frankly, I don't care whether they 'buy' anything or not- this foreign policy is strictly voluntary and shall remain so for the rest of my Presidency."

That evening, alone with Kathy, quietly sipping vodka *Martinis* by the fireside, Jack's 'hot line' rang.

"Jack ol' buddy this is José, and I'm sorry to bother you, but I have run up against a problem that I can't resolve by myself without your help. The 'drug lords', large and small, refuse to accept the bribes I have offered them to pack up their operations and retire to some little private island. The $50 billion you gave us for *Baja* doesn't even begin to satisfy their greed- they make that much in one year worldwide, and I have to assume that my military commanders are on the take and therefore cannot be trusted to carry out their 'elimination' orders. I think that by now, you have learned that the American market has become so large that my offers to these people have become laughable.

"My only remaining solution may seem somewhat drastic, but it is the best I can come up with at this point. I therefore must ask you to send in the 100,000 Hispanic-Americans currently training North of our border. This 'Gringo invasion' will no doubt bring an end to my short political career- either by popular vote or impeachment- but then again, like yourself, I am *not* a professional politician, just a 'citizen-politician' serving my country.

"I see this as a military operation designed to wipe out all the drug cartels in Mexico and the rest of Central America. Colombia and Bolivia will be quite another matter when the time comes. Although this is essentially a land operation, I don't think that it will hurt if your Caribbean Fleet were to be anchored in Vera Cruz. When our combined land troops have spotted all the locations of drug cartel operations, your aircraft carrier warplanes; and helicopter gunships, and laser satellites can go into action as a first strike, followed by ground troops to kill or capture the enemy.

"One last thing Jack, I would appreciate it if you would 'lend' me one of your Aleutian Island Marine camps to accommodate those we do not kill. I believe that just the prospect of spending year after year in the Arctic will prove to be a great deterrent to drug production and drug trafficking in the near future." Jack was quick to respond:

"Jose, you've just stolen my own 'game plan'- have you been hacking into my government computers, or are we just two men of the same mind?"

"The latter Jack, the latter. When can you move?"

"Would two days be soon enough? I've been waiting for your call for the past several weeks. See you soon, *amigo*, and I'll tell my Marines in the Aleutians to get ready for some new 'bad guys' to fill those bunk beds we emptied when we sent 300,000 men to protect American interests abroad. I guess you must have learned a lot at UCLA, when you got your Doctor's Degree in International Economics a few years ago. The spectre of spending many years in the Aleutians has become a great deterrent to drug dealing on the 'retail side' here in America, which is exactly what I explained to the American Congress before they passed my 'Drug Act' a few months ago.

"The only answer is to eliminate the wholesale providers South of our border, and the retail on my side. Sooner or later, the 'consumers' will understand that if they want relief from the realities of everyday living, they must look to their family doctors, 'shrinks', or corner taverns. I have no idea how many years this will take, but America has risen to every challenge during my administration, and I will do everything within my power to bring an end to our 'drug disease'.

"To sum up our agreement, 100,000 Latino-American troops will move South at dawn in two days in armored personal carriers, accompanied by 500 of our latest tanks, just in case we need them. At the same time, our Caribbean Fleet in Guantanamo will sail today and anchor off Vera Cruz, with 20,000 Marines and their equipment."

That same evening Jack addressed the nation:

"My fellow Americans, our *American Commonwealth* neighbor to the South, Mexico, has requested our help in ridding their country of drug cartel private armies. President Jimenez would not have asked for our support unless it was absolutely necessary. This will not be another 'one-day war', but rather an extended military campaign to eliminate the sources of illegal drug products entering our country.

"At the same time, I will ask the Congress to approve new and more severe legislation regarding American illegal drug distribution and consumption. This will include a mandatory minimum sentence for *convicted* drug dealers of 10 years in our Aleutian criminal camps, and a minimum sentence of 2 years for *convicted* illegal drug users.

"I assure you that the Aleutian Islands are not a pleasant place to live, but there are 200,000 empty bunk beds provided by those African- Americans who volunteered for military service in Africa, and another 100,000 left empty by those Hispanic- American volunteers who will now march South to wipe out the sources of illegal drug production.

"In closing, I remind you that these are *not* actions taken only for the protection of American adults, but rather for our children and grandchildren. Goodnight, and may God bless us all in this endeavor."

When Jack returned to his residence quarters, Kathy had his double single-malt Scotch awaiting him, and some poignant observation about his speech:

"Honey, you have just given the most somber speech of your presidency- there wasn't a single note of optimism."

"Darling, I can't tell you how depressed I feel about this whole drug business- Mexico is just the tip of the iceberg. There's no telling how many problems we'll find in the rest of Central America. Once we have started our move South, there will be no turning back- and in the case of Colombia, I don't think there will be any invitation forthcoming. We will probably have to take over the country to smash the epicenter of world- wide cocaine production.

"Before this is over, I expect there to be many ugly moments, and there is no assurance that we will be successful in stamping out American drug usage- anymore than *Prohibition* was able to stop alcohol consumption. On the other hand, it may be that our home-grown marijuana will be enough to satisfy our drug users. For the time being, I will not propose any new legislation regarding 'pot'; gambling; or prostitution, but will leave these matters in the hands of our towns to legalize, or not."

Chapter Nineteen

In mid-June, the rest of the Fitzgerald family was treated for the first time to a long ride on *Air Force One*; landed in Florence 10 hours later; picked up their personal cars; unloaded the bullet-proof Presidential limousine and black security guard vans; and were escorted to their villa by the Italian Secret Service, just in time to see the sunrise- and the American flag flying high over the villa rooftop.

Ursola, the cook and housekeeper, and Giorgio, the vineyard keeper and estate manager, were both there at the front door to greet them, while the rest of the villa staff were busy preparing everyone's quarters, and the 6 by 20 foot solid oak terrace dining table for a late breakfast. For security reasons, there had been no advanced notice, other than the phone call from the Florence airport one hour earlier.

Everyone in the family had noticeable 'jet lag', except for Caterina, who was now a 'terrible three' and ready to play in the pool and soak up the mid-morning Tuscan sun along with baby brother Jack; Mary; Nicky, and the family ever present nanny, Maria.

The elder boys made hurried phone calls to their Greve girlfriends, now attending the University of Florence, and found to their disappointment that each had acquired a new college boyfriend, and thus were not available. So Matt, Mark, and Stephen decided to skip the pool, and drive down to the central piazza in search of new, unattached Summer female companions. Everyone in town remembered them from previous years, and word spread like wildfire as the three young men sat down at their favorite outdoor café .

Within ten minutes, three tall, well-dressed 'town fathers' approached the boys. They were all middle-aged gentlemen, and their leader stepped forward and spoke in perfect English:

> "My name is Carlo Bonnini, the Mayor of *Greve in Chianti*, and on behalf of our town, I welcome you back. These two gentlemen are City Councilmen Giorgio Garavaglia and Umberto Minotti. We understand that you wish to meet new female companions for your Summer vacation. I think that together we can find appropriate escorts for you in a couple of hours. We know your reputations with our young women, and that you can be trusted." Mark spoke for the three brothers:

> "*Sindaco* Bonnini, we are most grateful for your kind intervention in this matter, and shall leave everything in your capable hands until your return."

> "What's going on?" Stephen asked, to which Matt replied:

> "Let's just wait and see. My best guess is that they will parade the tallest, prettiest young girls in town, all with impeccable reputations, and will have already decided the couplings. It certainly beats spending all day and all evening trying to hook up with someone who will not embarrass mom and dad."

As the town's church bells chimed out noon, the three elder men approached the Fitzgerald boys. Mayor Bonnini advanced first, while the three brothers rose to their feet:

"*Signorino* Stephen, I would like to present my eldest daughter Silvana, who will be your classmate at Harvard in September."

Stephen was awestruck by her beauty- tall; long blond hair; blue eyes; statuesque figure; swan-like neck; and long shapely legs- a princess gazing at her favorite knight. For several seconds he stood motionless, but then advanced slowly to take her extended arm, kissed her hand, and mumbled almost inaudibly:

"*Un grande piacere, Signorina* Silvana." To which she replied:

"*Il piacere è tutto mio,* Stephen." He could not believe his eyes- he stood before a goddess, looked straight into her eyes, and felt as if he had just been struck by a lightning bolt. His brothers had the same reaction to their almost six- foot tall young ladies- auburn haired Graziella Minotti for Matt, and brunette Carla Garavaglia for Mark. Graziella was headed for Bologna University, and a Degree in Biology, and Carla for the University of Milan, and a Degree in Business Management. Then came the expected return for these favors.

Mayor Bonnini turned to Stephen, and asked if he would be willing to play center forward on Greve's Class C amateur soccer team for a few pre-season practice games during the Summer:

"Stephen, you are the greatest striker ever to come out of English prep schools, and were offered millions of

290

dollars to play professionally for *Manchester United; Chelsea; Milan;* and *Inter*. I think I know why you declined these offers, but at the same time I believe you could teach a lot to our local soccer boys." Stephen did not hesitate:

"Mister Mayor, it's the least I can do for having your beautiful daughter as my Summertime companion." The mayor continued:

"The second favor I ask is that you boys introduce all of us to your parents." Mark responded quickly:

"How about dinner this evening with your wives and these beautiful young ladies? Cocktails are at eight and dinner at nine. We'll see you all then." The three young men reluctantly waved goodbye, sat down and stared silently in disbelief at their good fortunes.

The three local families arrived that evening and were promptly shown to the outdoor terrace, where they all introduced themselves to the rest of the Fitzgerald family, including Mary and Nick, who, although still in their late twenties, had become international celebrities as world-renowned operatic singers. Jack offered *Monte Cristo* cigars and single malt Scotch to the men, while Kathy made vodka *Martinis* for herself and the ladies. As host, Jack opened the conversation:

"First of all, you may all call me 'Jack', and my wife is 'Kathy', and I shall call you by your first names as well-this is an American home, and as you probably have heard, Americans are not known for adhering to strict formalities once we get to know you. Carlo, why don't you tell us what you did for a living before you became mayor."

"I own and managed a lumber, farm vehicles, and hardware business, which is now being run by my eldest son." The President then turned to Councilman Garavaglia:

"How about you, Giorgio?"

The middle-aged gentleman took a long sip of his Scotch, and a long drag on his cigar before responding:

"I was Chief physician at our local hospital. My eldest son is also a doctor, fresh out of his residency at Florence General Hospital, and has taken over my private practice offices." Umberto Minotti spoke next, without prompting:

"Jack, like your father, I am the town 'vet', and also grow a few acres of *Chardonnay* from saplings I imported from *Sonoma Valley* more than 20 years ago. I brought along a couple of bottles this evening for you to taste on some other occasion. Carlo also brought a couple of bottles of *Champagne*, to celebrate our meeting tonight, and Giorgio brought a couple of bottles of 'boutique' single-malt Irish whisky which I think you might enjoy as a change of pace from time to time."

"Gentlemen, this is a very gracious gesture on your parts. I'd like you to sample all three vintages of my *Chianti Riserva* at dinner this evening, and let me know which year you prefer." Jack then took a long drag on his cigar, and a hefty swallow of Scotch before continuing:

"I'm curious to learn about your local politics here in Greve, so that I may compare them with town leadership in America." Carlo spoke for the three of them:

"To tell you the truth Jack, our last elections four years ago were quite uneventful, because many younger people, perhaps more talented than we, chose *not* to offer themselves as candidates. For example, the three of us volunteered to serve our town and were substantially unopposed- a situation that continues to this day- but we all hope that new candidates from the younger generations will come forth in our general elections this November, now that they have learned that there is a very big difference between old-time *'career politicians'* and *'citizen politicians'* like ourselves." Jack responded:

"It may interest you gentlemen to know that the same phenomenon exists today in America. The corruption; ineptitude; and self-interest associated with politics in general has had a stigmatic effect on our 'best and brightest', especially our younger generations. My best guess is that it will take many years to eradicate this stigma, and bring forth new blood, dedicated to the people they represent, as provided for in our common Constitution."

After a superb six-course dinner, featuring local white truffle shavings atop milk-fed veal *filet mignon,* and *crêpes suzettes* as dessert, the party split up- men with cigars and *cognacs*; ladies with green *Crème de Menthe*. Jack led the Mayor to a quiet spot at the far end of the huge patio, and asked:

"Carlo, how have you managed your town's finances?"

"Each year we have run a small budget surplus, and as yet have not been obliged to touch our Federal T-bonds, which we are keeping for the proverbial 'rainy day'. We receive more than enough tax dollars from the sale of our wines and other farm products, and from the many Summer tourists who visit our *Renaissance* art collections on their road trips between Florence and Siena. Stated simply, we run our town at a surplus and will continue to do so."

"Any problems with the illegal boat people from North Africa and the Middle East?"

"The only Muslims here in Greve are the daytime tourists to or from Florence, but on the Federal level, President Cecchi has a much bigger problem, and his policy has been to send our Coast Guard to divert African boats back to their ports of departure. For the one-half million African Muslims who are already here, he has done exactly what you have done with your illegal Mexican 'foreign invaders'- give them a one-way ticket back home.

"Italy is smaller than your State of California; and we have an ancient Christian culture that dates back nearly 2,000 years. In short, we don't have the land, nor the resources to absorb multitudes of non-Italians.

"There is no *Statue of Liberty* in any Italian harbor, because we have no sparsely populated 'waving fields of grain', and we definitely don't need the aggravation and possible terrorism associated with what you call *'Muslim Crazies'* who might slip through along with the refugees.

"Look at it this way Jack, we have just emerged from near social and economic disaster, and only your vision for Italy has now made us the vanguard of European prosperity. We are definitely not going to screw up this opportunity for national rebirth- much less let any bunch of foreigners try to screw it up for us. It may seem harsh not to have America's 'open- arms' for new permanent residents, while at the same time having wide open arms for 30 million tourists every year.

"Although they may not admit it, this same policy is now being followed by almost every other country in Europe, especially Switzerland."

While Jack and Carlo talked politics, the Fitzgerald boys and the elder generation were busy dancing to Frank Sinatra songs with their companions at the other end of the terrace, under a full silvery moon. Stephen and Silvana were the first to split off discreetly, and head down the terrace steps to the swimming pool area. Matt and Graziella followed a few minutes later and headed for the tennis courts. Mark and Carla descended to the swing overlooking the back garden.

Silvana spoke first as she and Stephen sat down outside the pool house:

"Stephen, I suppose you'll be studying for the Harvard Law School, and as a matter of fact, so will I, unless I change my mind. Will you also be playing soccer this Fall?

"As long as it doesn't interfere with my studies Silvana, because I plan to finish undergraduate school in 3 years. That means taking two extra courses every semester, and missing afternoon practice the day before exams and term papers. How about you?"

"I think I'll try the same thing, and if the girl's basketball coach doesn't permit it, I'll play volleyball instead."

"That's a great idea. If my soccer coach doesn't go for it, I'm sure I can persuade the football coach to let me do the place-kicking. So you see, we can just play them off one against the other, and see who blinks first. Then in the Spring, I can do the same thing with the baseball and tennis coaches, while you play off the field hockey coach against the track coach."

"How did you know about field hockey and track?"

"I took aside your father while you were freshening up in the powder room. He also mentioned your tennis game, so why don't we get together tomorrow morning, play a couple a sets, and then hit the swimming pool?"

"Sounds lovely, Stephen", as she inched closer to him, put her arms around his neck, and gave him a warm, long, passionate kiss which he promptly returned.

"Aren't I the one who should normally make the first move?"

"Normally, yes. But I am not a 'normal' young woman, and you are definitely not a 'normal' young man. Now I'll say goodnight and rejoin my parents. I need a good night's sleep if I am going to beat you tomorrow in tennis at 10."

Silvana rose from her seat, and strode away calmly, as if nothing had happened, while Stephen remained seated and simply mumbled *'buona sera'* as she climbed the terrace stairs-the moonlight still shining on her now silvery hair like an angel's halo.

Next morning, all three couples were on the two tennis courts-Stephen and Silvana played singles, while his elder brothers played doubles for one set, and then they switched partners and places for the next hour, before heading to the swimming pool.

If these tall beauties looked great in tennis garb, they looked absolutely spectacular in their *bikini* bathing suits. All three brothers looked at each other as Matt remarked:

"How can one little town of 25,000 people produce three prime 'Las Vegas chorus girls'?"

For the next hour, the family watched six talented swimmers vie with each other in individual and mixed medley races, during which the girls performed almost as well as the boys. The competition was interrupted when Ursola and her crew descended the terrace steps with trays of luncheon goodies and glasses of champagne.

Jack and Kathy had observed this mating scene, and were astounded by the selections made by the Mayor and his two Councilmen. In their minds, these Summertime companions might just as well have been sent from Heaven. Jack commented during lunch:

> "You young ladies are a delightful addition to my family this Summer, and since I must visit Pope Luke in *Castel Gandolfo* this coming weekend, I would be quite pleased if you and your parents would accompany my family, and be blessed by Pope Luke. We will all gather here, and leave after breakfast, and return after Mass on Sunday morning. While I am in conference with the Pope Saturday afternoon, I think you will find many points of interest to visit in his ancient castle."

The Fitzgerald 'caravan' was greeted by the Pope's *Camerlengo*, Monsignor Casey, and their castle guide, Sister Margarita. Jack and O'Brian excused themselves, and proceeded to the Pope's private study.

> "Jack my son," said Pope Luke as he embraced the President. "I can't tell you how happy I am to be with you once more, and to share some good news. It's taken four years of hard work in Vienna, but we have finally united every Christian Church, and are now working out the details of a common liturgy. We have also persuaded the more important Islamic sects to join us for an Interfaith Council, to be held in Istanbul before the end of this year.
>
> "We would consider it a great personal favor if you would attend this opening meeting between Christians

and Muslims, because the *American Commonwealth* embraces both religious. We have also invited the High Priest of the Jewish Temple in Jerusalem.

"Lastly Jack, the Council of Christian Churches has asked me to express our eternal gratitude for the protection of our Missions in Africa. The number of Missionary Priests and Nuns has doubled since you began your African Campaign. When do you think you will be allowing the Central African countries to join the *American Commonwealth?*" To which Jack replied:

"Just as soon as we have wiped out the last of the 'Muslim Crazies', and the terrorist tribal chieftains-which should bring me to the end of my first term if all continues to go well." Jack continued:

"Much the same story goes for Central and South America, except that our fighting is against private drug cartel armies who refuse to accept bribes to retire permanently from their production activities. However, on the consumer side, I have had reasonable success by sending convicted 'distribution network operators' directly to nasty little islands in the Aleutians, to be drilled by our Marine D.I.s. The same treatment goes for convicted 'drug users'. All and all, I expect us to have almost one million reserves to eventually reinforce our campaigns in Africa, Central and South America. After a year or more in the Aleutians, I could get these convicted felons to volunteer for *anything*- even a space mission to Mars. On the domestic consumer side, more than half of our towns have elected to legalize marijuana; gambling; and prostitution, but with iron-clad regulations regarding these three 'sins'."

During Sunday Mass the following morning, Mary sang *Ave Maria* with a small choir from the village and Nicky sang the *Lord's Prayer* with the entire congregation. After Mass, the Pope pulled Jack aside and whispered:

> "I understand that Mary and Nicky will be singing once again at *La Scala*, in a charity performance for *St. Luke Academy*, which is now under construction on your family's farmland. It would give me great pleasure to see and hear my two favorite operas- *La Boheme* and *Turandot*, next Saturday and Sunday evenings."

> "*Your Holiness*, nothing will give my family greater pleasure than to share the Royal Box with you."

Pointing to the lightweight Irish linen, double breasted suit he wore on unofficial occasions. The Pope observed:

> "I trust that this simple garment will fit the occasion."

> "Absolutely, Your Holiness- no one in my group will be wearing anything but blue suits and discreet evening dresses. These will be unscheduled charity performances, with no advanced publicity, except for the outdoor *La Scala* wall signs which will go up on Monday morning."

> "Jack, tell me how the Academy construction is coming along."

"As in everything I set my mind to, and considering that this is the harvest season in Cissna Park and the rest of Iroquois County, we are proceeding at a fast pace. So far, we have converted one of the small barns into a Chapel to serve the local Catholic community of about 60 families; hired a Chicago construction company to build the simple country-style solid stone Church, and have given them instructions that their laborers be chosen from the Irish; Polish; and Italian neighborhoods on the Southside of Chicago, because some workers' families may decide to settle in Cissna Park.

"Starting in September, our pre-school and elementary school will be open in another of our renovated large barns, with playground equipment; a Little League baseball field, and a football/soccer/lacrosse field. Phase two will include permanent structures-student dormitories; preschool and elementary school buildings; indoor gymnasium for basketball; volleyball; and ice hockey; with an elevated running track above. Finally, we will construct the best college preparatory school that money can buy, complete with ivy-covered walls.

"Outdoors, we will have an athletic complex second to none, including an Olympic swimming pool with diving platforms; a multi-purpose football/soccer/lacrosse/track and field lighted stadium with expandable spectator seating; and lighted full-size and Little League-size Baseball Parks with stands.

"These athletic facilities will be open to everyone in Cissna Park. Most importantly, I would expect Father

O'Malley and Sister Mary Elizabeth to recruit the 'Best and the Brightest' of young Jesuit Priests and Dominican Nuns seeking a new adventure in building Catholicism in the heartland of Protestant America."

Chapter Twenty

Early Tuesday morning in late July, Cynthia Adams landed her corporate two engine jet in Florence, and had her co-pilot and personal bodyguard off-load her classic red *Testa Rossa Ferrari* three liter, two-seat roadster onto the tarmac. She hopped in, waved goodbye to her copilot, and headed South to *Villa Americana*- phoning ahead to announce her arrival. Jack and Kathy were there to meet her at the front door, while Ursola grabbed her bags and headed to the upstairs bedroom and patio- overlooking the vineyards, farm houses, and far hills between the villa and the Mediterranean Sea. Jack and Kathy led her to the living room's outside terrace, to embrace the magnificent view.

"Welcome to our peaceful retreat from the real world." Jack commented. To which Cynthia replied:

"Now you know how I feel about my Montana ranch." Jack observed:

"You call four million acres a 'ranch'?"

"Well, Montana is a *very* big State." Cynthia responded.

"What can we offer you to drink?" Kathy inquired.

"Well, the sun is about to go over the yardarm, so I guess I'll try some good ol' straight Kentucky Bourbon on ice. It's been a long flight- 12 hours- and I've got the fastest two engine jet they build. Dave, my co-pilot and bodyguard is an art buff, and has decided to spend the next few days in Florence, since you've got plenty of Secret Service guards around here. Are those your kids I see down below in the pool, and on the tennis courts? And who are those tall young 'fashion models' I see them with?"

"Just local young women headed for Harvard and other colleges this September- but you'll meet them all at lunch." Kathy replied.

"Hey Jack, this extraordinary whisky can't be from Kentucky!"

"You're right Cynthia, it's a *boutique* whisky gifted by the father of one of those girls- 20 year-old Irish single-malt whisky- and smooth as silk. Let me tell you about the program for this week. Today and tomorrow we'll be staying around the villa, except for a short side trip to Cortona to see this medieval town; have dinner, and then watch the musical program conducted by Andre Rieu, his symphony orchestra, and his opera singers. We have been invited to share the Mayor's balcony seats in the main piazza.

"Thursday, we'll be traveling to Milan in my 'caravan', unless you want to see how fast that *Ferrari* of yours can really go at the Monza Formula One racetrack, because on Friday I've been invited once again by media billionaire Silvio Berlusconi to try beating my own amateur record set four years ago, in their F1 number three backup car.

"Friday afternoon and early evening is 'girls' day', when Kathy, you and the other young women get private showings at the world's best Italian fashion houses on *Via Montenapoleone*, to select your Fall fashions. Saturday, we can have a tourist day visiting the *Duomo* Cathedral; *Sforza* Castle; and Leonardo da Vinci's *Last Supper fresco* in the small church of *Santa Maria delle Grazie*.

"Later on Saturday, we will have an early evening dinner at *Alfredo's*, next door to the world-renowned *Galleria* on *Via Vittorio Emmanuelle*. Then off the back exit out the *Galleria*, across *Piazza alla Scala,* and seating in the Royal Box to see Mary and Nicky perform *La Boheme* in an unscheduled charity event for my St. Luke Academy in Cissna Park.

"After the performance, we have all been invited for a St. Luke Academy charity ball, at the home of Silvio Berlusconi at his town manor. All and all Cynthia, it should prove to be a very busy weekend for you, and who knows what interesting gentlemen you may encounter."

"Jack, I prefer to drive up to Milan in my little red *Ferrari,* and 'have a go' at the Monza race track, as long as you have rented it for the morning. Let's say you go first, then I go, and after two flying laps, we switch cars. I should say that I've had this baby 'elaborated' with an old F-1 twelve cylinder engine, putting out 1,000hp at 18,000rpm. We'll have two test marks- one for overall time around the F-1 circuit, and the other for the fastest speed across the finish line."

Come Saturday morning, Jack and Cynthia showed up at the *Ferrari* pit lane garage at 9am for their personal 'race day'. Paolo, the *Ferrari* F-1 mechanic, rolled out his *Scuderia's* number 3 back-up car, fitted with Jack's special long seat and rolled him out for his warm up lap, then turned his attention to Cynthia's car.

"Good Lord, young lady! Wherever did you find these classic F-1 replacement parts?" To which Cynthia replied:

"Paolo, it's just a question of my passion for fast automobiles, and the money it takes to build them my way- which in this case are the engine and gearbox; the brakes; suspension, and transmission axle from Michael Schumacher's championship years at *Ferrari*."

"Okay lady, the track is yours."

She proceeded down pit lane just as Jack was completing his practice in a warm up lap at 200mph. Cynthia exited in first gear at 100mph, and then slowed to 50mph before navigating the front *chicane*, then shifted into 2nd gear and exited onto the straightaway at 200mph, before tapping her brakes for the upcoming *Lesmo* long right turn onto the mile-long North straightaway at 210mph in 7th gear; geared down to 100mph for the sharp exit right hander; navigated the back straightaway *chicane* at 80mph; then geared up to 210mph for the remainder of the back straightaway, before gearing down to 5th upon entering the *Parabolic curve* and the front straightaway, where she crossed the finish line at 230mph.

Their second timed lap was much a repeat of the first- Jack's F-1 was definitely superior in maneuverability, so his time was 10 seconds better than Cynthia's- but she had an engine almost twice the size of Jack's turbocharged 1.6 liter new formula. When they pulled into pit lane Jack approached Cynthia.

"How in the world did you do that? Let me look at that machine you're driving!"

"It's really quite simple, Jack, when the FIA changed the formula a few years back, I shipped my *Testa Rossa* back to the factory in Maranello and had them 'transplant' the engine and other parts from Michael Schumacher's previous F-1 car. So, in round two of our competition you will essentially be driving the same car once driven by the greatest champion in Formula One history- and I'll be driving a new Formula One for the first time in my life. Let's do a warm-up lap, and then as before two running laps."

Jack exited pit lane, and by the time he had navigated the front straightaway *chicane,* he had a pretty good idea that he was driving the fastest street car ever created for road travel, although the braking and ultra-tight suspension were just a notch below the F-1 factory car, and lacked the front wing and back aerolon downforce for the curves and *chicanes.* However, the straightaway pure power was exhilarating, as he crossed the finish line of his second running lap at 250mph, while Cynthia crossed at 220mph- but was 7 seconds faster around the circuit on her last lap.

"Well Jack, how did you like riding my *half-breed*, which I have named after my father *Mike*?" Jack simply shook his head and responded:

"If there were any place in America to drive it, I would order up a duplicate from the *Ferrari* factory. When do you ever get a chance to drive this little jewel?" To which Cynthia replied:

"Jack, it takes a lot of overland driving to keep track of 100,000 head of cattle; and hundreds of mines and oil rigs, and I own most of the private roads in my part of Montana. Thus there are no 'speed limit' signs; however, I have put up hundreds of 'no hunting, private property' signs to protect the gaming animals from poachers."

Teatro alla Scala was packed to the rafters that Saturday evening to witness for the first time in four years their beloved operatic couple, Mary Fitzgerald and Nicky Verenko, who proceeded to put on the best performance of *La Boheme* in living memory. The net proceeds, after substantial costs and the 10% tax, was destined for St. Luke Academy.

Pope Luke, in plain white suit and skullcap, and President Fitzgerald in a dark blue suit, sat front and center in the Royal Box, which seated 6, with standing room for another half dozen members of their *entourage*. The vast audience rose to their feet spontaneously for these two great leaders, moments before conductor Kurt Wilhelm struck his baton for the first note. Between Acts, those in the Royal Box were served *Champagne* and caviar by agents of the Vatican Swiss Guard, while the

Italian and American Secret Services guarded the rest of the opera house.

Later that evening at Silvio Berlusconi's city mansion, his charity ball got underway, as Nicky took the microphone and announced:

> "Tonight, Mary and I have selected a medley of popular Broadway numbers by composer Richard Rodgers and lyricist Oscar Hammerstein II- *Shall We Dance; Some Enchanted Evening; Hello Young Lovers,* and *If I Loved You.*" Then turning to the conductor, Nick nodded:

Cynthia was fully concentrated on the singing, when she heard a lovely baritone voice whisper in her ear:

> "In case you haven't noticed, we are the only two people in this place without dancing partners." Cynthia turned, looked up from her seat, and was surprised to see a tall, very handsome stranger extend his hand in invitation.

She followed his lead onto the dance floor and slid easily into his arms, while placing her cheek against his. Neither said a word for several moments- they simply gazed into each others' blue eyes, while their bodies molded together as one. The tall young man then spoke:

> "I'm Gianni Savoia, unattached bachelor, and you are?"
>
> "I'm Cynthia Adams, unattached spinster."
>
> "How very fortunate for both of us."
>
> "Yes, isn't it." As they continued to gaze only at each other with smiles that said everything.

Cynthia couldn't make up her mind whether Gianni looked more like *Cary Grant* without the chin dimple, or a much taller *Tyrone Power* because of his thick dark eyebrows. At the same time, Gianni made no such comparison because in his eyes Cynthia had a distinct beauty like no other young woman he had ever seen-on screen or off.

When the first number was completed, Gianni and Cynthia remained on the dance floor awaiting Mary to sing *Hello Young Lovers* from *The King and I*.

"What do you do, Gianni?"

"I manage my family's lands and other properties. And you?"

"For several years after my father died, I did the same thing, but for the last six years I've been serving in government- first as a Congresswoman from Helena, and now as junior Senator from the State of Montana, specializing in Foreign Affairs and traveling abroad a great deal. Over the years, I've recruited outstanding CEOs to run my family's enterprises on a day-to-day basis."

"So have I, except that I cannot get involved in politics."

Right in the middle of Mary's *Hello Young Lovers*, Gianni once again whispered into Cynthia's ear:

"Do you believe in 'love at first dance'?"

"Not before tonight, how about you?"

"I feel that I shall never let you go."

"Neither shall I, even though we have known each other for less than one hour. We have everything to learn about each other."

"Learning about each other promises to be an extraordinary adventure." Without saying another word Gianni turned his face to her, sought out her lips, and found them to be the softest he had ever known.

"My darling Gianni, how can this be happening to us?"

"Cynthia my love, I never argue with God."

After Mary and Nicky had finished their last number, *People Will Say We're In Love*, Gianni suggested that they leave the ball for a splendid view of *Piazza del Duomo* lit up at night. Cynthia was desperately in love for the first time in her young life, and simply followed Gianni's suggestion, though conventionally she would have offered to introduce him to Pope Luke, Jack and Kathy, and others in the Royal Box. 'Well, there'll be plenty of time for that', she thought to herself, 'and I know he just wants to be alone with me, as I do with him'.

Their cab pulled up at the front entrance to the *Grand Hotel Duomo*, and they entered to the bows and curtsies of the hotel staff and went directly to Gianni's private penthouse elevator. Minutes later, they were standing on the top terrace overlooking a floodlit Cathedral, *Galleria*, and central piazza fountain statues. Cynthia allowed her curiosity to speak out:

"Gianni, why did the staff in this hotel show us such deference when we entered?" Gianni responded:

"I might say that it's because my family owns this hotel, which is true, but that would *not* be the whole truth. My full name is Gianni Vittorio Emmanuele Savoia, *Principe di Piemonte*. My great-grandfather was the last King of Italy."

"Gianni, you're the *Prince of Piedmont*, and presumptive heir to the throne, if there was a throne. Now I know why you are precluded from taking any part in politics- it's the deal your Royal Family made to retain your properties after your family narrowly lost the *referendum* in 1948."

"How is it that you know so much about Italy and its history?"

"I spent the Spring semester of my sophomore year at the Harvard program in Florence, as I had done since age 10 during my Summer vacations in other countries, to learn foreign cultures and languages.

"My father knew that the 21st century would require firsthand knowledge of our future trading partners around the globe, and that *Adams' Industries* would be left in my hands. But enough of family obligations. Let's just enjoy our love affair, and let the world go 'round, because we have all our lives ahead of us. How many children would you like to have?"

Gianni gazed out upon the Cathedral in front of them before responding:

"I would say a minimum of three; and a maximum of five. How does that sound to you?"

"I'm already 33 and not getting any younger, so perhaps we should get started tonight."

"Another coincidence! I'm also 33, and your suggestion is absolutely lovely. First thing tomorrow morning, I'll have the owner of *Cartier* open his store so we can pick out your engagement ring. Then, let's drive over to my family's country estate in the hills just West of Turin, so we can have a long talk with my grandfather before Sunday dinner with the rest of my family, when I will announce our engagement. Am I moving too fast for you, *amore mia*."

"Not at all, my love. Once I make up my mind about something, I prefer to move as quickly as possible, which is why I suggested that we spend the night together. So let's finish our *Champagne* and then go make lots of love."

Chapter Twenty-One

Cynthia suggested that Gianni drive her *Ferrari* to his family's Summer estate, and they talked mostly about race cars during the two hour trip.

"Speaking of Monza, my family owns the entire Monza Park which surrounds the F-1 race circuit, but we rarely go there for anything except to play golf on one of the Park's courses- it's only ½ hour from my first floor offices in the *Grand Hotel Duomo*. Now let me tell you a little about my grandfather, Vittorio Emanuelle, who looks exactly like famous film actor/director Vittorio DeSica- tall; thick white hair; blue eyes; and most of all, very sharp-witted.

"He was once a charter member of the 'International Jet-Set', which included many prominent celebrities of the mid-20th century, such as Aristotle Onasis; Jackie Kennedy; Maria Callas; Gianni Agnelli, and other 'playboys' and 'playgirls'. Needless to say, his notoriety in the tabloids caused much anxiety within our family, because it threatened to nullify the 'pact' we had made with the Italian government in 1948, which included 20 years of exile to the small seaside resort town of Estoril, just North of Lisbon, Portugal; no Italian political Party connections, and staying out of the 'limelight'- all of which he promptly ignored; made the front cover of every European 'scandal magazine'; and abdicated his royal title to my father, Giovanni. Other than that, I think you'll find him to be a very entertaining fellow."

"Gianni, you have a lovely British accent, and speak the English language beautifully."

"Well Cynthia, after ten years of schooling at Eton, Oxford, and the London School of Economics for my Doctorate Degree, I should certainly hope so. It's been a family tradition that all the young men be educated in England, and all the young women in Switzerland. You've mentioned Harvard?"

"Also a family tradition, since the days of my ancestor President John Adams- who helped write our *Declaration of Independence* and our *Constitution*. I also have another direct ancestor, President John Quincy Adams, his son. Now, Jack Fitzgerald wants me to replace John McCall as his Vice President, and has promised to support me if I should choose to run as the first woman President of the United States."

"Sounds to me like the two of you are very close. Have you ever been lovers?"

"No Gianni, that could never happen. I must admit that I had a schoolgirl infatuation with him for a while- but never more than that. In fact, he told me that I would fall in love at first sight with someone like you, so here we are Gianni, exactly as Jack Fitzgerald predicted."

"Jack must be quite a guy, and has been dead right on so many decisions during the last three years. Where does America find such men like Jack and such women like you?" Cynthia answered promptly:

315

"From the Atlantic Coast to the farmlands of the Midwest, to the Great Plains of the Northwest, and most any other place in between. We Americans are God's new 'Chosen People', and are always at our very best when things are at their very worst, because great leaders like Jack Fitzgerald always appear at the right time." Gianni then turned the *Ferrari* right, onto the tree lined lane leading to the front door of the enormous mansion, where his family was waiting to greet him:

"Grandfather, I would like to present my fiancée Cynthia Adams, Senator from the State of Montana in America."

Vittorio, just turned 80, thought he had seen everything, but the beautiful young woman standing before him was a complete surprise, as was Gianni's announcement of their engagement. The old man was almost, but not quite, left speechless for one of the few times during his long life. He stepped forward, took her hand; kissed her long slim fingers, and proclaimed in a clearly audible baritone voice:

"My dear Cynthia, welcome to our family. This is a very special moment in my life, and I cannot wait to greet my first great-grandson on the day of his birth. *Bravo* Gianni, *bravissimo*! But tell me, where on earth did you two lovers meet?" Gianni stepped in:

"Yesterday evening, at the Charity Ball given for the President of the United States, Jack Fitzgerald. The proceeds will be used for the construction of a school complex, to be named *St. Luke Academy*, in honor of our Pope, who was also present."

"So Gianni, if I understand you correctly, you both fell in love while dancing together, and spent the rest of evening getting better acquainted. Well, I must say that you are the handsomest couple to come upon the international scene in many decades- reminds me of my youthful days with your late grandmother. Tell me Cynthia, how do you and Gianni plan to reconcile the U.S Senate with Gianni's responsibilities as CEO of our family holdings?"

"Good question, Vittorio. I am also responsible for my family's holdings- 4 million acres of Montana land with 100,000 head of cattle; gold mines; silver mines; copper mines; uranium mines; oil wells; natural gas; and the conversion facilities connected to these natural resources- meat packing plants; gold and silver facilities; oil and liquid natural gas refineries; leather tanneries and a few dozen other enterprises, including hotels and apartment buildings in our downtown capital city of Helena.

"Like Gianni, over the years I have recruited the best CEOs money can buy to run these operations. Other than this, we're both quite tall; have dark brown hair; blue eyes; are very much in love, and plan to raise 3-5 children as quickly as we can, so you can stop worrying about your future great-grandchildren, or about the fortunes they will inherit from both sides of their family. The only problem I can foresee will come up late next year, when we have our next general elections, and I will have to decide whether or not to continue serving my country. In the meantime, Gianni and I will figure it out as we go along."

After dinner, while toasting the couple's engagement, Vittorio asked Gianni:

"Have you set a wedding date?"

"Yes grandfather, Cardinal Montini has agreed to marry us tomorrow morning at 10 'o clock in the Cathedral. Right afterwards, we will be leaving on our honeymoon for several weeks. Sorry about the short notice, and the lack of a formal wedding reception, but we simply want to be alone together."

"And where will you make your home?" Vittorio asked:

"For now, we will be living in the Georgetown manor Cynthia purchased from Jack Fitzgerald when he moved into the White House. We have made no definite plans beyond that, except for Summer vacations, which we will be spending here in Italy, with our baby, or babies, as the case may be. If you agree, we would like to use our family's mountain lodge up in Sestriere as our home base-popping down the mountain from time to time to dine with all of you."

The Monday morning papers had just one headline- "Italian Prince Gianni Weds American Heiress/Senator", with subtitle, *Italian head of ex-royal family chooses Cynthia Adams as his bride,* and below that, 'President Fitzgerald and family attend wedding in Turin Cathedral'. Below the headlines came the love story that they had met at a Charity Ball on Saturday night; were engaged and met the groom's family on Sunday, and were married this morning by Cardinal Montini.

The couple then disappeared in the bride's *Ferrari*- destination unknown. While the press and everyone else assumed that they were bound for the harbor in Monte Carlo, and the Royal Yacht for a Mediterranean cruise. Gianni was correct in suggesting that they go straight up the mountain to his familys' lodge in Sestriere, and only emerge 10 days later to go back down the mountain to the Florence airport; hop on Cynthia's private jet; land on her private airstrip outside Georgetown, Virginia, and spend the rest of the month before Labor Day in their manor hideaway.

Tuesday morning after Labor Day, Cynthia and Gianni had breakfast together, during which she told Gianni:

> "Darling, why don't you take over my study, which looks out upon the back garden, and arrange it as you wish. At 2pm, I'll be meeting with the rest of Jack's 'inner circle' for the latest updates." At that meeting Cynthia spoke as she received everyone's congratulations:

> "Excuse me if I make a couple of personal requests before we get started. First, I would appreciate it if no one in this room, and no one in our Administration for that matter calls me 'Princess', or calls my husband 'Prince'.

> "My name is not Grace Kelly, and I am not moving to Monaco or anywhere else in Europe. My name is Cynthia Savoia and his name is Gianni Savoia.

Secondly, you are all invited to my post-wedding reception this coming Saturday evening-cocktails at 6, and dinner at 8. I guess that's all for now, and please pass the word along about my disdain for royal titles." Jack took his clue and began:

"Admiral Brown, why don't you bring us up to date on what's happening in the Americas and Africa."

"You've all no doubt read my daily briefings with regard to our Latino convict/volunteers in the Americas, and our African-American convict/volunteers in Africa.

"After 'cleaning-up' the drug cartels in Central America, we have moved our troops across the Panama Canal and are currently stationed on the border of Colombia, Bolivia, and Venezuela, awaiting invitation by their governments to assist them. To date, those invitations have not been forthcoming, but we have added another 50,000 Latino-American troops to our forces, bringing the total to150,000 men and 1,000 tanks- plus our Caribbean Fleet, with two aircraft carriers and 300 warplanes and helicopter gunships.

"Central Africa is much the same story. After wiping out terrorists in Somalia, Kenya, and Nigeria, most of the 'troublemakers' South of our 'belt' have become surprisingly quiet. During the Summer we have added another 50,000 Aleutian convict/volunteers just in case, bringing our total level of African-American troops to 250,000- plus 300 carrier warplanes and helicopter gunships on our Persian Gulf Fleet, stationed off the Eastern Africa coast. Barring any new uprisings in countries we have already stabilized, or requests from other African governments, we are just sitting and waiting."

Jack went around the table, but there were no suggestions from anyone that an imminent crisis was on the horizon, in either foreign or domestic affairs. America was growing by leaps and bounds, as were most members of the *American Commonwealth*- full employment; new housing; rising exports, especially oil and LNG to Europe, replacing their Russian imports; payoff of foreign debt; budget surpluses; new cures for cancer; stable prices; renovated infrastructure, including *Super Bullet* railway extensions to most of our larger cities, and revival of American trans-Atlantic/ trans-Pacific passenger shipping lines. Jack was uneasy, because he sensed a gathering storm- no facts to back up his feelings- just a general belief that things were going much too smoothly.

Chapter Twenty-Two

"Jack, you Americans have a very poignant expression- 'if you can't beat 'em, join 'em'," the Russian President said calmly upon Jack's arrival in the Kremlin. "My country is about to default on our foreign debt, and I have no alternative left but to ask you to accept us a member of the *American Commonwealth*- which would cut our budget by about one-third, which is the cost of maintaining our current military establishment at its present levels. We are in the same position today that our former Prime Minister Gorbachev found himself during his negotiations with President Reagan in the 1980's. Bottom line, I can no longer sustain the Russian economy without substantial basic changes."

Jack was suspecting anything but this capitulation by 'hard-liner' Mikhail Varishnikov, but deep down had great sympathy for the plight of the average Russian, so he decided to provide the best solutions he could generate on the spot:

"On behalf of myself and the American Congress, we welcome you and your people, but as you know, you must first conduct a national *referendum,* and then conduct general elections." The Russian leader responded:

"In that regard, neither I nor my Central Committee members, will be running for office. We're all approaching 70 years of age, and it's time to leave the future of Russia in younger hands."

"What do your colleagues say about all of this?"

"Jack, you know as well as I that they have no say in these important matters. As it was with Reagan and Gorbachev, only two men, eyeball-to-eyeball, can make these kinds of monumental decisions. In short, nothing has changed in 'Mother Russia' since the days of Josef Stalin, and our agreement will prove to be the greatest revolution in Russia since Tsar Nicholas II was deposed in 1917- except it will be a peaceful revolution, as was the case in your country three years ago."

"Mikhail, we must first resolve your foreign debt problem- and no, we will not 'bail you out', because we don't even bail out our own people, or our own companies anymore. Your country has more natural resources than mine, and many of these riches will need to be sold to large private sector companies.

"Secondly, you need to put hundreds of thousands of ex-military personnel to work, and there is no larger private enterprise I can think of than building a *Russian Super Bullet,* that will take passengers from Moscow to Vladivostok in 12 hours- instead of three days. Local infrastructure-decaying roads, tunnels, buildings and bridges- should provide daily jobs for everyone else who is likely to find themselves unemployed when your bureaucracy is cut.

"In short, you will find that private enterprise will lift you from near bankruptcy to full economic health within about three years, and provide budget surpluses within about 5 years. In the meantime, as with all *American*

Commonwealth nations, our Treasury Department will guarantee your foreign debts- that's how confident I am in our American system of Constitutional law, plus private enterprise economics."

"Jack, where is your beautiful Russian-speaking Senator, Cynthia Adams?"

"As you may have heard or read, she is quite busy nurturing her three- month-old embryo Vittorio, and cannot travel during her pregnancy, because he will be her husband's heir come late May. And yes, I miss her greatly when talking with foreign leaders such as yourself, but even a President cannot argue with a lovely Princess."

Jack's New Year's Eve *State of the Union Address* was unusually upbeat:

"Ladies and gentlemen of the Congress; Justices of the Supreme Court; honored guests, and my fellow Americans viewing at home and abroad. This evening, I am pleased to report that 2019 has been an exceptional year for America and the *American Commonwealth,* because our long-standing military adversary, Russia, has now become a key member of our team in bringing peace to the world. And soon, I expect them to become one of our most important trading partners.

"This past year, the nations of Central America have joined our *Commonwealth,* and I expect the nations of South America to be applying for membership during the coming year, as will quite a few nations in Central

Africa, once they fully understand the economic importance of stabilizing that Continent, militarily and economically.

"On the home front, everyone seems to be making a good living, which means that our towns' administrators are indeed doing their job in taking care of their townspeople, as was the case during the era of our *Founding Fathers*. However, many men and women with demonstrated abilities to 'run things' are still reluctant to step forward and serve as town leaders, for fear of being labeled 'politicians'. Therefore, I once again put on my *'Uncle Sam's'* wartime *top hat with the stars and stripes*, and point my finger at them and state empathically, *"Your Country Wants YOU!"*, and you all know who you are.

"Next month, I will propose to the Congress that the State of California be divided into *North California,* and *South California*, and that Puerto Rico be granted Statehood.

"I'll close now by wishing each of you an ever more prosperous New Year."

In mid-January, Jack flew to the Conference of Christian/Islamic Churches in Istanbul, as he had promised Pope Luke, and was invited to make the opening address:

"Every country, and every person within that country, has some amount of prejudice- preference for one person or group over another. I consider this to be normal behavior, because we are all human beings, and therefore have our likes and dislikes.

"Hateful discrimination is quite another matter entirely, which is why it is outlawed by the *American Constitution*. I wish all of you the best of success in finding common ground between your two major religions, which represent almost 3 billion members worldwide.

"Therefore gentlemen, I charge this gathering to come up with a common Christian/Muslim prayer- something like the Christian *The Lord's Prayer*, which begins with the words "Our Father, Who art in Heaven"- one that can be spoken aloud in both Church and Mosque. If you can do this one thing only, I believe you will be well on your way to a successful Inter-Faith Conference."

Pope Luke whispered to Jack as he left the podium:

"Let's meet in your suite after my afternoon session, and have a couple of cocktails while I tell you how your 'Common Prayer' went over with the Muslim clergy. By the way, I thought your opening address was Heavenly-inspired."

"Indeed it was, *Your Holiness*, indeed it was, and I have no idea why I have been chosen to be His messenger."

Pope Luke was elated as he sat down late that afternoon:

"Jack, you won't believe this, but our Muslim friends have accepted the *Lord's Prayer*, a perfect piece of theological poetry, as our interfaith common

Christian/Muslim prayer, changing only *'Amen'* to *'Insha'Allah'*." Pope Luke took a long drag on his *Monte Cristo* cigar, and a long swig of his single malt Irish whiskey before continuing:

"We spent the rest of the afternoon discussing all the similarities between *The Bible* and *The Koran,* and discovered that, with the exception of Islamic *Jihad* and *Sharia Law*, the same fundamental message is conveyed- 'love God, and love thy fellow man, and you shall enter the Kingdom of Heaven. You were absolutely right- come up with even a 'Common Prayer', and everything else will follow." The Pope then switched topics and asked:

"So what's happening back in D.C.?"

"Just this afternoon, I learned that several South American governments have been threatened by the drug cartels, and have asked for our military assistance in quelling their rebellious private armies. In response, I have ordered my Latino-American convict/Marines to wipe them out within the next week.

"At the same time, rebellious tribal chieftains, and *'Muslim Crazies'* in Central Africa have threatened to overthrow several unstable governments, so I have ordered our *African Belt* African-American convict/Marines to move South and 'take out' all rebellious elements. In short, we are on the move on both Continents, and it's not going to be a pretty picture at the end of these conflicts.

327

"Once upon a time, when I first took office, I vowed that the United States would never become the *'World's Policeman'* during my presidency, but that was wishful thinking, as everyone has witnessed. The reality is that America has become the "only cop on the block", and if America cannot bring about world stability, then we are all lost! Your *Holiness*, we are both American pioneers, traveling on uncertain roads, in uncharted lands."

"Indeed we are Jack, and I'm certain that the Lord looks down upon us both as His Earthly shepherds, protecting and guiding His flock."

On his way home, Jack felt like a kid waiting for Christmas day- except that in this case he couldn't wait to discuss the results of the Inter-Faith Conference with Kathy, and to witness the expression on her face.

"Jack, how did you come up with this idea? It's so beautiful, yet so simple."

"I can't explain it Kathy, it just came to me out of the blue, as I gazed out at a roomful of clerics in their finely-woven religious garments, and for a brief instant felt that Jesus Himself was speaking to them through me."

Three weeks after Cynthia delivered a healthy new Italian Prince at Bethesda Naval Hospital, Jack called her to the Oval Office:

"There is no doubt in my mind that you are the first qualified female Presidential material in history, and I will stand by my previous offer made before you met your charming Prince- which by the way, I predicted you would- but I never suspected it would be a 'Real Prince'. Will baby Vittorio have American or Italian citizenship?"

"Jack, Gianni and I had our first 'marital tiff' several months ago. He insisted that he be born in Italy, because of Savoy family tradition, and any possibility of a future position for the Italian Monarchy. I reminded him that the chances of this happening under Italy's new Constitution is zero, and furthermore argued that only American- born citizens came become President of the United States.

"He quickly rebuffed my argument by stating that the *'House of Savoy'* dated back to the Crusades, almost one thousand years ago, and that his family had substantial properties on the French side of the Alps as a result of his *'Knights Templar'* ancestry.

"I then rebutted by telling him my ancestors include two early Presidents of the United States; that my family fortune was more than twice his; and that our children will be raised as Americans, and not as Italian nobility- no English education for them- it shall he *Harvard* and not *Oxford*. I also reminded him of my service obligations to my country.

"Oh Jack, it was absolutely horrible." Jack responded sympathetically:

"I am deeply sorry for the grief it must have caused you, so let's agree to this- between now and the end of the year, when I must declare my candidacy for a second term, we'll just see how you can manage your service to our country; your oversight of the Adams' family fortune; and most importantly, your duty as a wife and mother. If you can, all well and good, and you will be the next Vice President of the United States come this January first when John McCall's resignation becomes effective.

"If you cannot, I only ask that you let me know as soon as possible. I might add that as far as Kathy and I are concerned, nothing in the world is more important to us than our marriage and our children, who were fortunately in their teens when I was named to the Supreme Court, so I never found myself in your position." Cynthia quickly switched the subject.

"Speaking of family, Gianni and I would like you to be Godfather to Vittorio, and Kathy to be his Godmother, when we have him baptized at St. Patrick's Catholic Church here in Washington."

"Cynthia, of course we will be honored. Now let me tell you what happened with Mikhail, who specifically asked for you, by the way. I would like to say it was a stroke of genius on my part, but it was entirely otherwise- the Russians are broke, and only we can save them from default by guaranteeing their foreign debt, and also allowing them to reduce their military costs by one-half."

"You did the right thing, Jack- the Russian people have such a big heart, and yet are so simple- they just want to be like us! You have given them this opportunity, and we can only hope that they find the *'town leadership'* you have so often called for in America. Don't be surprised if many Russian notables end up on voting ballots in the General Elections. Until proven otherwise, they all have a long history of *Machiavellian* subterfuge."

At the Baptismal reception, Jack took Gianni's elbow and led him out to the rear garden for a private discussion.

"How much has Cynthia discussed with you about her political future?" Gianni replied:

"We have never kept any secrets from each other, except for official 'classified' information, of course. I understand that you have chosen her to be your Vice President when John McCall retires at the end of this year, but only if she can handle the pressure of family; Adam's Industries, and Government responsibilities.

"Before I met her, I would have said that this would be an impossible task for *any* woman, but after 10 months of marriage, I have learned that she is unlike any other woman I have ever met, in every respect. What everyone can see, of course, is a beautiful body. What they don't see, is a brain that is like a steel trap- her ability to analyze situations and make decisions is astounding, as I'm sure you have come to realize.

"She has also told me that you have given her until the end of the year to learn whether or not she is able to handle babies; husband; family fortune; foreign affairs, and next year's political campaign schedule. My answer to you is that if she cannot, then no one else alive- man or woman- can tackle this degree of multitasking- or even come close.

"For my part, I will hold our Royal engagements down to the bare minimum, and would ask you to do the same with regard to her foreign travel. Other than that, it seems to me that we'll both have to just see what happens during the next several months."

On that note, Jack and Gianni shook hands firmly, and returned to the reception.

Chapter Twenty-Three

As the Summer of 2019 drew to a close, the Fitzgerald family were together again in the White House preparing for the Fall academic semester to begin; the *Met* season to open, and The Congress to reconvene. Jack took his sons aside to learn of their comportment, and degree of affection for their summertime female companions. Mark spoke for he and Matt:

> "No Dad, there has been no sexual intercourse- just a lot of kissing and necking- we all know your rules of conduct regarding gentlemanly behavior with the town's girls. At the same time, like you, Matt and I have had a number of sexual encounters in college, and have always taken precautions." Stephen was obliged to add:

> "Dad, I have fallen in love with Silvana, and I can't help myself. Sooner or later, I believe we will have a formal engagement, and then be married."

> "Stephen, you could not have picked a lovelier girl for your future wife, and I heartedly approve-once you both graduate, and I assume both enter Harvard Law School. Her father has given outstanding public service to the town of Greve, has been elected Governor of the State of Tuscany, and I expect him to be elected President of Italy in the next general elections of 2022. In the meantime, I expect her to be a virgin on her wedding night."

> "Yes Dad, I understand completely."

When Cynthia and Gianni arrived for cocktails and dinner, Jack drew Cynthia aside for a private conversation.

"Cynthia, I've just received word from our Ambassador in Beijing that China has just woken up to the fact that we have encircled their country with *American Commonwealth* nations- on the West and North with Russia; and on the East with Korea; Japan; Taiwan, and the Philippines.

"For guys that think ahead quarter centuries instead of corporate quarters, they are all of a sudden behaving rather strangely. As a result, China has asked for a sit-down to be held in Beijing, which can only mean one thing- capitulation to the *'real-politik'* of American dominance.

"So, my dear, we have a brand new ball game. I hadn't planned to deal with China or any of the rest of Asia before my second term. But as always, we are driven by world events, not the other way around."

"I would like to have you and Rollie at my side to 'triple- team' them- I'll take on Chairman Chang; while Rollie takes on their Secretary of Foreign Affairs, and you handle their Finance Minister. Afterwards, all six of us will get together and review in detail what I hope will be a tentative agreement. We should be in and out in about 3 days.

"That should work out perfectly Jack, because Gianni has been itching to take a close look at my Montana cattle ranch and other operations. What timeframe are we looking at?"

"Late September should give us time to meet with the rest of the inner circle, and to prepare our questions. I want to strike while the iron is hot."

Tuesday morning after Labor Day, Jack reported to his team that China had approached him secretly, through Italian President Dino Cecchi, on the occasion of his recent State visit.

"It's clear to me that whatever they have to propose, we should keep it to ourselves. The only thing for publication is that I will be making a State visit to Korea and Japan early next week, together with my Secretary of State and Senator Savoia, who will be representing The Congress. Until we get back Admiral, I want to refrain from any unusual military activity in the Far East. Any questions? Good, because I don't have the foggiest idea of what these guys are up to. It can't be about money, because we have already liquidated our $1.5 trillion debt to them."

Air Force One landed at Beijing's Military Airport in the middle of the night, the following Tuesday, and its occupants were promptly escorted in secrecy to their deluxe accommodations at Government Headquarters. At the same time, a repainted civilian Boeing 777 *Dreamliner* landed at Tokyo International Airport, and debarked Hollywood actor look-alikes of the President; Secretary of State; Chairman of the Senate Foreign Relations Committee, and were escorted to the Presidential suite at the Tokyo Hilton hotel.

Jack, Cynthia, and Rollie were fully rested for Wednesday afternoon's meeting. The Chinese leader spoke first:

"It's been a long time since Camp David, and it seems to me that the world has changed greatly in the meantime. Good to see you again."

"Same here Chang, but why all the secrecy?"

"Simple Jack, ' *the natives are restless* ', because our centralized government control has proved to be wrought with incompetency, graft, and nepotism- human errors which in past generations could have gone unnoticed. However today, with modern communications technology, *nothing* goes unnoticed, regardless of tight central government censorship."

"Let me understand this correctly, Chang. You've stolen our intellectual property for the past 20 years and have now realized that technology is a 'two-edged sword'."

"Something like that Jack, but the main point I'm trying to make is that over the past 4 years you have demonstrated that the *American Commonwealth* relationship between nations brings greater prosperity to everyone- and China can no longer compete with your vision of the 21st century 'New World Order'.

"Some years ago Chang, China came to realize that individual private enterprise was the key to what Mao once called *'The great leap forward'*, and you have successfully competed with all countries, including ours. Now you tell me that this fundamental change to capitalism is not sufficient, even though China has had a fair share of the new markets our *American Commonwealth* has created for you. You have come to realize that centrally controlled national economic growth does not work nearly as well as individual entrepreneurship. Am I correct?"

"Yes Jack, that's about the sum of it. We now have a new, well-educated middle class that is in a position to take over control of their own destinies- and they instinctively know it. My Central Committee is also aware of a better path to China's future prosperity, and have concluded that your American Constitutional Law; American dollar, and American military protection is the best solution. We therefore request that your Congress admit China as the newest member of the *American Commonwealth*." Jack replied:

"Chang, I don't think that will be too difficult as long as you agree to abide by all our laws, including those related to the theft of intellectual property, and the hacking of computer files. We send people to prison when convicted for that kind of thing, and will expect you to crack down as well. The same applies to Global Free Trade and the new minimum wage that is an integral part of that agreement- we only do business with countries whose people can afford to buy our American products."

Early next morning, the meeting was joined by Cynthia and her counterpart; Rollie and his counterpart; the American Ambassador to China, and the other members of the Chinese Central Committee. Jack opened the meeting:

"On behalf of the Executive Branch of my Government I accept your request for membership in the *American Commonwealth*, and will submit the question to Congress upon my return to Washington. Now, I would like to ask Senator Savoia to give us her understanding of China's current financial condition."

"Gentlemen, I am pleased to report that my review yesterday afternoon revealed that at the moment China is in the best financial position of any foreign nation we have thus far admitted to our *Commonwealth*- there is ample hard currency foreign exchange reserves, including the $1½ trillion we have just credited them with in redemption of their T-Bonds- this should be ample for internal currency circulation, replacing their *yuans* at whatever exchange rate chosen.

"My principal negative finding is that Chinese GDP has been falling steadily over the past 10 years, from 12% in 2009 to just 2% so far this year- while claiming it to be 6%. In short, China is headed for a recession very soon, should it fail to take drastic action. At the same time, I also believe that their GPD can rise substantially with membership in the *American Commonwealth*- and is the primary reason for this conference. We must all keep this to ourselves, because I believe that otherwise it will have a profound negative effect on world markets." Jack spoke once more.

"Thank you Cynthia, and thank you Mister Treasury Secretary for bringing out the truth of China's current economic dilemma. Because of the consequences

Cynthia has mentioned, we Americans will not breathe a word to anyone, and suggest you gentlemen do likewise- the last thing we all need is another worldwide economic shock like the one we had 11 years ago. I am confident that your GDP growth will indeed be 6% by this time next year, and will eventually rival the American economy's 10% target GDP growth rate. In closing, I wish to thank all of you for your kind hospitality, but most of all for your openness and truthfulness. This is the kind of honest foundation that leads to permanent trust between nations."

Chang remained silent, because he knew that Jack knew the reality of the Central Committee's decision to go with the *American Commonwealth*. It was simply a multi-millennial question of 'saving face'.

As they boarded *Air Force One*, seated themselves in the conference room, and distributed a well-deserved and much-needed alcoholic beverage, Jack announced a surprise:

"Gang, we desperately need some R&R, so I'm inviting you to spend the next few days at my vacation home. We can all relax and figure out the best solutions to solve this 'Chinese puzzle'. Rollie, you haven't been to my vacation home."

"No Jack, but Cynthia has told me all about it, and I'm quite anxious to see it for myself; have a little wine-tasting; do a few laps in the pool; play a little tennis, and sample Ursola's great home cooking." Jack responded:

"That's what we should all do, but in the meantime, I'm going to phone John McCall and give him a press release that goes something like this- 'the Chinese government have asked our country to accept them as a member of the *American Commonwealth,* because their leaders have recognized that the future prosperity of the Chinese people can improve at a faster pace than that under Central Government control. Ten minutes later Jack returned to his 'troupe':

"While I'm on the subject of the Vice President, I should tell you now that after many decades of service to our country, he has decided to retire at the end of this year, and therefore will not be my running mate in 2020. His military and political service to his country has been a great inspiration to myself and anyone else who knows him well. He has served our country for most of his adult life as a Naval pilot; as a representative of the people of Arizona, and today as my Vice President, with more executive power than any other Vice President in our history, but at age 79 he has decided to enjoy his final years in leisure, writing his memoirs.

Chapter Twenty-Four

"Kathy, what would you think if I told you that I am seriously considering making mine a one-term Presidency?" Kathy was caught completely by surprise- they had never discussed this before.

"What about the Asian Campaign? And who could possibly take your place?"

"Now that China has joined *The Commonwealth*, I believe the rest of Asia, from Pakistan to Indonesia, will follow suit within the next 4 years, as will the remaining African and South American nations. That would only leave those nations which prefer to keep operating under *Sharia Law*, which I maintain is basically incompatible with our American Constitution.

" The only reason I would have for a last minute run for a second term would be if I thought that everything I have put together here in the States and abroad was about to become 'unglued'. As for my successor, it all depends on whether Cynthia manages to handle home; baby; husband, and job between now and the end of this year, when I will nominate her to become my new Vice President.

"My basic idea is to spend at least the next four years doing other things that will make us both happy together. After all, we are both still relatively young- I'm 49 and you're 47. I need a break in the action and nothing would preclude me from returning for a second term should my countrymen need me, that is, if Cynthia should get into a 'mess' she can't handle, and Americans want me back to clean it up. I would serve a second term, but I seriously doubt that this would be the case- she is much too talented to get into a 'mess' in the first place, but a man like me can never put himself into the mind of a woman like her."

"Jack, I assume you're talking about operating out of our villa in Greve. Darling, there are an infinite number of new places we have not yet visited, and people to see as former American celebrities, including spending a lot more time with our children, either at their homes or in Tuscany. And don't forget, we still have to finish St. Luke Academy." Jack interrupted:

"Kathy, we've always spent a lot of time with our children- every one of Mark's and Matt's college football games; many of their baseball games; most of Stephen's soccer games; many of his baseball games; and all of Mary's operatic performances at the Met. However, you're right about St. Luke Academy- I would like to see the progress made to date, and be there when it is finished." Kathy came right back:

"Then there is always the standard 'Around the World' luxury cruise to the *American Commonwealth* nations. I am particularly curious to see what changes you have brought to the poorest people on this planet. By the way dear heart, I am still ovulating, so if we want to make a new baby, I wouldn't say no."

Vice President McCall announced his resignation on Thanksgiving Day in the Rose Garden, with President Fitzgerald at his side:

> "Every man and woman who has served our great country for as many years as I, realizes that advanced age takes its toll. The time has now come for me to step down from my position as Vice President as of the end of this year, and yield it to someone of the next generation. I refer specifically to the Chairwoman of our Senate Foreign Relations Committee- Senator Cynthia Adams Savoia from the State of Montana- in my opinion the most talented woman ever to serve our country."
> Jack stepped forward and seconded John's nomination. McCall then added:

> "It has been a privilege for most of my life to serve my country, from young Naval Aviator to elderly Vice President, a position which has now become one of great importance and power. I shall now do my outmost to enjoy my remaining years in leisure with my family. Farewell, and may God continue to bless and guide America."

In his *State of the Union Address* on New Year's Eve, Jack was entirely upbeat, with an emphasis on bringing lasting peace and prosperity to every nation on Earth. He ended with the words:

> "We Americans are indeed blessed by God-never for a moment think otherwise. He has been by my side to help me lead you to a position of world dominance never before witnessed by any nation in the history of our planet. With this leadership of world affairs we now

have a great responsibility to assure that no person on Earth is left destitute.

"With this said by your Commander-In-Chief, I once again commend the American people for your support, and our brave warriors for their victories. I wish you all an even more prosperous new 'election year' in 2020, and call upon all of you who have demonstrated the ability to 'get things done' to offer your services to your fellow citizens at every level of government.

"This new year will also bring forth a new President to continue my design for 21st century America. This may seem unusual for a man of 49, and I suppose it is, but I have given my beloved America absolutely everything my mind and body had to offer. As in my *Illini* football and baseball days some 30 years ago, there is that inevitable letdown after winning the *National Championships* in football and baseball. I have had the same feeling for the past several months, after Russia and China joined our *American Commonwealth.*

"On a personal note, Kathy and I will be starting a new life next November with a new baby girl, just to keep us 'on our toes'. Also, looking forward to next year, I will be giving my *Farewell Address* and have my much-belated *Victory Parade* on July 4th down Pennsylvania Avenue and will be nominating your next President at the mid-August Republican National Convention."

A few days later, Jack and Kathy invited Gianni and Cynthia to a private family dinner in their quarters. Jack led off:

"Next August, I will personally nominate you, Cynthia, as the first woman President of the United States, at our Party convention. Gianni, how do you feel about your wife becoming the most powerful person on Earth at 10am on November 15th?" Gianni was quick to comment:

"I'll have a better idea when we meet at your villa during Easter vacation. By that time, Cynthia's pregnancy will be quite noticeable. She is now carrying *Prince* Giovanni, who is due to arrive on the 4th of July." Kathy then observed:

"Cynthia, no one would guess that you are already at the end of your first trimester- you hardly show a thing. Of course, neither do I with our new baby Christina."

"I didn't show much with *Vittorio* either, until the last two months. By the way, your Godson has gone from 'crawler' to 'toddler', and is now speaking his first words. Gianni and I would like you and Jack to also be Godparents to Giovanni." Jack answered for them both:

"Of course, we will again be quite pleased and honored- you have both become part of our family, like a younger brother and younger sister, and would like you to reciprocate by accepting to be Godparents to Christina. I have another favor to ask of you, Gianni- it involves you serving your 'adopted country' in a formal capacity, as *Ambassador-at-Large* to Europe, with a mandate to carry out 'special missions' as they should develop from time to time.

"Your first mission would be to represent the United States as an 'observer' at the European Central Bank, starting right after your meeting tomorrow with Treasury Secretary, Johnnie Diamond.

"Find out what inside information he would like to obtain with regard to the current, and the forecasted financial position of the European Central Bank, and each of its member nations. With your Doctorate in International Finance from the London School of Economics, I don't think you will find yourself 'in over your head', but rather in an interesting position which will give me, and eventually Cynthia, an independent view when the time comes for certain European countries to apply for membership in the *American Commonwealth*. Gianni, this is strictly your decision- and if you find it not to be your 'cup of tea', you are free to 'bow out' at any time." Gianni suddenly realized the purpose of Jack's proposal:

"Jack, are you asking me to become a 'financial spy', covering all of Europe, Great Britain and Russia?"

"Gianni, at one time or another, everyone connected with our government is asked to collect information of one stripe or another- and in your case, it is financial and economic information- so the term 'spy' is hardly appropriate.

"Your name is Gianni Savoia, *not James Bond*- you are no longer a bachelor playboy; you *do not* carry deadly weapons; you *are not* required to kill people, and you report directly to me- not to *'M'* at MI-6 in London.

"Our meetings will be held in the Oval Office, and will include Cynthia; Secretary of State Rollie Giordano, your 'nominal' boss, and Treasury Secretary Johnnie Diamond. In short, an economic 'Gang of Five', as opposed to my dozen-member 'inner circle group'.

"Your supporting staff in Europe will include the local CIA Station Chief and his field operatives for any background *dossiers* you may require regarding the people you will be meeting with. By the way, your standard Ambassadorial salary is $5 million- which includes all personal travel and entertainment expenses you will incur during your missions.

"Since you are an experienced, licensed multi-engine aircraft pilot, I might suggest that you use Cynthia's twin engine jet for your travels, and I will have Mike McMahon, our CIA Director, arrange for qualified co-pilots/bodyguards. Any questions?

"Jack, if my 'missions', as you call them, are to be without danger, why would I need to have a bodyguard?"

"Gianni, when it comes to my 'younger brother', I will always prefer to err on the side of caution. Also, I want you to take three day weekends off here at home to keep Cynthia and your family happy, and to meet briefly with our 'Gang of Five'."

True to Jack's expectations, Gianni Savoia would prove to be the conveyor of invaluable information from the heart of the financial; political; industrial, and Royal circles of European 'movers and shakers'.

On July 4, 2020, Jack had his 'Victory Parade' down Pennsylvania Avenue, in the company of Kathy, their new baby Christina; their four grown children; Nicky; their granddaughter, Caterina, and their new baby grandson, 'little Jack'. Cynthia was in labor at the hospital, giving birth to her second boy, Giovanni.

The parade came to a halt in front of the White House, and Jack proceeded to give his Address on the South Lawn podium.

> "About four months from today, I will be handing the keys to the White House over to our next President, but today belongs to us all, as we celebrate the birthday of our great nation.

> "It seems that the last few years have gone by in a 'blink', but when I look at what our nation has accomplished- beginning with the return of domestic power to *We The People*, to the establishment of a peaceful and evermore prosperous planet- I can't help but take pride in myself and my countrymen, who stood behind me when I ordered the elimination of ominous threats to global stability.

> "Those threats- 'rogue' nuclear nations, Islamic terrorism, and drug cartels are now behind us- and a bright new day has dawned, not only for America, but for the entire *American Commonwealth*, and other democratic nations around the globe.

"We Americans are now in a position to fuel the world with our huge surpluses of oil, gas, and coal. We are also in a position to feed the world with our giant surpluses of wheat, corn, soybeans, and rice. No one on this planet need ever again worry about their energy supply, or their food supply.

"In resolving our domestic and international crises, I have learned that the Office of *The Presidency* has been substantially changed. The demands now placed upon my Office in this 21st century of American Leadership plus World Leadership has become literally overwhelming.

"After four years, although I may still be tall and strong on the outside, I must admit that I am completely 'drained' on the inside- I've given my country everything I have to offer. I did not plan it this way, but I shall *not* seek a second term as your President, but will be nominating my Vice President Cynthia Savoia at next month's Republican National Convention. Suffice it to say that during the past four years I have taught her everything I know, and that her God-given talents go well beyond my tutelage.

"To conclude our July 4th celebration, I have asked my eldest daughter and her husband to sing my two favorite patriotic songs- *"God Bless America"* and *"America The Beautiful"*."

Jack had always felt that victory celebrations are not exclusive to the inauguration of a President, who must then go on to fulfill his political campaign promises- but perhaps more appropriate after winning the *big game*. Thus, his invitation cards for that evening bore the title 'Victory Ball', where *Dom Perignon* would flow like water. Mary and Nicky volunteered to again sing a medley of Broadway musical classics by Rogers and Hammerstein, which made the evening complete. Kathy then took the mic and expressed the everlasting gratitude of the American people, and the invited guests:

> "This day would not be complete without expressing what I, and all American patriots hold to be true, and that is- my husband Jack Fitzgerald is the greatest leader our Republican Party has produced since its founding by Abraham Lincoln a century and a half ago. He will be revered in the same breath as President Ronnie Reagan, who won the 50-year 'Cold War' against Russia and Communism."

During the following three months Jack would fulfill his promise to Cynthia by nominating her at the Republican Convention, and then campaigning at her side before the general elections. She was then elected by a majority popular vote of 70%.

On November 15, 2020, a typically brisk Washington Autumn day, Jack would have another 'Victory Parade' down Pennsylvania Avenue, in the company of his family and new President Cynthia Savoia. He would then participate in Cynthia's Presidential Ball, after handing her the keys to the White House, and reclaiming his Georgetown manor at the same price she had paid him four years earlier.

That evening at Cynthia's Inauguration Ball, she and her guests demanded that Jack say a few words. Jack reluctantly stepped to the podium:

> "I find myself incapable of saying 'farewell'. So I shall borrow a salute from our Italian friends by bidding you *arrivederci-* which means 'until we meet again'.

Six months later, the two families met for Easter vacation at Jack's villa in Tuscany, where Cynthia laid bare her heart:

> "Jack, I have little to give or create for America that you haven't already thought of- it's been more a question of 'tweaking' a few of our laws. This Office that the Constitution designed primarily for Domestic Administration, has become far too complex for any one person, when the *American Commonwealth* is added. In short, you have constructed a 21st century American Presidency that only you can administer." Cynthia continued:

> "I know you didn't do this on purpose- you expected others of your caliber to fall in line behind you, but I must tell you that there *are* no others- including myself, that can do the job you have laid out for future Presidents.

> "I don't know what the answer is, but I *do know* that even a very talented person like myself can never fill your large shoes. Therefore, I have decided *not* to run for a second term, and unfortunately I have not chosen, in Tom Akers, a Vice President who can take my place, much less yours." Jack responded sympathetically:

"I'm surprised to hear that Cynthia, because he seems to possess all the qualities necessary to be your Second in Command- two-term Governor of Texas; still in his mid-forties; very likable personality, and certainly what women would call handsome. So where has it all gone wrong?"

"Jack, to put it simply, he doesn't have a lot of brain power, and absolutely no creativity. During our 'inner circle' meetings he has never offered one original thought. In short, he has turned out to be an 'old school politician', but not particularly well-read, even in our American history.

"Now that we've got a number of smaller European countries knocking at the door for entry into the *American Commonwealth*, this would normally mean to me a heavy foreign travel schedule. However, I am reluctant to leave domestic matters in Tom's hands while I am gone, because the few decisions he has been called upon to make thus far reflect poorly on his judgment."

"Got the picture, Cynthia. Looking back, the only person that made my 'short list' before I chose you, was a young Congressman from Milwaukee, named Pat Rowan, who at the time was working on the House Ways and Means Committee, and was quick to understand the logic behind the new tax system I had formulated. He was later talented enough to put my tax ideas into legislative language; sell it to the bi-partisan Committee; and with a lot of 'push' from former

President O'Hara, got it passed in the full House with Democrat support, and then through the Senate.

"In my opinion, he was the most talented Congressman in the House when it came to 'numbers', but unlike you, had no experience in foreign matters. The rest is history- he was elected Speaker of the House five years ago at age 33- the youngest Speaker in history. As far as personality goes, he can be fiery and passionate about what the Federal Government spends its money on, but otherwise is a soft spoken, and very thoughtful man whose intelligence and creativity is truly exceptional.

Jack and Cynthia were interrupted by her Secret Service bodyguard, who entered the study, leaned down and whispered into Cynthia's ear. Her expression quickly turned to visible disbelief, as she uttered the words "Good Lord, I can't believe it!" She then turned to Jack and the others:

"Tom Akers just died from a massive heart attack while playing tennis at a private country club in the 'boondocks' 30 miles outside Washington. No one at the club or at the hospital was able to revive him. Gianni and I must return to the White House immediately." Jack replied:

"If you don't mind Cynthia, Kathy and I would like to accompany you- during the next few days you're going to need all the help you can get, especially in soothing Tom's family. Also, I have great respect, as you know, for the Office of the Vice President, ever since I made it so powerful in domestic affairs."

"Of course you may Jack, and I am very grateful to have a strong arm to lean on during my first big crisis."

After an elaborate funeral ceremony in Arlington National Cemetery, Cynthia approached Pat Rowan, and asked him to follow her back to the White House. She also invited Jack to join them. When all three were seated comfortably in the Oval Office, Cynthia came straight to the point:

"Pat, I have asked Jack to sit in because he has worked longer with you than I have, and I implicitly trust his judgment when it comes to recognizing unique leadership talent. As Speaker of the House, you now have a very important position, but as my Vice President you would have greater responsibility, because you would be in charge of my domestic Administration during my travels abroad, and during my vacations.

"In addition, I would give you the responsibility for clearing out the remaining 'dead wood' in the Federal government. This includes redundant agencies and sub-agencies which were not eliminated during Jack's Presidency. It would also include convincing the few remaining elderly 'career politicians' to yield their Offices to the younger generation."

Pat was clearly unprepared for Cynthia's proposal, and could only utter *sotto voce*:

"Why me?" Jack stepped in:

"Funny you should say that Pat, because those were exactly the same words that Cynthia said to me about two years ago, when I proposed she take over for John McCall as my Vice President.

"America is still a relatively young country as nations go, and requires younger generations to guide our nation- that was, and still is, my vision for the 21st century. Cynthia is now 37, and you are 38. More importantly, I believe you both share this vision, and have the same respect for our Constitution- which today remains the *only written contract* between *We The People* and our Federal Government." Cynthia then intervened:

"Quite eloquent, Lord Fitzgerald. What say you now, *Sir Rowan?*" To which Pat replied:

"How could any man refuse his *Queen's* command?" Cynthia, with a smile on her face replied:

"Pat, I was only 'joshing' you, to see if you had a quick wit and a sense of humor, by referring to my ancient ancestors' land of birth- England. Every person should have a sense of humor, and I'm happy to see that you are not an exception. At the same time, we shall never forget that we are now the *servants* of the American people- the '*D.C. Mafia*', as Jack is prone to call it, as well as the local political 'Little Mafias' are at last *"Gone With The Wind"*.